Queer Engagements with International Law

This book explores times, spaces and imaginings relating to international law through the lens of queer theory.

For some time now, queer theorists and legal scholars who think with queer theory have asked, what happens when queer theory moves out of its home base of gender and sexuality? The chapters in this book begin to answer this question by applying insights from queer theory to a diverse array of international law topics, from *travaux préparatoires* and international judging to the environment, oceans and outer space. While some contributions maintain a focus on gender and sexual diversity, all are characterised by a shift away from questions about LGBTIQA+ people towards wider discussions about power, normality, difference and liberation in international law. Through these engagements, the book demonstrates how queer theory can provide insights into a range of international law issues by allowing us to 'make strange' the taken-for-granted and contributing to a broader practice of reading for difference rather than dominance. The book engages with contemporary challenges in international law, from the climate crisis to new military technologies, such as automated naval vessels. It also showcases the diversity of approaches to queering international law that are emerging, with some authors drawing attention to the violence of (neo-)colonial international law and others engaging in more utopian and reparative thinking.

This collection of queer theoretical engagements with international law will be invaluable to scholars of international law and international relations with an interest in critical approaches to these areas, as well as to researchers, activists and practitioners working in cultural, gender, queer and/or postcolonial studies.

Claerwen O'Hara is Lecturer at La Trobe Law School, La Trobe University, Australia.

Tamsin Phillipa Paige is Senior Lecturer at Deakin Law School, Deakin University, Australia.

Part of the FEMINIST AND QUEER INTERNATIONAL LAW Series
Series Editors Gina Heathcote, *Newcastle University, UK*
Vanja Hamzić, *SOAS University of London, UK*

A GlassHouse book

Queer Engagements with International Law

Times, Spaces, Imaginings

Edited by Claerwen O'Hara and Tamsin Phillipa Paige

Routledge
Taylor & Francis Group
a GlassHouse Book

First published 2025
by Routledge
4 Park Square, Milton Park, Abingdon, Oxon OX14 4RN

and by Routledge
605 Third Avenue, New York, NY 10158

Routledge is an imprint of the Taylor & Francis Group, an informa business

A GlassHouse book

British Library Cataloguing-in-Publication Data
A catalogue record for this book is available from the British Library

Library of Congress Cataloging-in-Publication Data
Names: O'Hara, Claerwen, editor. | Paige, Tamsin Phillipa, editor.
Title: Queer engagements with international law : times, spaces, imaginings / edited by Claerwen O'Hara and Tamsin Phillipa Paige.
Description: Abingdon, Oxon [UK] ; New York, NY : Routledge, 2025. | Series: Feminist and queer international law | Includes bibliographical references and index.
Identifiers: LCCN 2024025954 (print) | LCCN 2024025955 (ebook)
Subjects: LCSH: Sexual minorities—Legal status, laws, etc. | Gender identity—Law and legislation. | Homosexuality—Law and legislation. | Sex and law. | Feminist jurisprudence. | International law and human rights.
Classification: LCC K3242.3 .Q435 2025 (print) | LCC K3242.3 (ebook) | DDC 341.4/85—dc23/eng/20240612
LC record available at https://lccn.loc.gov/2024025954
LC ebook record available at https://lccn.loc.gov/2024025955

ISBN: 978-1-032-64322-9 (hbk)
ISBN: 978-1-032-64534-6 (pbk)
ISBN: 978-1-032-64533-9 (ebk)

DOI: 10.4324/9781032645339

Typeset in Sabon
by Apex CoVantage, LLC

Contents

Notes on Editors and Contributors

Caitlin Biddolph (she/her) is Postdoctoral Research Fellow in Gender and Global Governance in the School of Social and Political Sciences at the University of Sydney, Australia. Her doctoral research explored discourses and logics of gender, sexuality, civilisation and violence at the International Criminal Tribunal for the former Yugoslavia (ICTY). Caitlin is currently researching the global governance of transitional justice through queer decolonial perspectives. More broadly, she is interested in queer, feminist, postcolonial and decolonial approaches to global politics, particularly global governance, international law and transitional justice. She has recently published articles in *International Studies Quarterly* (forthcoming), *International Feminist Journal of Politics* (forthcoming) and *Millennium: Journal of International Studies*.

Vanja Hamzić (he, his/no pronouns) is Reader in Law, History and Anthropology at SOAS University of London, United Kingdom. Vanja's work principally considers colonial, postcolonial and decolonial subjectivity making – with a particular focus on gender nonconformity – in South and Southeast Asia, West Africa and Louisiana. Vanja's books include *Control and Sexuality: The Revival of Zinā Laws in Muslim Contexts* (with Ziba Mir Hosseini, 2010) and *Sexual and Gender Diversity in the Muslim World: History, Law and Vernacular Knowledge* (2016, 2019). Vanja's current book project addresses gender diversity and cosmological pluralism in eighteenth-century Senegambia as well as the ways enslaved gender nonconforming West Africans have survived the Middle Passage and the gender regime of colonial Louisiana. Vanja was a 2016/17 Member of the School of Social Science in the Institute for Advanced Study at Princeton.

Gina Heathcote (she/her/they) is Professor of Public International Law at Newcastle University, UK. Gina is the author of *Feminist Dialogues on International Law* (2019) and *The International Law on the Use of Force: a Feminist Analysis* (2012) and co-author, with Sara Bertotti, Emily Jones and Sheri Labenski, of *The Laws of War and Peace: a Gender Analysis Vol 1* (2021). Her current work examines the International Law of the Sea and develops a queer feminist analysis of ocean governance, nonhuman subjects and legal pluralism.

Emily Jones (she/her) is NUAcT Fellow based in Newcastle Law School, United Kingdom. Emily's research broadly examines modes of resistance and hope in relation to the theory and practice of public international law, drawing on feminist, queer, posthuman, postcolonial and critical disability studies with that aim. Emily's monograph, *Feminist Theory and International Law: Posthuman Perspectives*, was published with Routledge's GlassHouse series in 2023. Emily is the co-author of *The Law of War and Peace: A Gender Analysis, Volume One* (2021) and has co-edited two volumes: the *More Posthuman Glossary* (2022) and *International Law & Posthuman Theory* (2024).

Lucas Lixinski (he/him) is Professor at the Faculty of Law & Justice, UNSW Sydney, Australia. He researches and teaches across a range of fields of international and comparative law, particularly international cultural heritage law and international human rights law. Some of his current projects involve an exploration of the possibilities of applying queer theory to critical heritage studies, as well as a larger project on how international human rights adjudication shapes the way social movements engage with their own rights claims. His latest monograph is *A Research Agenda for Cultural Heritage Law* (2024).

Claerwen O'Hara (they) is Lecturer at La Trobe Law School, Australia, co-chair of the Australian and New Zealand Society of International Law (ANZSIL) Gender, Sexuality and International Law Interest Group, and Managing Editor of the *Australian Feminist Law Journal*. Their research spans the fields of international human rights law and international economic law, with a particular focus on queer and feminist approaches to international law, alternative internationalisms and law and political economy. They have published on these topics in *Law and Critique*, the *London Review of International Law*, the *Melbourne Journal of International Law* and the *Modern Law Review*, amongst other journals. They are currently working on their monograph, *Consensus in International Law: Critical History, Queer Reimaginings*.

Tamsin Phillipa Paige (she/her) is Senior Lecturer with Deakin Law School, Australia, co-chair of the Australia and New Zealand Society of International Law Gender and Sexuality in International Law interest group and periodically consults for the UN Office on Drugs and Crime in relation to Maritime Crime. Her work is interdisciplinary in nature, using qualitative sociological methods to analyse international law. She also does law and literature research using popular fiction to understand social perceptions of the law. Her work has examined (among other things) Somali piracy,

UN Security Council decision-making and conflict-based sexual violence. In a former life, she was a French-trained, fine dining pâtissier.

Danish Sheikh (he/they/no pronouns) is an activist-lawyer, playwright and lecturer at the La Trobe Law School, Australia. Danish's research focuses on the legal regulation of sexuality and gender identity and, conversely, how queer persons reshape the law through creative forms of resistance. In approaching these questions, Danish draws upon an array of methods from socio-legal scholarship and theatre and performance studies. A parallel strand of his research explores legal pedagogy, examining the training offered in the law school through the methods and materials that we use to teach and write and how that training might be approached differently. His first book, *Love and Reparation*, restaged the Section 377 litigation in India, blending courtroom transcripts with archival research and personal memoir. His research has been cited by the Supreme Court of India in its decision to decriminalise homosexuality and has also won multiple awards, including the Law, Literature and Humanities Association of Australasia's Early Career Researcher Article Prize in 2023 and the Melbourne Law School Graduate Student Research Prize in 2022.

Joanne Stagg (she/her) is a lecturer in the Griffith Law School at Griffith University, Australia. In addition to teaching core Torts and Contract courses, she designed and teaches Gender and the Law. Her current research interests include issues around law, gender and medicine. She is being lured into the international law community via research collaborations based on applying queer and feminist theory to queer issues and to the UN's Women, Peace and Security agenda.

Ruby Rosselle L. Tugade (she/her) is a lecturer in the University of the Philippines College of Law and the Ateneo de Manila University Department of Political Science, teaching international law, human rights, politics, legal method and legal ethics. She is also a practicing lawyer in the field of international criminal law and international human rights.

Cris van Eijk (he/him) is a Northern Bridge doctoral candidate at Newcastle University, United Kingdom. His research questions what it means to make space 'common' and how international law attempts to do so – which, it turns out, involves looking queerly at history with silly/disruptive questions. He holds a BA and LLM in Public International Law from Leiden University and a BA in Law from the University of Cambridge.

Acknowledgments

This book was edited on the stolen lands of the Wurundjeri People (in Naarm/Melbourne) and the Ngambri and Ngunnawal people (in Canberra) on the continent that many now call Australia. We acknowledge that the sovereignty of Aboriginal people over these lands and waters was never ceded, and we pay our respects to their elders, past and present.

This book was made possible by the dreaming, curiosity and critical thinking of the contributors. We are grateful for their enthusiastic engagement in this collective journey, as well as their timeliness and responsiveness to feedback, especially when our deadlines became stricter than expected. We also thank Dianne Otto for building this scholarly community and acting as a guiding light to us all as we explore new intellectual frontiers. In addition, we wish to thank all of the anonymous peer reviewers for their time and efforts – you are as much a part of this project and community as the contributors.

Thanks are also due to our excellent research assistant, Adrienne Ringin, whose attention to detail and copy-editing skills are what got this book and its queer sibling, *Queer Encounters with International Law: Lives, Communities, Subjectivities*, over the line by the due date. We are grateful to Deakin Law School for making Adrienne's research assistance possible.

This book and its sibling book originated with a workshop, *Queering International Law 2.0*, which the editors convened at Deakin Downtown in Melbourne in November 2022 with the generous financial support of Deakin Law School, the Institute for International Law and the Humanities (IILAH) at Melbourne Law School and La Trobe Law School. We are thankful to Jessica Costanzo (Deakin), Hayley Taylor (Deakin), Liz Nguyen (Deakin), Angela Hendley-Boys (Melbourne), Virginia Versace (La Trobe) and Amber Treseder Fitts (La Trobe) for all their help arranging the catering, brochures, travel bursaries, dinner booking, gifts and more. We could not have done it without you.

We gratefully acknowledge the contributions at the workshop. In particular, we thank those who presented papers for discussion that did not appear in these two edited books: Danny Bradley (MADRE), Lisa Davis (CUNY) and Iram Khan (South Asian University). We are also grateful to those who acted as discussants at the workshop: Holly Cullen (University of Western Australia and Deakin University), Maria Elander (La Trobe University), Julia Dehm (La Trobe University), Emma Genovese (University of Technology Sydney), Fleur Johns (University of New South Wales), Melanie O'Brien (University of Western Australia) and Honni van Rijswijk (University of Technology Sydney). In addition, we thank LJ Maher (University of Melbourne) for her delightful, queer poetry readings during the workshop.

Finally, we thank our partners, Melissa Kennedy and Daniel Myles, for their unwavering patience and support during this journey.

Foreword

Many before us have aspired to and struggled for emancipatory change in the conceptual architecture of international law, as well as in its practice. Postcolonial, feminist, Indigenous, TWAIL, critical race, Marxist and redistributive scholars and activists, amongst others, have all found ways to trouble the law's edifice and its many claims to foster international peace and global well-being. As I have discovered, these earlier efforts have left behind remnants or footholds in the law for us to (re)discover and reclaim in our efforts to recraft international law's adjudication of the 'normal' that stubbornly repeats and re-legitimates its hierarchies and violences. Separately and more powerfully together, the enduring fragments of these legacies of resistance have always offered me hope that deep change to the normal of international law may yet be possible.

As I write these words in early 2024, on the unceded lands of the Wurundjeri People of the Kulin Nation, keeping this hopefulness alive has become more difficult, as I'm sure it has for many others. But *Queer Engagements with International Law* and its sibling volume, *Queer Encounters with International Law*, have revived my optimism. The contributors remind me that it is not only possible but also imperative that we find ways to survive the lethal legacies – the wreckage – of contemporary international law and build a different kind of law capable of supporting a radically different world.

Doggedly moving against the grain of international law, the authors further enrich and empower our movements towards a post-normal kind of law, fostering new insights and energies and, especially, new solidarities. With the aid of queer theory and/or methodology, the accepted underpinnings, naturalised assumptions and normal practices of law are disrupted. Queer curiosity reveals the assemblages of cisheteronormativity that have served as the bedrock for the development of what passes as international legal rules and processes today. The false promises of the supposedly neutral and impartial conceptual structures of normal law are exposed, and the biases of its accepted practices of adjudication are made visible. From many vantage points, the queer gaze shakes the foundations of several bodies of settled law, including those concerning the environment, oceans, outer space, cultural heritage, international crime and empire, and troubles the justice promised by methods of legal interpretation, categorisation, judgment and education. More fluid and locally responsive legal imaginaries are fostered, inspiring transformative legal languages and practices aimed at ensuring that all life matters.

The resulting collection, with authors united in their determination to persist against the odds, is a cause for celebration in these bleak times. Queerly re-making international law challenges us all to dive into the wreck of false promises, hollow aspirations and broken commitments and bring to the surface the 'ab-normal' – those memories and knowledges of demonised communities and peoples that have been silenced and dismissed by those with power. Responding to injustice may necessitate law's fragmentation, contingency and instability because these are characteristics of life itself, and we deny life and its manifold possibilities by aiming to expunge or discipline this cacophony into homogeneous hierarchical order. We need to accept that what results may not be recognisable as law as we know it.

Dear readers, please join me in celebrating this gift of intrepid queer tenacity and the hope that fuels it. Together, we must dive deeply into the wreck and believe in the possibility of surfacing with the remnants of past struggles, which are now, for us, the treasure of new imaginaries of justice.

Dianne Otto
Professorial Fellow
Melbourne Law School

Chapter 1

Reaching Out Towards the Horizon

Queer Engagements with International Law Beyond Queer Theory's Site of Origin

Claerwen O'Hara and Tamsin Phillipa Paige

1. Unmooring Queer Theory from Its Home Base of Gender and Sexuality

For some time now, queer theorists and legal scholars who think with queer theory have been fascinated by the question: *what happens when queer theory moves out of its home base of gender and sexuality?*[1] This interest in moving beyond queer theory's site of origin is perhaps unsurprising given that queer theory has a long history of resisting confinement, critiquing from its beginning identarian and binary thinking and challenging disciplinary boundaries as it did so. Queer theory first emerged in the early 1990s as a critical response to a tendency in gay and lesbian studies and some strands of feminist theory to treat sexual and gender categories, such as 'homosexual' or 'woman', as innate and natural.[2] Would-be and early queer theorists saw this tendency as limiting the potential for radical change and began pouring their efforts into challenging assumptions about 'normal' and 'valid' constructions of gender and sexuality instead.[3] In this context, queer theorists contested the binaries of heterosexual/homosexual and man/woman and embraced a fluid and open understanding of 'queer'. As Eve Kosofsky Sedgwick put it in 1993:

> That's one of the things that 'queer' can refer to: the open mesh of possibilities, gaps, overlaps, dissonances and resonances, lapses and excesses

1 See, for example, Oishik Sircar and Dipika Jain, "New Intimacies/Old Desires: Law, Culture and Queer Politics in Neoliberal Times," *Jindal Global Law Review* 4, no. 1 (2012): 1–16, 3, in which Sircar and Jain, paraphrasing Janet Halley, ask: 'what happens to queer identity when it moves out of its home base of sexuality?'.

2 Martha Albertson Fineman, "Introduction: Feminist and Queer Legal Theory," in *Feminist and Queer Legal Theory: Intimate Encounters, Uncomfortable Conversations*, eds. Martha Albertson Fineman, Jack E. Jackson and Adam P. Romero (Surrey and Burlington: Ashgate, 2009), 4–5.

3 Claerwen O'Hara, "Queering the International Human Rights Framework Pertaining to Sexuality: Toward the Right to Relate," in *Worldwide Perspectives on Lesbians, Gays and Bisexuals*, ed. Paula Gerber, vol. 2 (Santa Barbara: Praeger, 2021), 61.

DOI: 10.4324/9781032645339-1

> of meaning when the constituent elements of anyone's gender, of anyone's sexuality aren't made (or can't be made) to signify monolithically.[4]

With its orientation now toward an 'open mesh of possibilities', queer theory itself opted to 'resist definition'.[5] Queer theorists described themselves as less interested in questions of what queer theory *is* and more interested in what queer theories *do*.[6] This focus on the 'doing' opened up the possibility of queer theory being applied to new topics. By the mid-1990s, Katherine Gibson and Julie Graham, who co-authored under the pen name J.K. Gibson-Graham, were drawing on insights from queer theory in the context of economic geography by relating what they called 'capitalocentrism' (a mode of thinking that privileges capitalist sites over non-capitalist ones) to heteronormativity.[7] Gibson-Graham argued that, just as many people would feel uncomfortable describing a particular country as 'heterosexual', notwithstanding the dominance of heterosexuality within that country, so too should we feel uncomfortable describing a country as 'capitalist', as such a description can erase a great many non-capitalist practices that continue to exist throughout the world, from housework to hunting to gift giving.

So what, then, can queer theories do that makes them applicable – even useful – beyond the context of gender and sexuality? What enabled Gibson-Graham to make this move? Given the plural and unfinished nature of queer thinking, it would not be very queer of us to use this introduction to seek to enumerate exhaustively all the things that queer theories can do. So, instead, we will focus on two things which are useful both within and beyond conversations about gender and sexuality. The first is queer theory's ability to 'make strange' ideas and practices considered to be 'the normal, the legitimate, the dominant'.[8] The second is its ability to prompt us to read for 'difference rather than dominance',[9] helping to reveal the alterity that may lie beneath a dominant practice or idea.

Let us begin with queer theory's capacity to make the normal seem strange. Originally meaning 'strange' or 'odd', 'queer' was once used as a pejorative

4 Eve Kosofsky Sedgwick, *Tendencies* (Durham: Duke University Press, 1993), 9.
5 Craig Gingrich-Philbrook, "Queer Theory and Performance," *Journal of Homosexuality* 45, no. 2 (2003): 353.
6 See, for example, Nikki Sullivan, *A Critical Introduction to Queer Theory* (Edinburgh: Edinburgh University Press, 2003), vi.
7 J.K. Gibson-Graham, *The End of Capitalism (As We Knew It): A Feminist Critique of Political Economy*, 2nd ed. (Minneapolis: University of Minnesota Press, 2006; first published 1996); J.K. Gibson-Graham, "Queer(y)Ing Capitalism in and Out of the Classroom," *Journal of Geography in Higher Education* 23, no. 1 (1999): 80.
8 David M. Halperin, *Saint Foucault: Towards a Gay Hagiography* (Oxford and New York: Oxford University Press, 1995), 62.
9 J.K. Gibson-Graham, *A Postcapitalist Politics* (Minneapolis: University of Minnesota Press, 2006), xxxi–xxxii.

term to describe people who engaged in sex and relationships with people of the same gender.[10] In the late 1980s and early 1990s, direct-action groups in the US, such as ACT-UP (AIDS Coalition to Unleash Power) and Queer Nation, began reclaiming the term 'queer' as a way to celebrate the anti-normal.[11] Queer theorists soon followed suit with the adoption of the term 'queer theory' in 1991.[12] Having embraced strangeness for themselves, queer theorists and activists then set about projecting ideas of strangeness back onto the 'normal', particularly as it applied to ideas about gender and sexuality. 'To queer', as a verb, came to mean 'to make strange, to frustrate, to counteract, to delegitimise, to camp up . . . heteronormative knowledges and institutions, and the subjectivities and socialities that are (in)formed by them and that (in)form them'.[13]

An early example of this mode of queering can be found in Eve Kosofsky Sedgwick's reflection on the strangeness of Western society's designation of gender as the defining feature of human sexuality:

> It is a rather amazing fact that, of the very many dimensions along which the genital activity of one person can be differentiated from that of another . . . , precisely one, the gender object of choice, emerged from the turn of the century, and has remained as the dimension noted by the now ubiquitous category of 'sexual orientation'.[14]

Another example is Judith Butler's argument that gender itself is an act or performance[15] and that the 'gender-bending art form'[16] of drag can be used to subvert this system of performativity by reflecting and undermining 'the mundane impersonations by which heterosexually ideal genders are performed and naturalized'.[17]

10 Lena Holzer et al., "An Introduction to International Law Dis/Oriented: Sparking Queer Futures in International Law," *Australian Feminist Law Journal* 49, no. 1 (2023): 5.
11 O'Hara, "Queering the International Human Rights Framework Pertaining to Sexuality," 61.
12 Teresa de Lauretis was the first person to use the term 'queer theory' in Teresa De Lauretis, "Queer Theory: Lesbian and Gay Sexualities An Introduction," *Differences* 3, no. 2 (1991): iii–xviii.
13 Sullivan, *A Critical Introduction to Queer Theory*, vi.
14 Eve Kosofsky Sedgwick, *Epistemology of the Closet*, 1st ed. (Berkeley: University of California Press, 2008), 8.
15 Judith Butler, *Gender Trouble: Feminism and the Subversion of Identity* (Abingdon and New York: Routledge, 1990).
16 "What Is Drag? A Primer on Drag Queens in Popular Culture," *MasterClass*, June 8, 2021, www.masterclass.com/articles/a-primer-on-drag-queens-in-popular-culture. This is the definition used by Claerwen O'Hara and Cris van Eijk, "On Straightening and Subversion: A Queer Feminist Exploration of International Space Law and Politics," this volume.
17 Judith Butler, *Bodies That Matter: On the Discursive Limits of Sex* (Abingdon and New York: Routledge, 2011), 243.

However, the idea of making the normal seem strange need not be limited to issues of gender and sexuality. This is because it can present an effective way to *dislodge* and *denaturalise* ideas that are taken for granted, whatever they may be, thereby facilitating critique and opening up alternative possibilities. Or, as Holzer, Schramm, Santos de Carvalho and Beury put it, 'making strange' can function as a general tool for 'dis-/re-orientation', in which, '[t]he familiar becomes strange' and the '[once-]strange becomes a new compass sparking new paths ahead'.[18]

For this reason, it should perhaps come as no surprise that 'making strange' is already a technique used by international legal scholars working with other critical theories, such as Marxian and Third World Approaches to International Law (TWAIL), albeit sometimes less explicit ways than in queer approaches. In her 2021 article, 'The Specter of Eurocentrism in International Legal History', for example, Ntina Tzouvala describes her aim as 'to *make strange something very familiar* to everyone in the field of international legal history' – the idea that 'Eurocentrism is a common and effective charge against one's intellectual opponents'.[19] Tzouvala then sets about achieving this aim by demonstrating how the term 'Eurocentrism' 'remains open-ended, and no amount of technically impeccable scholarly work can concretize its meaning'.[20] Likewise, in their 2022 article, 'Picturing Pedagogy: Images, Teaching, and Development', Jeremy Baskin and Sundhya Pahuja reflect 'on the way that teaching with images can help to *make strange the taken-for-granted*', their goal being 'not only to help students to think critically about the development project, but also to think about how they can develop ways of engaging with the world that are reflexive about both power and the politics of distribution'.[21] These two examples show that there is no single way to go about making the familiar seem odd, but instead, a range of tools and techniques, from demonstrating the emptiness or fluidity of a term to using images within the text-heavy discipline of international law.[22]

18 Holzer et al., "An Introduction," 8.
19 Ntina Tzouvala, "The Specter of Eurocentrism in International Legal History," *Yale Journal of Law & The Humanities* 31, no. 2 (2021): 416 [emphasis added].
20 Tzouvala, "The Specter of Eurocentrism," 416.
21 Jeremy Baskin and Sundhya Pahuja, "Picturing Pedagogy: Images, Teaching, and Development," *Osgoode Hall Law Journal* 59, no. 1 (2022): 80 [emphasis added].
22 For a similar use of image in the specific context of queer theory and international law, see, for example, Aeyal Gross, "Post/Colonial Queer Globalisation and International Human Rights: Images of LGBT Rights," *Jindal Global Law Review* 4, no. 2 (2013): 98–130. Other techniques for 'making strange' include emphasising context and contingency through a turn to history, providing a diversity of perspectives so as to disrupt the sense of a singular narrative and rendering visible and unsettling dominant narratives through recourse to film and literature, see Claerwen O'Hara, "On Making Law Strange and Other Pedagogical Lessons from Queer Theory," Paper presented at *Australasian Law Academics Association Conference: Evolution or Revolution? Challenging Legal Education and Scholarship*, Monash University,

Similarly, self-described queer engagements with international law that seek to make the normal seem strange have not only been concerned with the way international law constructs gender and sexuality or affects the lives of queer people – although this has been, and continues to be, an important use of queer theory, as our sibling edited collection, *Queer Encounters with International Law: Lives, Communities, Subjectivities*, shows. International legal scholars who think with queer theory have also sought to 'make strange' other objects or modes of thinking. On some occasions, the strangeness has been to reveal the hetero- or cis-normative thinking embedded in a particular idea or legal principle that, at first glance, seems to have little to do with gender or sexuality. As Dianne Otto explains in the introduction to her 2018 edited collection, *Queering International Law: Possibilities, Alliances, Complicities, Risks:*

> Just as feminist curiosity exposed international law's gendered framework, and postcolonial curiosity its European underpinnings, queer curiosity makes visible its [hetero]sexual ordering that is so taken for granted that it is considered 'natural'.[23]

An example of this mode of 'making strange' can be found in Otto's own work revealing how the nation-state is legally 'organised along the grid-lines of (patriarchal) heterosexual kinship relationships'[24] – from the international legal requirement that a state must have a permanent population to domestic systems of birth, sex and marriage registration.

On other occasions, the lens of strangeness has been applied to topics of international law that do not necessarily have a direct connection to hetero- or cis-normative thinking. An example is Claerwen's use of queer theory to 'make strange' the claims of sameness and agreement in the World Trade Organisation's (WTO) origin story and critique the intolerance of economic difference that such claims have generated.[25] While international trade law

Melbourne, July 7–9, 2022. For an example of the use of film to make the normal – in this case, the masculine gaze – seem strange, see Emma Genovese and Tamsin Phillipa Paige's "Life as Distinct from Patriarchal Influence: Exploring Queerness and Freedom through Portrait of a Lady on Fire," *Australian Feminist Law Journal* 50, no. 1 (2024). See also Tamsin Phillipa Paige, "'The Whore that Lost Everything': The Tyranny of Law and the Queer Feminisation of Soft Power as Explored in Black Sails," *Pólemos* 17, no. 2 (2023): 415–429, for the use of a television series to denaturalise and 'make strange' law and power relations.

23 Dianne Otto, "Introduction: Embracing Queer Curiosity," in *Queering International Law: Possibilities, Alliances, Complicities, Risks*, ed. Dianne Otto (Abingdon and New York: Routledge, 2018), 2.

24 Dianne Otto, "Resisting the Heteronormative Imaginary of the Nation-State: Rethinking Kinship and Border Protection," in *Queering International Law: Possibilities, Alliances, Complicities, Risks* (Abingdon and New York: Routledge, 2018), 241.

25 Claerwen O'Hara, "Consensus and Diversity in the World Trade Organization: A Queer Perspective," *AJIL Unbound* 116 (2022): 32–27.

does affect the way gender and sexuality are constructed, as well as the lives and health of queer people,[26] the object of strangeness in this particular work are the *economic* and *institutional* narratives surrounding the WTO rather than 'traditionally' queer issues.

Another way that queer theory can be applied beyond the context of gender and sexuality is through its capacity to prompt us to read for 'difference rather than dominance'. In addition to denaturalising the taken-for-granted, queer theory has long sought to reveal alterity and attend to the ways of doing and being of the Other. When queer theory first emerged, it was alterity in the context of sexuality and gender that it sought to make visible and the 'sexual subaltern'[27] upon whom it set its gaze. However, by the time Gibson-Graham coined the phrase 'reading for difference rather than dominance' in 2006, it was to describe their attempts to 'queer' the *economy* by looking beyond the hegemony of neoliberal capitalism to reveal the economic diversity that continues to exist throughout the world.[28]

Since then, there have been many attempts to use queer theory to draw our attention to forms of otherness that are not necessarily or primarily defined by gender or sexuality. One example is Doris Buss and Blair Rutherford's work casting the artisanal and small-scale miner as a queer figure and mining 'outlaw', whose practices are framed as a perversion against the norm of 'industrial' mining.[29] Another is Ilan Kapoor's article, 'The Queer Third World', which seeks to align the queer and Third World projects by pointing out that 'both result from the same orientalist hetero-normative discourse'[30] and 'operate from the margins, questioning normalising power mechanisms and social order, while upholding a deviant, non-conformist and non-assimilationist politics'.[31] In this piece, Kapoor then goes on to sketch a 'queer Third World' politics by calling for the Global South to revisit 'its

26 Claerwen O'Hara, "Queer Approaches to International Economic Law," in *Elgar Encyclopedia of International Economic Law: Expanded Edition*, ed. Krista Nadakavukaren Schefer and Thomas Cottier (Cheltenham: Edward Elgar, forthcoming 2024).

27 The term 'sexual subaltern' was coined by Ratna Kapur. See Ratna Kapur, "Law and the Sexual Subaltern: A Comparative Perspective," *Cleveland State Law Review* 48, no. 1 (2000): 15–23; Ratna Kapur, "Post-Colonial Economies of Desire: Legal Representations of the Sexual Subaltern," *Denver University Law Review* 78, no. 4 (2001): 855.

28 In their 2006 introduction to *A Postcapitalist Politics*, Gibson-Graham used this phrase to describe their method in *The End of Capitalism (As We Knew It): A Feminist Critique of Political Economy*, see Gibson-Graham, *A Postcapitalist Politics*, xxxi–xxxii.

29 Doris E. Buss and Blair Rutherford, "'Dangerous Desires': Illegality, Sexuality and the Global Governance of Artisanal Mining," in *Queering International Law: Possibilities, Alliances, Complicities, Risks*, ed. Dianne Otto (Abingdon, NY: Routledge, 2018), 35–52. However, note that Buss and Rutherford are still attentive to how sexual discourses help to render the small-scale and artisanal miner as Other.

30 Ilan Kapoor, "The Queer Third World," *Third World Quarterly* 36, no. 9 (2015): 1619.

31 Kapoor, "The Queer Third World," 1612.

political roots in non-alignment'[32] and embrace a position of difference so as to denaturalise the prevailing global economic system.

The chapters in this book continue this rich practice of applying queer theory beyond its home base of gender and sexuality. However, for the first time, they are not intermingled with other works that make a return back to queer theory's site of origin. Rather, this book constitutes the first collection in which *all* of the contributions take as their immediate object of inquiry or critique something other than gender, sexuality or queer communities, marking an important turning point in queer (legal) theory.

This is not to say that issues of gender and sexuality are absent from the collection. Far from it, analogies with gender and sexual diversity are used throughout the book to interrogate dominant understandings of international law and reveal alternative possibilities. Some of the chapters also take up the strategy of making the normal seem strange by rendering visible the gendered and heteronormative thinking that underpins a given legal concept or body of law that, at first, seems to have little to do with gender or sexuality, such as the militaristic and extractivist imaginaries that have framed human encounters with outer space,[33] or the neo-colonial practices of the United States' military empire.[34] Nevertheless, in all of the chapters, what is being 'queered' – that is, made strange or read for difference rather than dominance (or subjected to some other form of queering) – are not constructions of gender or sexuality themselves, but other concepts, logics or structures of power. In this way, this book can be seen as a celebration of the spirit of freedom and creativity that has informed queer theory from its beginning and which continues to grow – out towards the horizon.

2. Coming to This Collection

This book emerged from a two-day workshop held at Deakin Downtown in Melbourne, Australia, in November 2022 entitled *Queering International Law 2.0*. We organised this workshop from within the Gender, Sexuality and International Law Interest Group of the Australian and New Zealand Society of International Law (ANZSIL), of which we were and continue to be (at the time of writing) co-chairs. The workshop was generously funded by Deakin Law School, the Institute for International Law and the Humanities (IILAH) at Melbourne Law School and La Trobe Law School.

As the name '2.0' suggests, the idea for this workshop came from an earlier workshop convened by Dianne Otto in 2015 which went on to produce the

32 Kapoor, "The Queer Third World," 1621.

33 O'Hara and Van Eijk, "On Straightening and Subversion."

34 Ruby Rosselle "Ross" Tugade, "The Filipina in the Shadows of International Law: A Case Study of Philippine Court Decisions," this volume.

first book focused solely on queer approaches to international law: *Queering International Law: Possibilities, Alliance, Complicities, Risks*.[35] In our '2.0' workshop, we sought to revisit the project of queering international law, with a particular focus on changes that had occurred in international law in the seven years that had passed since Otto's foundational 2015 workshop, as well as the possibilities, alliances, complicities and risks held out by international law's future. We invited submissions from new and established scholars working with queer, feminist and postcolonial theories and practices in international law and related disciplines.

The interest in our call for papers far exceeded our expectations. At one point, we even looked into extending the workshop by a day to try to accommodate more papers, but unfortunately, we could not due to booking and funding constraints. In the end, scholars from across Australia, Brazil, France, India, Italy, the Philippines, Singapore, Switzerland, Thailand, the United Kingdom and the United States participated, and there were so many interesting papers that we were able to put together two different book proposals. And so came about this collection and its sibling collection, *Queer Encounters with International Law: Lives, Communities, Subjectivities*. Although separate entities, for us, the two books remain connected through the bonds of queer kinship – two genderqueer 'chosen' siblings who, while having slightly different conversations, continue to refer to one another and cannot be fully known or understood in the absence of the other.

When we recall the context from which this book emerged, it is even more significant that all of its chapters apply queer theory to aspects of international law that are not solely, or even primarily, related to gender or sexuality. The fact that we were so easily able to find a book's worth of papers that used queer theory in this way from a workshop that did not have this as its specific focus is a testament to how the project of queering international law (and queering more generally) is changing. For at least half of the people that attended the workshop, queering constitutes a methodological approach with an inbuilt freedom that can be used to question and unpack a range of topics beyond queer theory's site of origin.

Indeed, the idea that we should be queering more than just constructions of gender and sexuality played into the organisation and running of the workshop itself. We were not the first to seek to apply insights from queer theory to an academic workshop or even an academic workshop specifically focused on international law. A year before our workshop, in 2021, Bérénice K. Schramm, Juliana Santos de Carvalho, Lena Holzer and Manon Beury, supported by the Graduate Institute of Geneva, had organised a virtual workshop entitled, *International Law Dis/Oriented: Queer Legacies and*

35 Dianne Otto, ed., *Queering International Law: Possibilities, Alliances, Complicities, Risks* (Abingdon and New York: Routledge, 2018).

Queer Futures, which we both attended; Claerwen as a presenter and Tamsin as a discussant. This workshop later produced a special issue in the *Australian Feminist Law Journal*.[36]

In the lead-up to *International Law Dis/Oriented*, Schramm, Santos de Carvalho, Holzer and Beury thought deeply about how to queer the academic workshop, holding multiple Zoom discussions with potential participants and scholars involved in the field and reflecting on the process through an article in *AJIL Unbound*.[37] For them, queering an academic event meant both creating a 'site of collective contestation'[38] to disrupt and challenge the normal practices of legal academia, and creating an 'everyday utopia' in which the networks and spaces that constitute daily life could be performed in 'a radically different fashion'.[39] In these two gestures, we see both modes of queering described earlier at work: queering as contesting and 'making strange' the normal,[40] and queering as prioritising radical difference over dominance.[41]

Inspired by these efforts, we too sought to queer our Melbourne-based workshop, from adopting COVID-safe measures when these had fallen out of favour in legal academia (despite still being needed)[42] to scheduling poetry and play readings during the academic proceedings as a way to play with genre and allow creativity and emotion in. In the final chapter of this book, 'Repairing (The) International Law (Conference): The Affordances of Theatre', Danish Sheikh reflects on how the reading of his play, *Contempt*, at the workshop represented another form of queering – 'repair' work[43] – and how

36 "International Law Dis/oriented: Sparking Queer Futures in International Law," eds. Manon Beury, Lena Holzer, Juliana Santos de Carvalho and Bérénice K. Schramm, *Australian Feminist Law Journal*, 49, no. 1 (2023).

37 Bérénice K. Schramm et al., "Doing Queer in the Everyday of Academia: Reflections on Queering a Conference in International Law," *AJIL Unbound* 116 (2022).

38 Schramm et al., "Doing Queer in the Everyday of Academia," 17.

39 Schramm et al., "Doing Queer in the Everyday of Academia," 17. Here, Schramm et al. are drawing on Davina Cooper, *Everyday Utopias: The Conceptual Life of Promising Spaces* (Durham, NC: Duke University Press, 2013).

40 In seeking to make their conference a 'site of collective contestation', Schramm et al. note that they 'were particularly interested in queer theory's radical potential to destabilize the normal'; see Schramm et al., "Doing Queer in the Everyday of Academia," 17.

41 Schramm et al. state, '[f]or us, queering the everyday practices of international lawyers—including scientific exchanges—meant imagining a utopian space where the process of knowledge production involves drawing on the *differences* and *multiplicity* of queer voices, approaches, and strategies in international law', Schramm et al., "Doing Queer in the Everyday of Academia," 17 [emphasis added].

42 In this way, we followed Schramm et al. in placing 'care at the core' of our queered workshop, prioritising '*caring* for ourselves, *caring* for each other and *caring* for our planet', see Schramm et al., "Doing Queer in the Everyday of Academia," 18 [emphasis in the original].

43 This form of queering is derived from Eve Kosofsky Sedgwick's notion of 'reparative reading', see Eve Kosofsky Sedgwick, "Paranoid Reading and Reparative Reading, or, You're So Paranoid, You Probably Think This Essay Is About You," in *Touching Feeling: Affect, Pedagogy, Performativity*, ed. Eve Kosofsky Sedgwick (Durham: Duke University Press, 2003).

the reparative ethos of this collective activity helped to build and nurture community.[44] In this way, our workshop (and academia more generally) became another topic not directly related to gender or sexuality to which we could apply queer theory, another object for queer experimentation and curiosity.[45]

3. The Structure of the Collection: On Times, Spaces and Imaginings

In moving beyond queer theory's site of origin, the chapters in this book broadly reflect on international law's times, spaces and imaginings. As such, we have broken the book into four parts, three of which correspond to these themes, followed by a final part, which reflects on queering international legal academia itself. However, in true queer form, the structure of the collection does not follow the order of the book's subtitle, beginning with a part on 'spaces' rather than 'times'. Many of the chapters in each part also engage in conversations that intersect with the themes of other parts. For example, the chapters in Part 1, which are focused on queering new spaces in international law, also pick up on themes of temporality and imagination. Nevertheless, we have sought to arrange the chapters in such a way as to highlight the new and exciting directions in which queer approaches to international law are traveling as they tackle topics beyond gender and sexuality.

Part 1 is entitled 'Queering New Spaces in International Law: The Environment, Oceans and Outer Space' and is concerned with applying insights from queer theory to areas of international law hitherto underexplored by this theoretical lens. We have framed this part around the idea of 'spaces' because the contributions within it take as their object concepts or entities traditionally thought of as open areas in this world or beyond it – specifically, the environment, the ocean(s) and outer space – in a way that often decentres humanity. However, it should be noted that, despite this framing, the contributors to Part 1 do not necessarily conceive of their objects as mere 'spaces'; instead, they queerly read subjectivity and agency into them. Part 1 begins with a chapter from Emily Jones, which applies queer theories of the nonhuman and kinship to international environmental law in a way that addresses critiques of the anthropocentric and heteronormative tendencies of this area of law. Jones argues in favour of international law embracing a queer notion of kinship, which centres around multiple human and nonhuman connections.

Jones' intervention is followed by Gina Heathcote's chapter focused on the ocean(s) – something traditionally thought of as a subset of the global 'environment'. Drawing on the hydrohumanities and critical ocean studies,

44 Danish Sheikh, "Repairing (The) International Law (Conference): The Affordances of Theatre," this volume.
45 On queer curiosity, see Otto, "Introduction: Embracing Queer Curiosity."

Heathcote accepts the ocean as agential and considers 'it as resolutely queer in its nonlinear temporality and fluid resistance/existence'.[46] Heathcote's chapter critiques how the regulation of 'ghost fleets' of automated naval vessels to date has reproduced colonial imaginaries and heteronormative statehood and juxtaposes this mode of thinking with indigenous and Pacific traditions of knowing the sea differently. In doing so, Heathcote hopes to provide new 'apertures for re-imagining legal subjectivity and, ultimately, international law'.[47] Part 1 concludes with a chapter by Claerwen O'Hara and Cris van Eijk on international space law. O'Hara and van Eijk begin with the proposition that outer space holds radical imaginative potential, arguing that, through its vastness, queerness and infinite diversity, outer space can 'help to disrupt human regimes of normativity and make earthly hierarchies seem small, strange, and irrelevant'.[48] At the same time, they obverse that the imaginary underlying international space law is strikingly limited, being structured around gendered, extractive and militarised logics with their roots in the Cold War. O'Hara and van Eijk argue the projection of dominant imaginaries onto outer space can be seen as an exercise in what Sara Ahmed would call 'straightening', aimed at bringing the disorienting, queer effects of space into line with earthly power relations. However, engaging with the work of Judith Butler, they also contend that the spectacular nature of this exercise can help to reveal power relations on Earth, opening up opportunities for subversion.

The book then moves onto the theme of time(s) in Part 2, which is entitled 'Queer Encounters with Temporality and Coloniality in International Law'. This part begins with a chapter from Vanja Hamzić, which seeks to disrupt the Western progress narratives that permeate histories of international law by reconceiving the past and future of international law in a temporal *otherwise* – that is, through a sense of time that is geontologically diverse and allows for the temporalities of multiple lifeworlds, including those that were distemporalised through colonial and capitalist forces and have since been 'forgotten' by international law. To do this, Hamzić focuses on 'proto-colonial' eighteenth-century Senegambia and the example of the gender-nonconforming Mande griots (*jeliw*), who, as storytellers, had as their chief domain temporality due to a social understanding of oral histories 'as both the history of today and the history of tomorrow'.[49] The *Jeliw* also performed a diplomatic and legal function by acting as negotiators and messengers between warring polities. Through this example, Hamzić advocates for a 'sustained, queerer focus on the local and the particular'[50] as a way to

46 Gina Heathcote, "Oceans versus Ghost Fleets," this volume.
47 Heathcote, "Oceans versus Ghost Fleets."
48 O'Hara and Van Eijk, "On Straightening and Subversion."
49 Vanja Hamzić, "International Law, Coloniality and the Temporal Otherwise," this volume.
50 Hamzić, "International Law, Coloniality and the Temporal Otherwise."

challenge the dominant past and trouble what or who is rendered 'recent', and what or who 'distant' in international law.

This is followed by a chapter from Lucas Lixinski, which seeks to queer an area of international law deeply informed by time and our relationship(s) to history: international cultural heritage law. Lixinski does this by explaining how he went about rewriting the International Criminal Court's decision in *Prosecutor v Al Mahdi*,[51] which addressed the destruction of cultural heritage, for the 'queer judgments project'.[52] Lixinski's queer re-imagining of international cultural heritage law understands heritage not as a thing but as an affective relationship, which matters to communities first and foremost. As such, his rewritten judgment sought to recentre the voices and lived experiences of the local community affected by the destruction of the cultural heritage in question. Lixinski also suggests that the experience of rewriting a judgment from a queer perspective forces normative commitments that can further the influence of queer insights for the practice of international law. Part 2 concludes with a chapter from Ruby Rosselle L. Tugade, which engages with issues of temporality and coloniality through an examination of Philippine court decisions concerning violence against women and queer people by United States military officers. Tugade troubles the idea of colonisation as a thing of the past by showing how these cases bring 'to the fore the continuing struggle of the Filipina beneath the shadows of the United States' military empire'[53] Tugade's chapter also highlights the gendered and sexual nature of this form of (neo)colonialism, arguing that 'part of what fuels modern-day conquest is the subjugation of bodies in the post-colony'.[54]

In Part 3, we move onto the theme of international law's imaginaries, with a particular focus on its myths and methods.[55] Beginning with its myths, Part 3 opens with a chapter from Caitlin Biddolph challenging international criminal law's claim to bring 'certainty' to situations of violence. Biddolph does so by engaging in a queer reading of the International Criminal Tribunal for the former Yugoslavia (ICTY), which allows her to reveal and revel in the uncertain, the paradoxical and the contingent practices of international criminal law. Her chapter destabilises the assumed certainties of the law/violence

51 Judgment and Sentence, *Prosecutor v Al Mahdi*, International Criminal Court Trial Chamber VIII, ICC-01/12–01/15 (September 27, 2016). See also 'Reparations Order,' *Prosecutor v Al Mahdi*, International Criminal Court Trial Chamber VIII, ICC-01/12–01/15 (August 17, 2017); and Judgment on the appeal of the victims against the 'Reparations Order', *Prosecutor v Al Mahdi*, International Criminal Court Appeals Chamber, ICC-01/12–01/15 A (March 8, 2018).

52 Nuno Ferreira, Maria F. Moscati and Senthorun Raj, eds., *Queer Judgments* (Coventry: Counterpress, forthcoming 2024).

53 Tugade, "The Filipina in the Shadows of International Law."

54 Tugade, "The Filipina in the Shadows of International Law."

55 This part is entitled 'Queering International Law's Imaginaries: Reflections on Legal Myths and Methods'.

binary and the straight, cis-gender legal subject, among others. By embracing the certain and the uncertain, Biddolph re-imagines international law as a site that is violent but can be animated by queerness. Next up, we have a chapter from Cris van Eijk, which engages in a similar queering of (un)certainty in international law, but this time in relation to its interpretive methods. More specifically, van Eijk attempts to understand what *travaux préparatoires* (a term usually used to refer to negotiation records) is and does as a tool of treaty interpretation from the perspective of queer theory. Asking a series of questions about the normative boundaries of *travaux préparatoires*, van Eijk shows how 'these "rules" are at best ambiguous, often obscure and at times even absurd'.[56] However, in his account, this is not necessarily a problem. Rather, van Eijk is of the view that we should openly embrace the messy fluidity that is *travaux préparatoires*.

Part 3 ends with another chapter on legal methods and international law – this time, one by Joanne Stagg focused on queer judging. For Stagg, '[a] judge does not need to be a member of the QUILTBAG+[57] community to engage in queer judging'.[58] Instead, queer judging involves 'applying the methods and spirit of queer theory to the process of judging' by, *inter alia*, 'valuing non-normative members of society, challenging cis-heteronormative thinking, re-evaluating the place of emotion in public life, and prioritising justice over form'.[59] Stagg then goes on to detail what this might look like in the context of international law, focusing on the two main models of judicial decision-making in this field: consensus and dissensus models of judging.

The final part of the book, Part 4, is entitled 'Queering Ourselves: Experimenting with Genre in Legal Academia' and consists only of Danish Sheikh's chapter. As noted above, in this chapter, Sheikh reflects on how the reading of his play, *Contempt*, helped to queer the workshop that led to this collection (and its sibling, *Queer Encounters with International Law: Lives, Communities, Subjectivities*) by allowing emotions and vulnerability into an academic space, thereby facilitating the participants' ability to inhabit reparative positions. Sheikh concludes that genre experiments with academic forms, such as theatre, could ultimately help us to build and nurture a more collegial scholarly community.

56 Cris van Eijk, "Uncloseting *Travaux*," this volume.
57 Queer, undecided, intersex, lesbian, trans, bisexual, asexual, gay/genderqueer plus.
58 Joanne Stagg, "Queer Judging, Straight Up: The Queer Judge and Judicial Systems," this volume.
59 Stagg, "Queer Judging, Straight Up."

Part 1

Queering New Spaces in International Law: The Environment, Oceans and Outer Space

Chapter 2

Challenging International Environmental Law's Heteronormativity and Anthropocentrism

Towards Queer Kinship

Emily Jones[1]

1. Introduction

This chapter applies queer theories of the nonhuman and of kinship to international environmental law, proposing an alternative vision of the subject of international environmental law, one that transcends the subject/object binary. International environmental law has been critiqued for being anthropocentric, centring the human subject and prioritising elite human interests. This anthropocentrism ultimately renders international environmental law ineffective at providing the solutions needed to tackle environmental degradation adequately. International environmental law also contains certain heteronormative values, this being exemplified by the idea that the law should protect the environment for the sake of future generations – a concept that imagines the future of humanity and the entire world as being in the hands of human children, centring human reproductive futures.

Queer theories of the nonhuman argue that queer subjects have never had full access to the category of 'humanity', often being marked as inhuman or less-than-human. Links are subsequently drawn in this body of thought between the inhuman queer subject and scholarship that examines the less-than-human status of other human subjects, drawing on Black and postcolonial studies, crip theory and feminist theory. Queer theories of the nonhuman also highlight the links between the inhuman queer subject and the subjugated status of many nonhuman subjects, including the environment

1 Thank you to everyone at the Queering International Law 2.0 Workshop held in Melbourne in November 2022 for their comments and feedback, with special thanks to Julia Dehm for her insightful feedback as my panel's respondent. Thank you also to Rahul Rao for his comments on an earlier draft of this chapter and to my anonymous peer reviewer for their extremely helpful feedback. With thanks to Ronit Matar for her invaluable research assistance when finalising this chapter. Finally, a big thank you must go to the collection editors, Tamsin Phillipa Paige and Claerwen O'Hara. Thank you, not only for the useful feedback on my chapter but also for fostering an important and nurturing space for us to think together.

DOI: 10.4324/9781032645339-3

and nonhuman animals. These theories thereby call for the nonhuman to be embraced, arguing for the need to re-centre nonhuman subjects while holding the question of the nonhuman alongside the continued need to tackle inequalities between humans. However, until now, most queer theories of the nonhuman have remained within the theoretical realm, primarily emerging from philosophy and literary studies. This chapter applies these theories to some of the core principles and ideas in international environmental law, focusing primarily on the subject of international environmental law.

In the meantime, kinship has long been a core concept in queer studies, where scholars argue for the need to move beyond heteronormative models of family, highlighting the importance of chosen family and solidarity beyond blood ties. This chapter puts the concept of queer kinship into conversation with queer theories of the nonhuman, calling for a post-anthropocentric queer model of kinship that embraces both human and nonhuman subjects. It is argued that this model of kinship, and the subject position it is based upon, can be used to queer international environmental law, in turn providing for a post-anthropocentric and less heteronormative basis for this body of law. Such a paradigm shift, it is argued, will be required if international environmental law is to tackle the core environmental challenges of our times adequately.

The chapter is organised as follows: first, an overview of the anthropocentrism that underlies international environmental law is provided. Given that this problem has already been extensively discussed in critical scholarship on international environmental law, this overview is brief, focusing on three main examples from international environmental law that subsequently become the central focus of the chapter. These examples are the principle of the common heritage of humankind, rights as applied to environmental issues – including human rights and the environment and the rights of nature – and the responsibility owed to future generations. These examples were chosen purposefully, with each having been framed in environmental law literature as potentially providing hope for addressing the urgent issues posed by environmental degradation. However, and as argued in this section, each of these examples is underpinned by anthropocentrism. Despite this, these examples were chosen as opposed to some of the more traditional, and traditionally critiqued, principles of international environmental law, such as the so-called 'uber' principle of sustainable development,[2] precisely because their framing provides some scope for re-imagining international

2 Stephen Humphreys and Yoriko Otomo, "Theorizing International Environmental Law," in *The Oxford Handbook of the Theory of International Law*, eds. Anne Orford and Florian Hoffman (Oxford: Oxford University Press, 2016), 800. For critiques see: S. Adelman and L. J. Kotzé, "Environmental Law and the Unsustainability of Sustainable Development: A Tale of Disenchantment and of Hope," *Law and Critique* 34, no. 2 (September 2022): 227–248; Ruth Gordon, "Unsustainable Development," in *International Environmental Law and the Global South*, eds. Shawkat Alam et al. (Cambridge: Cambridge University Press, 2015),

environmental law, providing a basis to analyse whether international environmental law can, in some instances, be queered. In other words, they were chosen for their queer potential, with concepts like sustainable development arguably being so deeply embedded in the problems critical scholars have identified with international environmental law that the only way to queer them is to abandon them.

The chapter subsequently moves on to provide a summary of queer scholarship of the nonhuman, drawing on the work of authors such as Dana Luciano, Mel Y. Chen and Gloria Anzaldúa. This literature broadly argues that the queer has never been human, noting points of solidarity between multiple less-than-human *human* subjects and the nonhuman. The following section then outlines some queer theories of kinship, proposing queer kinship as a means to better connect these points of solidarity between less-than-human *human* subjects and the nonhuman. Drawing on this framework, the chapter then returns to its three examples: the principle of the common heritage of humankind, rights as applied to environmental issues and the concept of future generations. These examples are analysed from a queer perspective, further unpicking the anthropocentrism and heteronormativity underpinning both these specific examples and international environmental law more generally. The chapter next draws on queer theories of hope as a framework to provide some preliminary thoughts on how each example could potentially be re-framed or 'queered' using queer kinship models. Overall, it is argued that a queer notion of kinship, one that centres around multiple human-nonhuman connections, may be used to queer international environmental law. The chapter concludes with a reflection on the risks and potentials of queering international environmental law.

2. The Anthropocentric Subject of International Environmental Law

Globally, groups are declaring that we have reached a 'climate emergency'. Yet despite the increasingly dire warnings about biodiversity loss, environmental degradation and climate change, international environmental law has failed to produce necessary solutions.[3] International law is part of the current environmental crisis: its anthropocentric underpinnings work to prioritise human interests, and primarily human economic interests, over the interests of the environment itself.[4] For example, while international environmental

50–73; Usha Natarajan and Kishan Khoday, "Locating Nature: Making and Unmaking International Law," *Leiden Journal of International Law* 27, no. 3 (July 2014): 589.

3 Will Steffen et al., "Planetary Boundaries: Guiding Human Development on a Changing Planet," *Science* 347, no. 6223 (January 2015): 1259855.

4 Julia Dehm and Usha Natarajan, eds., *Locating Nature: Making and Unmaking International Law* (Cambridge: Cambridge University Press, 2022).

law is often plagued by enforcement issues, with many of the key instruments of international environmental law being soft law provisions that are therefore more difficult to enforce, in contrast, international economic law has much stronger structures of both adjudication and enforcement, thereby creating incentives to comply with the latter when these two bodies of law clash.

Critical international environmental law scholars have exposed the anthropocentrism inherent in many of the core principles that make up international environmental law.[5] Overall, these scholars highlight the fact that the central subject of international environmental law is the human subject, the environment being deemed to be a commodity as opposed to a subject itself.[6] Furthermore, that subject is very much white, male, able-bodied, cis and heterosexual.[7]

5 See, for instance, Vito De Lucia, "Anthropocentrism and International Law," in *The Routledge Handbook of International Law and Anthropocentrism*, eds. Vincent Chapaux, Frédéric Mégret and Usha Natarajan (Abingdon and New York: Routledge, 2023), 84–101; Emily Jones, "Posthuman International Law and the Rights of Nature," *Journal of Human Rights and the Environment* 12 (December 2021): 75–101; Sam Adelman, "A Legal Paradigm Shift Towards Climate Justice in the Anthropocene," *Oñati Socio-Legal Series* 11, no. 1 (February 2021): 44–68; Anna Grear, "Anthropocene, Capitalocene, Chthulucene': Re-encountering Environmental Law and Its 'Subject' with Haraway and New Materialism," in *Environmental Law and Governance for the Anthropocene*, ed. Louis J. Kotzé (Oxford and Portland, OR: Hart, 2017), 77–95; Anna Grear, "Human Rights and New Horizons? Thoughts Toward a New Juridical Ontology," *Science, Technology, & Human Values* 43, no. 1 (January 2018): 129–145; Frédéric Megret, "The Anthropocentrism of Human Rights," in *The Routledge Handbook of International Law and Anthropocentrism*, eds. Vincent Chapaux, Frédéric Megret and Usha Natarajan (Abingdon and New York: Routledge, 2023), 35–60; Jasmijn Leeuwenkamp, "Will Human Rights Save the 'Anthropos' from the 'Anthropocene'? Limitations of Human Rights Strategies in Responding to the Climate Crisis," in *International Law and Posthuman Theory*, eds. Matilda Arvidsson and Emily Jones (Abingdon and New York: Routledge, 2023): 279–304; Marie-Catherine Petersmann, "In the Break (of Rights and Representation): Sociality Beyond the Non/Human Subject," *International Journal of Human Rights* (July 2023): 1–25; Usha Natarjan, "The Global Commons: Deep Sea, Outer Space and Beyond," *Ocean Yearbook Online* 37, no. 1 (May 2023): 1–16; Usha Natarajan and Julia Dehm, "Introduction: Where Is the Environment? Locating Nature in International Law," in *Locating Nature: Making and Unmaking International Law*, eds. Usha Natarajan and Julia Dehm (Cambridge: Cambridge University Press, 2022), 1–18.

6 Grear, "'Anthropocene, Capitalocene, Chthulocene'."

7 See, for instance, Sumudu A. Atapattu et al., "Intersections of Environmental Justice and Sustainable Development: Framing the Issues," in *The Cambridge Handbook of Environmental Justice and Sustainable Development*, eds. Sumudu A. Atapattu et al. (Cambridge: Cambridge University Press, 2021), 1–20; Global Greengrants Fund, "Why the Environmental Justice Movement Must Include Persons with Disabilities," *Global Greengrants Fund*, March 18, 2019, www.greengrants.org/2019/03/18/disability-and-environment; Sawkat Alam et al., *International Environmental Law and the Global South* (Cambridge: Cambridge University Press, 2015); Usha Natarajan, "Third World Approaches to International Law (TWAIL) and the Environment," in *Research Methods in Environmental Law: A Handbook*, eds. Andreas Philippopoulos-Mihalopoulos and Victoria Brooks (Cheltenham and Northampton, MA: Edward Elgar, 2017), 207–235; Emily Jones, *Feminist Theory and International Law:*

The anthropocentric subject of international environmental law is exposed when examining certain key principles and concepts in the law, such as the principle of the common heritage of humankind (tellingly originally referred to as 'mankind').[8] This principle has mostly been invoked in relation to resources within international territories not owned by one state alone, such as certain parts of the sea,[9] Antarctica[10] and outer space,[11] with invocation being most prominent notably in relation to resources in the deep seabed. Key to this principle is the idea of benefit sharing, particularly between Global North and South states.[12] The principle has therefore been used to call for the profits of extraction in these areas to be shared more equally between Global North and South states, thereby representing, in itself, an alternative vision for international law, one which seeks to tackle some global inequalities.[13] However, despite this, the principle enforces other inequalities, primarily through its anthropocentrism. Not only is this principle anthropocentric in that it focuses on *humankind's* heritage, thereby excluding the interests of the nonhuman subjects that live in and rely upon these areas,[14] but it is also

Posthuman Perspectives (Abingdon and New York: Routledge, 2023); Katie Woolaston, "Wildlife and International Law: Can Feminism Transform Our Relationship with Nature?" in *Research Handbook on Feminist Engagement with International Law*, eds. Susan Harris Rimmer and Kate Ogg (Cheltenham and Northampton, MA: Edward Elgar, 2019), 44–62; Anne Rochette, "Transcending the Conquest of Nature and Women: A Feminist Perspective on International Environmental Law," in *International Law: Modern Feminist Approaches*, eds. Doris Buss and Ambreena Manji (Oxford and Portland: Hart, 2005), 203–235.

8 For a queer feminist critique of this term in the context of international space law, see Claerwen O'Hara and Cris van Eijk, "On Straightening and Subversion: A Queer Feminist Perspective on International Space Law and Politics," this volume.

9 See, for instance, Convention on the Law of the Sea, 1833 UNTS 397 (December 10, 1982), Article 136; United Nations General Assembly, Resolution 2749 (XXV) Declaration of Principles Governing the Seabed and the Ocean Floor, and the Subsoil Thereof, beyond the Limits of National Jurisdiction (December 17, 1970); Agreement Relating to the Implementation of Part XI of the United Nations Convention on the Law of the Sea of 10 December 1982, 1836 UNTS 3 (July 28, 1994).

10 See, for example, Zou Keyuan, "The Common Heritage of Mankind and the Antarctic Treaty System," *Netherlands International Law Review* 38, no. 2 (May 2009): 173–198.

11 See, for example, The Treaty on Principles Governing the Activities of States in the Exploration and Use of Outer Space, including the Moon and Other Celestial Bodies, 610 UNTS. 205 (January 27, 1967), preambular para. 1 and Article 1; Agreement Governing the Activities of States on the Moon and Other Celestial Bodies (The Moon Agreement), 1363 UNTS 3 (December 5, 1979) Article 11. The US has recently contested the notion of space as a global commons, and the applicability of the Moon Agreement: see Exec. Order No. 13914, 85 FR 20381 (April 6, 2020), paras. 1–2.

12 Convention on the Law of the Sea, Article 144.

13 Surabhi Ranganathan, "Ocean Floor Grab: International Law and the Making of an Extractive Imaginary," *European Journal of International Law* 30, no. 2 (May 2019): 573–600.

14 Emily Jones, Cristian van Eijk and Gina Heathcote, "The Common Heritage of Kin-Kind," in *International Law and Posthuman Theory*, eds. Matilda Arvidsson and Emily Jones (Abingdon and New York: Routledge, 2023).

anthropocentric in terms of how the environment is conceptualised by this principle: the environments governed by the common heritage of humankind are defined as resource areas to be extracted for economic exploitation.[15] This is possibly best exemplified by ongoing discussions at the International Seabed Authority that are seeking to authorise deep-sea mining of areas that are deemed to be the common heritage of humankind.

Another example of how the anthropocentric basis upon which the environment is governed in international law is the field of human rights and the environment. Human rights have long been criticised for being anthropocentric,[16] and this body of law is now increasingly being applied to environmental issues. The intersections between human rights and the environment are wide-ranging, from the issue of environmental refugees to the environmental impacts of conflict.[17] One of the most promising and rapidly developing convergences between human rights and the environment is to be found in the right to a healthy environment. The human right to a healthy, clean and sustainable environment was recognised at the global level for the first time by the Human Rights Council in October 2021.[18] The right was then subsequently recognised by the UN General Assembly in July 2022.[19] While neither the Human Rights Council nor the UN General Assembly defined the right, the UN Special Rapporteur on Human Rights and the Environment, taking stock of the way the right has been defined regionally

15 Matt Craven, "'Other Spaces': Constructing the Legal Architecture of a Cold War Commons and the Scientific-Technical Imaginary of Outer Space," *European Journal of International Law* 30, no. 2 (May 2019): 547–572; Jones, van Eijk and Heathcote, "The Common Heritage of Kin-Kind"; Surabhi Ranganathan, "Ocean Floor Grab: International Law and the Making of an Extractive Imaginary," *European Journal of International Law* 30, no. 2 (May 2019): 573–600; Isabel Feichtner and Surabhi Ranganathan, "International Law and Economic Exploitation in the Global Commons: Introduction," *European Journal of International Law* 30, no. 2 (May 2019): 541–546; Natarajan, "The Global Commons."

16 See, for instance, Grear, "Human Rights and New Horizons?"; Mégret, "The Anthropocentrism of Human Rights"; Leeuwenkamp, "Will Human Rights Save the 'Anthropos' from the 'Anthropocene'?"

17 The relationship between the enjoyment of rights and the quality of the human environment was first recognised in 1968. See, for instance, United Nations General Assembly, Res. 2398 (XXIII) (December 3, 1968). On environmental refugees, see "Climate Change and Disaster Displacement," *UNHCR*, accessed March 23, 2024, www.unhcr.org/uk/climate-change-and-disasters.html; On the environmental impacts of conflict, see Eliana Cusato, "International Law, the Paradox of Plenty and the Making of Resource-Driven Conflict," *Leiden Journal of International Law* 33, no. 3 (June 2020): 649–666; Karen Hulme, *War Torn Environment: Interpreting the Legal Threshold* (Leiden: Brill, 2004); Eliana Cusato, *The Ecology of War and Peace: Marginalising Slow and Structural Violence in International Law* (Cambridge: Cambridge University Press, 2021).

18 UN Human Rights Council, Resolution 48/13, Doc. A/HRC/48/13 on the Human Rights to a Clean, Healthy and Sustainable Environment 18 (October 18, 2021).

19 UN General Assembly, Resolution A/76/L.75 The Human Rights to a Clean, Healthy and Sustainable Environment (July 26, 2022).

and domestically, has noted that the right to a healthy environment includes many elements, including 'the right to breathe clean air, [and to have] access to clean water and adequate sanitation, healthy and sustainable food, a safe climate, and healthy biodiversity and ecosystems'.[20] While the right is potentially transformative, providing a more integrated means by which a locality and its overall 'health' can be protected, the right remains limited in its framing. This is because the right protects *human* rights to *live* within a healthy environment. The right does not protect the rights of the environment, therefore, to its own health, nor the rights of animals to live in a healthy environment. This means that environmental damage that does not (at first glance) impact on humans but may, for example, impact on other species or cases where environmental damage is occurring a long way from human occupants is not addressed by the right in its current framing.[21]

Yet, while at the global level, the right to a healthy environment has generally been framed in an anthropocentric way, there is one exception to this tendency. The Inter-American Court of Human Rights (IACtHR) has argued that the right should also be used to protect the rights of 'forests, river and seas', meaning that:

> it protects nature and the environment, not only because of the benefits they provide to humanity . . . but because of their importance to the other living organisms with which we share the planet that also merit protection in their own right.[22]

This provides a central example of human rights law being shaped in ever more transformative ways by courts and institutions in the Global South, demonstrating what can happen when Eurocentric visions of human rights are rethought. At the same time, the project of granting rights to nonhumans also has its limitations, as I discuss in more detail below.

However, overall, the IACtHR jurisprudence is an exception. The field of human rights and the environment is primarily set up in a way that protects human interests in relation to their environments. Therefore, while this

20 UN Human Rights Council, Resolution 48/13, para. 17.

21 This is a point Neimanis has raised, albeit in relation to the right to water. See Astrida Neimanis, "Bodies of Water, Human Rights and the Hydrocommons," *TOPIA: Canadian Journal of Cultural Studies* 21 (Spring 2009): 161, 173.

22 *The Environment and Human Rights*, Advisory Opinion OC-23/17, Inter-Am. Ct. H.R. (Ser A) No. 23, 15 November 2017, para. 62.

This approach was later confirmed in the 2020 case, Fondo, Reparaciones y Costas, *Comunidades Indígenas Miembros de la Asociación Lhaka Honhat (Nuestra Tierra) v Argentina*, Sentencia, No. 420, Inter-Am. Ct. H.R. (ser. C) 6 February, 2020) [Merits, Reparations and Costs, *Case of the Indigenous Communities of Lhaka Honhat (Our Land) Association v Argentina*], (ser. C) No. 420 Inter-Am. Ct. H.R. (February 6, 2020).

field is indeed one of the most promising areas of global environmental protection, it, like international environmental law more broadly, continues to promote human interests and is marked by the deep anthropocentrism that pervades international law.[23]

A third example of international environmental law's anthropocentrism is the idea of needing to protect the environment for 'future generations'. This concept has its origins in the 1972 Stockholm Declaration, which uses the concept of future generations twice, noting the 'responsibility to protect and improve the environment for present and future generations',[24] the need to safeguard natural resources 'for the benefit of present and future generations'.[25] The concept was later picked up in 1987 when the World Commission on Environment and Development published the Bruntland Report. In this report, the idea of sustainable development was put forward and defined as needing to meet 'the needs of the present without compromising the needs of future generations to meet their own needs'.[26] Since then, the need to protect the environment for future generations has come to the fore in multiple international fora, this language being used, for example, in the Rio Declaration in 1992[27] and by the International Court of Justice in the *Gabčíkovo-Nagymaros* case in 1997.[28] More recently, as actors globally have come to reckon with the urgent need to tackle climate change, the concept has risen in prominence, with the UN Secretary General António Guterres centring this concept in his 2021 Report entitled *Our Common Agenda*, in which he calls for a new Declaration on Future Generations.[29] The recent request by the UN General Assembly of the International Court of Justice for an Advisory Opinion on the obligation of states in respect of climate change also includes the language of future generations – the court being asked to reflect on several questions, including what obligations states have 'under international law to ensure the protection of the climate system . . . for present and future generations'.[30]

23 For a wider discussion of the anthropocentrism of human rights, see Grear, "Human Rights and New Horizons?"

24 UN General Assembly, Resolution 2994/XXVII, 2995/XXVII and 2996/XXII Declaration on the Human Environment (December 5, 1972) principle 1.

25 UN General Assembly, Resolution 2994/XXVII, 2995/XXVII and 2996/XXII, principle 12.

26 World Commission on Environment and Development, *Our Common Future* (Oxford: OUP 1987).

27 UN General Assembly, Resolution 2994/XXVII, 2995/XXVII and 2996/XXII, principle 13.

28 Judgment, *Gabčíkovo-Nagymaros Dam Case (Hungary/Slovakia)*, 1997 ICJ 7 (September 25, 1997), para. 140.

29 U.N. Secretary General, *Our Common Agenda*, E.21.1.8. (2021), www.un.org/en/content/common-agenda-report/assets/pdf/Common_Agenda_Report_English.pdf.

30 United Nations General Assembly, *Request for an Advisory Opinion of the International Court of Justice on the Obligations of States in Respect of Climate Change*, UN Doc. A/RES/77/276 (2023), 3.

Interestingly, the concept has also been taken up in domestic environmental litigation,[31] where it is often framed in terms of the *rights* of future generations and subsequently paired with existing human or constitutional rights, such as the right to a healthy environment. This is well exemplified by the 2018 Colombian case *Future Generations v Ministry of the Environment and Others*. Here, 25 young plaintiffs sued various Colombian governmental bodies that were operating in the Amazon rainforest for violating various international environmental agreements and their human rights, including their right to food, to a healthy environment and to water. The Supreme Court of Justice ruled in favour of the plaintiffs, recognising also, for the first time, the Colombia Amazon as itself having rights.[32]

While the concept of future generations challenges the anthropocentric presentism of how the environment is framed elsewhere in international environmental law as a resource to be extracted for economic gain, the idea that the environment must be protected for future generations remains anthropocentric in that future generations are very much envisaged as *human* future generations – the concept is certainly not framed in a way that encompasses nonhuman future generations. Furthermore, this legal principle also embeds a heteronormative vision of human reproductive futurity into the law, with the human child being posed as inherently good and as the future of the entire planet – a point I will return to and apply a queer lens to later in this chapter.

Overall, international environmental law reproduces a problematic subject/object binary under which humans are the central subject of the law and 'the environment' is a mere object.[33] This remains the case both when the environment is being protected (where it is still seen as an object) and when it is being exploited, i.e., as an economic resource. Nonhumans and the environment thus range along a 'spectrum of objectifications'.[34] However, international environmental law is not only deeply anthropocentric, but it also upholds, through concepts such as the rights of future generations, a heteronormative vision of the future, one that problematically centres the human child as inherently good.

31 See *Oposa v Factoran*, G.R. No. 101083, 224 S.C.R.A. 792 (July 30, 1993).

32 *Future Generations v Ministry of the Environment and Others*, Radicación no, 11001-22-03-000-2018-00319-01, Supreme Court of Justice of Colombia (April 5, 2018).

33 Grear, "'Anthropocene, Capitalocene, Chthulucene'" 77–95; Marie-Catherine Petersmann, "Response-Abilities of Care in More-Than-Human-Worlds," *Journal of Human Rights and the Environment* 12 (December 2021): 102–124; Emily Jones, "Posthuman International Law and the Rights of Nature," *Journal of Human Rights and the Environment* 12, no. 0 (December 2021): 76–101; Emily Jones, *Feminist Theory and International Law: Posthuman Perspectives* (Abingdon and New York: Routledge, 2023).

34 Grear, "'Anthropocene, Capitalocene, Chthulucene'" 87.

3. Queering the Nonhuman

While international environmental law can be shown to be based upon anthropocentric underpinnings, broadly protecting human interests, primarily economic interests, over the interests of the environment, queer theories of the nonhuman, in contrast, hold the potential to better account for the interests of the nonhuman, including those of the environment itself and nonhuman animals. In this section, I outline some of the core ideas within this emerging field of scholarship before, in the following sections, moving on to apply these theories to provide a queer re-imagination of some of the principles in international environmental law.

When most people think of queer theory, they do not, initially at least, tend to think of the nonhuman. Queer studies, despite being associated with the 'antinormative',[35] emerged from struggles against the discrimination of LGBTI+[36] people – this seemingly having little to do with the nonhuman. However, there is now a strong body of work which applies queer theories to the question of the nonhuman; these theories broadly start with the premise that 'LGBTQ+ people have historically been placed on the side of the unnatural'.[37] These theories thereby embrace the inhuman or the nonhuman as a site for radical transformation. Queer theories of the nonhuman argue that engagements with the environment must not be underpinned by gendered binaries such as nature/culture, but, rather, there is a need to actively seek to dismantle this gendered binary as part of queer environmental politics.[38]

There are many strands of thought within what can be termed queer theories of the environment, including theories of queer ecology that call for the 'opening up of environmental understandings to explicitly non-heterosexual forms of relationship, experience and imagination' as a means to transform 'entrenched sexual and natural practices'.[39] This body of work also includes literatures that link queerness to the nonhuman or inhuman as a positive relation and resource.[40] Other such scholarship similarly seeks to challenge heteronormative assumptions in discussions of nature,[41] noting, for exam-

35 Annamarie Jagose, "The Trouble with Antinormativity," *Differences: A Journal of Feminist Cultural Studies* 26, no. 1 (May 2015): 26–47.

36 Lesbian, gay, bisexual, transgender, intersex plus.

37 Rosi Braidotti, *Posthuman Feminism* (Cambridge: Polity Press, 2022), 160.

38 See Catriona Mortimer-Sandilands and Bruce Erickson, "Introduction: A Genealogy of Queer Ecologies," in *Queer Ecologies: Sex, Nature, Politics, Desire*, eds. Catriona Mortimer Sandilands and Bruce Erickson (Bloomington: Indiana University Press, 2010), 1–48.

39 Mortimer-Sandilands and Erickson, "Introduction: A Genealogy of Queer Ecologies," 3.

40 See, for example, Dana Luciano and Mel Y. Chen, "Has the Queer Ever Been Human?," *GLQ: A Journal of Lesbian and Gay Studies* 21, nos. 2–3 (June 2015): 183–207.

41 See Nicole Seymour, *Strange Natures: Futurity, Empath, and the Queer Ecological Imagination* (Champaign: University of Illinois Press, 2013).

ple, the diverse sexualities of animals.[42] Another research approach focuses on the queer politics of coalition building in and across the environmental movement.[43]

However, another somewhat distinct strand of thought within this field falls under what can be termed queer theories of the nonhuman.[44] These theories can be understood by looking at the work of Dana Luciano and Mel Y. Chen, who argue that there is little gain to be found for queer people in seeking to be included in the category of so-called 'humanity', which has always been exclusionary and based around the heterosexual, white, middle class, male subject. They thereby argue for a queer focus on nonhuman configurations as a site of disruption to the 'human' subject.[45] What needs to be transformed, in other words, is the very idea and ideal of the human and the kind of recognition and equality that can emerge within this notion. The counter-figuration of the nonhuman queer is thereby deeply tied to theories which note that some people have never been able to fully access the dominant vision of humanity.

More broadly, beyond queer theory, the turn to the nonhuman in critical theory has been criticised by some who warn of the risks presented in merely adding the nonhuman to the frame of the liberal subject.[46] This is a conversation that has a much longer history, however, in debates around animal rights, with some arguing that human inequalities need to come first, calling for strategic speciesism to ensure this.[47] This move is something that Claire Jean Kim has termed the 'sanctification of species difference', noting that the African-American civil rights movement heavily invested in this strategy to

42 Bruce Bagemihl, *Biological Exuberance: Animal Homosexuality and Natural Diversity* (New York: St Martin's Press, 2000).

43 Katie Hogan, "Undoing Nature: Collation Building as Queer Environmentalism," in *Queer Ecologies: Sex, Nature, Politics Desire*, eds. Catriona Mortimer-Sandilands and Bruce Erikson (Bloomington: Indiana University Press, 2010), 231–253; Kathryn Yusoff, "Queer Coal: Genealogies in/of the Blood," *Philosophia* 5, no. 2 (2015): 203–229.

44 See, for instance, Noreen Giffney and Myra J. Hird, eds., *Queering the Non/Human* (Abingdon and New York: Routledge, 2008). This work also has a long history. For example, in 1991, Sandy Stone linked the dissonances formed around the transsexual body to Donna Haraway's promise of monsters. See Sandy Stone, "The Empire Strikes Back: A Posttranssexual Manifesto," in *Body Guards: The Cultural Politics of Gender Ambiguity*, eds. Julia Epstein and Kristina Straub (New York: Routledge, 1991), 280–304; Susan Stryker, "My Words to Victor Frankenstein above the Village of Chamounix: Performing Transgender Rage," *GLQ: A Journal of Lesbian and Gay Studies* 1, no. 3 (November 1993): 237–254; Judith M. Halberstam and Ira Livingston, *Posthuman Bodies* (Bloomington: Indiana University Press, 1995).

45 Luciano and Chen, "Has the Queer Even Been Human?," 184.

46 Zahi Zalloua, *Being Posthuman: Ontologies of the Future* (London and New York: Bloomsbury, 2021).

47 Will Kymlicka, "Rethinking Human Rights for a More-than-Human World," in *More Than Human Rights*, ed. César Rodríguez-Garavito (NYU MOTH Project, 2024).

combat dehumanisation.[48] In short, as Alison Suen puts it, it appears through this strategy that there is no way to 'curb racism without throwing the animal under the bus',[49] or on the other hand, that we have no way to defend nonhuman rights without discarding the rights of those humans who have historically been treated as less-than-human.

What sets *queer* theories of the nonhuman apart, however, is their retained focus on *both* human inequalities *and* the inequalities upheld between humans and nonhumans: in short, queer theories of the nonhuman refuse to 'throw' any human or nonhuman subject 'under the bus'. It is vitally important that these multiple vectors of inequality are held together and not separated precisely because, as such theories highlight, these issues are deeply entwined. This has been noted by multiple queer scholars of the nonhuman. For example, similarly to decolonial thinker Sylvia Wynter's analysis that many people have never had full access to humanity, including racialised and gendered subjects,[50] Chicana feminist and queer theorist Gloria Anzaldúa links the queer to difference. Noting the 'heterosexual tribe's fear' of the queer subject, Anzaldúa analyses how the queer subject becomes marked as 'sub-human, inhuman, non-human'.[51] Anzaldúa thus proposes a mode of resistance through what she terms 'mestiza consciousness', making links between marginalised subjects and the land and fostering material connections between the human and the nonhuman,[52] thus forming the 'onto-epistemology' of her New Mestiza.[53] Anzaldúa thereby sees 'dehumanization as an opportunity to reconstruct what it means to be human'.[54]

48 Claire Jean Kim, "Moral Extensionism or Racist Exploitation? The Use of Holocaust and Slavery Analogies in the Animal Liberation Movement," *New Political Science* 33, no. 3 (July 2011): 311–333.

49 Alison Suen, *The Speaking Animal: Ethics, Language and the Human-Animal Divide* (London and New York: Rowman and Littlefield, 2015), 99.

50 Sylvia Wynter, "Unsettling the Coloniality of Being/Power/Truth/Freedom: Towards the Human/After Man, Its Overrepresentation – An Argument," *The New Centennial Review* 3, no. 3 (Fall 2003): 288. See also, Sylvia Wynter and Katherine McKittrick, "Unparalleled Catastrophe for Our Species? Or, to Give Humanness a Different Future: Conversations," in *Sylvia Wynter: On Being Human as Praxis*, ed. Katherine McKittrick (Durham: Duke University Press, 2015), 9–89; Sylvia Wynter, "On How We Mistook the Map for the Territory, and Re-Imprisoned Ourselves in Our Unbearable Wrongness of Being, of Désêtre: Black Studies Toward the Human Project," in *Not Only the Master's Tools: African-American Studies and Theory in Practice*, eds. Lewis R. Gordon and Jane Anna Gordon (London: Paradigm Publishers, 2006), 107–169.

51 Gloria Anzaldúa, *Borderlands/La Frontera: The New Mestiza*, (San Francisco: Aunt Lute Books, 2012), 40.

52 Anzaldúa, *Borderlands/La Frontera*.

53 Carlos Gallego, *Chicana/o Subjectivity and the Politics of Identity: Between Recognition and Revolution* (New York: Palgrave, 2011), 74.

54 Luciano and Chen, "Has the Queer Ever Been Human?," 186.

The onto-epistemology of Anzaldúa's New Mestiza focuses on how humans are all an inherent mix of human and nonhuman. Anzaldúa thereby writes, 'You're all the different organisms and parasites that live on your body and also the ones who live in a symbiotic relationship to you . . . So who are you? You're not one single entity. You're a multiple entity'.[55] In this figuring of the queer subject, the human is not only unsettled but new possibilities are created. Many have never been fully human, including many racialised, gendered, sexualised, disabled and classed people. Queer theories of the nonhuman thus add another element to the inhuman and nonhuman paradigm, pointing out that humans were never all or solely human. Such a position challenges dominant hierarchies and accounts of the human, providing new ways of envisaging both humans and human-nature connections.

To summarise, the defining features of a queer approach to the nonhuman includes several key strands, starting from the need to challenge gendered binaries such as nature/culture and subject/object. Next comes a focus on the generative connections between humans and nonhumans. Alongside this, the need to more adequately account for, and even reclaim, the nonhuman – i.e., all those who do not match the dominant vision of the human – are centred, both as a subject (with this new vision of the subject transcending the subject/object binary) and as a site of knowledge. This does not, however, mean positioning the nonhuman as somehow beyond the human. This kind of slippage would risk the reintroduction of the very 'Eurocentric transcendentalism this movement purports to disrupt'.[56] After all, as Luciano and Chen reflect:

> If we accept the framing of the nonhuman turn as a move 'beyond' the merely human concerns of identity and alterity, we overlook how the very possibility of making a distinction between human and nonhuman has, historically, been constructed by the kind of actions and processes that we have named dehumanization.[57]

Therefore, as Zakiyyah Iman Jackson notes, there is a need to be careful of appeals to merely move 'beyond the human', noting that such appeals, detached from the critiques of humanism made by Black peoples, risk reinforcing racism and Eurocentric ideas of transcendentalism, asking '*whose* conception of humanity are we moving beyond?'[58] Jackson, however, does not

55 Gloria Anzaldúa, quoted in Mikko Tuhkanen, "Queer Hybridity," in *Deleuze and Queer Theory*, eds. Chrysanti Niganni and Merl Storr (Edinburgh: Edinburgh University Press, 2009), 96.

56 Zakiyyah Iman Jackson in José Esteban Muñoz et al., "Theorizing Queer Inhumanisms," *GLQ: A Journal of Lesbian and Gay Studies* 21, no. 2–3 (2015): 209–248, p. 215.

57 Luciano and Chen, "Has the Queer Ever Been Human?," 195.

58 Zakiyyah Iman Jackson, "Outer Worlds: The Persistence of Race in Movement 'Beyond the Human'," *GLQ: A Journal of Lesbian and Gay Studies* 21, no. 2–3 (2015): 215–218, p. 215.

see these two positions as inherently contradictory. Rather, she argues that 'any movement towards the nonhuman' must inherently be simultaneously 'a movement towards blackness, as blackness constitutes the very matter at hand'.[59] Queer theories of the nonhuman maintain a similar position, holding postcolonial, decolonial and critical race approaches together alongside other bodies of critical thought, such as feminist, queer and crip studies, with the aim of queering the subject. In this sense, queer theories of the nonhuman warn against merely adding a new subject to existing paradigms, noting instead the need to challenge and rethink, to queer, those existing paradigms.

What becomes clear through queer theories of the nonhuman, therefore, is that rather than focusing solely on the nonhuman, there is a need for legal discourse to note the interconnections between nonhumans and those humans deemed to be less-than or inhuman. This extra layer of complexity can result in highlighting points of solidarity between the nonhuman and the less/more/other/-than-human, without conflating their differences of location and power. In short, queer politics cannot be satisfied by simply looking beyond the human, as doing so would risk silencing 'the very histories of dehumanization too often overlooked in celebratory posthumanisms'.[60] A focus on the status of dehumanised humans, moreover, is a necessary corrective to theories and practices that pose equality as the only possible form of recognition for nonhuman entities. Queer theories of the nonhuman do much more than just displace the human but, rather, they explore the multiple new forms of interconnection between and across the inhuman or nonhuman categories in a manner that avoids dialectical oppositions. The in/non/post-human, in other words, should not become an anti-humanity. This allows for multiple struggles by turning these categories into various and variable vectors of the inhuman, the nonhuman, the less-than-human and beyond human to be held together without conflation. This can result in a plurality of political positions, creating a politics of 'being-with'[61] or, to use Haraway's language, a companion species politics of kin and kind.[62]

4. Queering Kinship in International Environmental Law

Queer theories of the nonhuman have a lot to contribute to critical environmental law scholarship. First of all, these theories speak back to the need to

59 Jackson, "Outer Worlds: The Persistence of Race in Movement 'Beyond the Human'," 217.
60 Luciano and Chen, "Has the Queer Ever Been Human?," 196.
61 José Esteban Muñoz in José Esteban Muñoz et al., "Theorizing Queer Inhumanisms," *GLQ: A Journal of Lesbian and Gay Studies* 21, no. 2–3 (2015): 209–248, p. 210.
62 See Donna Haraway, "Companion Species, Mis-Recognition, and Queering Worlding," in *Queering the Non-Human*, eds. Noreen Giffney and Myra J. Hird (Abingdon and New York: Routledge, 2016), xxiv.

focus on human inequalities, addressing some of the concerns raised with a more universalist approach to international environmental law that does not pay attention to the differing ways that environmental destruction and climate change are impacting different people, with the Global South paying the biggest price for the impacts of climate change – those impacts having been primarily caused by the Global North.[63] However, in addition, while focusing on the different vectors of oppression within the category of humanity, these theories also bring to the fore questions of the nonhuman. This is central, especially given the anthropocentric nature of international environmental law.

Yet, until now, most queer theories of the nonhuman have remained within the theoretical realm, primarily emerging from philosophy and literary studies. This section thereby attempts to apply these theories to some of the core principles and ideas in international environmental law, focusing primarily on the subject of international environmental law. As noted above, critical environmental law scholars have critiqued the subject/object binary at the heart of environmental law. Noting this, the subject is thereby re-defined here in a way that transcends the subject/object binary to include within its purview both traditional 'subjects' and those previously deemed to be 'objects', including the environment itself. Through this application, I seek to show how international environmental law may be queered, working to dismantle hierarchies between humans and fostering connections between the human and the nonhuman in a way that may, I argue, radically transform how international law manages and views the environment and nonhuman animals.

As I argued above, international environmental law is all too human, centring human interests and promoting, through concepts such as the rights of future generations, a notion of the future of humanity that is deemed to rest upon the shoulders of the human child. In contrast, queer studies and queer practice have long centred an anti- or post-heteronormative idea of kinship;[64] this model of kinship, as Dianne Otto notes, holds much potential when it comes to queering some of the core tenets of international law.[65] For example, anthropologist Kath Weston, in her book *Families We Choose*, explores how queer subjects construct their own bonds of kinship beyond biological

63 Alam et al., *International Environmental Law and the Global South*; Natarajan, "Third World Approaches to International Law (TWAIL) and the Environment," 207–235.

64 See, for instance, Tyler Bradway and Elizabeth Freeman, eds., *Queer Kingship: Race, Sex, Belonging, Form* (Durham: Duke University Press, 2022); Elizabeth Freeman, "Queer Belongings: Kinship Theory and Queer Theory," in *A Companion to Lesbian, Gay, Bisexual, Transgender, and Queer Studies*, eds. George E. Haggerty and Molly McGarry (Oxford: Blackwell Publishing, 2007), 293–314; Judith Butler, *Undoing Gender* (New York: Routledge, 200), 102–130.

65 Dianne Otto, "Queerly Troubling International Law's Vision of 'Peace'," *AJIL Unbound* 116 (2022): 22–26.

ties.[66] Marlon M. Baily likewise examines queer concepts of kinship in Ballroom culture in the US, where participants are affiliated with a house, forming an alternative queer family,[67] while Leah Lakshmi Piepzna-Samarasinha has shown how queer disabled people of colour foster communities of care.[68] These concepts of queer kinship encapsulate many ideas and practices, including the building of non-blood families when queer people are alienated from their blood relatives. Central, however, is the idea that the queer subject inherently disrupts the nuclear family as being the central organising body of the nation-state.[69] For example, noting that marriage is implicated in various structures of power, playing a role in border controls, access to healthcare and in taxation, queer theorists have argued that, rather than seeking to gain access to marriage equality, queer people should instead reject the idea of marriage as a way of ordering society.[70]

Queer theorist Lee Edelman argues that society's focus on the figure of the child as the embodiment of the future fosters an idea of the queer subject as the antithesis of that future. The queer subject thereby becomes positioned as both having and representing 'no future'. However, rather than calling for assimilation, and in a similar fashion to the queer scholars who reject marriage as a way of structuring society, Edelman does not call for the queer subject to embrace the child or gay parenting. Rather, he notes the potential of the queer subject to disrupt dominant heteronormative narratives of what the future should and can be. In this sense, the power of the queer subject lies in its disruption, in its refusal and its ability to foster social and political futures otherwise.[71]

Returning to international environmental law, concepts such as the rights of or the need to protect for the sake of future generations produce a

66 Kath Weston, *Families We Choose: Lesbians, Gays, Kinship* (New York: Columbia University Press, 1997).

67 Marlon M. Bailey, *Butch Queens Up in Pumps: Gender, Performance, and Ballroom Culture in Detroit* (Ann Arbor: University of Michigan Press, 2013).

68 Leah Lakshmi Piepzna-Samarasinha, *Care Work: Dreaming Disability Justice* (Vancouver: Arsenal Pulp Press, 2018).

69 Otto, "Queerly Troubling International Law's Vision of 'Peace'," 22–26; Dianne Otto, "Resisting the Heteronormative Imaginary of the Nation-State: Rethinking Kinship and Border Protection," in *Queering International Law: Possibilities, Alliances, Complicities, Risks*, ed. Dianne Otto (New York: Routledge, 2018); Bina Fernandez, "Queer Border Crossers: Pragmatic Complicities, Indiscretions and Subversions," in *Queering International Law: Possibilities, Alliances, Complicities, Risks*, ed. Dianne Otto (New York: Routledge, 2018).

70 Dean Spade, "Marriage Will Never Set Us Free," February 6, 2016, www.deanspade.net/wp-content/uploads/2021/10/Marriage_Will_Never_Set_Us_Free.pdf; Tyler Bradway and Elizabeth Freeman, "Introduction Kincoherance/Kin-Aesthetics/Kinematics," in *Queer Kinship: Race, Sex, Belonging, Form*, eds. Tyler Bradway and Elizabeth Freeman (Durham: Duke University Press, 2022), 6–8.

71 Lee Edelman, *No Future: Queer Theory and the Death Drive* (Durham: Duke University Press, 2004).

heteronormative and anthropocentric vision of the future, one that centres on the human child. Edelman's work in unpicking the heteronormative assumption that the human child is the future is useful in helping to queer the heteronormative assumptions made by and in international environmental law. However, through his rejection of reproductive futurity, Edelman also rejects futurity, calling for the queer subject and its inability to reproduce, at least in the heteronormative sense, to embrace their negative position in society. Edelman thus calls for a queer refusal of the future and of 'hope' in the future,[72] proposing, instead, to use the words of Jack Halberstam, a 'relentless form of negativity' in which 'death and finitude are the very meaning of queerness'.[73] If queer studies is, indeed, anti-normative, then at one level, the rejection of futurity as the only queer option makes sense. However, as Halberstam likewise notes,[74] there is a worryingly depoliticising note to Edelman's work. While indeed rejecting a certain model of the future, one which relies upon heteronormative reproduction or, I would add, models of capitalism, colonialism, racism, anthropocentrism and patriarchy, does indeed resonate strongly with queer study's anti-normativity, this is not the same as rejecting, as Edelman does, all futurity. Rather, rejecting specific, normative, violent and oppressive modes of governance *must* come with hope, a hope that a different world can be created.

Edelman's queer negativity is only one perspective on queer futurity, with other queer theorists finding, in contrast, a potentiality in queerness. In *The Queer Art of Failure,* Halberstam reclaims failure, arguing that, in a world that measures success in heteronormative and capitalist terms, failure can provide hope, a way of doing things otherwise.[75] Muñoz provides an equally more hopeful way to understand queer theory. For Muñoz, queerness is 'an ideality' based in 'potentiality', one that allows us 'to see and feel beyond the quagmire of the present'.[76] Thus, Muñoz continues, '[q]ueerness is essentially about the rejection of a here and now and an insistence on potentiality or concrete possibility for another world'.[77]

The notion of queer hope and the possibility of thinking the world otherwise is potentially transformative when seeking to imagine international environmental law beyond its current anthropocentric and heteronormative constraints, providing a means by which to move beyond the quagmire of

72 Edelman, *No Future: Queer Theory and the Death Drive*. Indeed, in the introduction he rejects hope all together.

73 Jack Halberstam, *The Queer Art of Failure* (Durham and London: Duke University Press, 2011), 106.

74 Halberstam, *The Queer Art of Failure*, 118.

75 Halberstam, *The Queer Art of Failure*.

76 José Esteban Muñoz, *Cruising Utopia: The Then and There of Queer Futurity* (New York: New York University Press, 2009), 1.

77 Muñoz, *Cruising Utopia*, 1.

the anthropocentric present. Queer concepts of kinship can be used as one of the tools to seek queer environmental futures in international law. While the concepts of chosen family and queer futurity provide a different notion of kinship, one that moves beyond heteronormative models of reproduction and blood ties, queer theories of the nonhuman provide yet another model of kinship, arguing that queer and other dehumanised subjects are deeply connected to nonhuman subjects, who have likewise been subjugated. This model of kinship is similar to models of kinship found elsewhere. For example, the term and idea of kinship is also central in many Indigenous philosophies, kinship being used to denote the deep connections and entwinements between humans *and* between humans and more-than-human kin.[78] Donna Haraway has likewise used the term 'kin' throughout her work, noting the need for humans to foster relationships with and better understand kin – this term once again being used to represent all entities other than oneself, including human and nonhuman subjects.[79] These uses of kin find resonance with queer ideas, not only queer theories of the nonhuman that likewise centre human-nonhuman links but also broader queer theories of kinship and chosen family. Bringing these bodies of thought together helps provide a concept of kinship that is based upon solidarity for *all* planetary beings, thereby challenging both heteronormative ties of kinship and anthropocentric models.

For example, as I have argued with others elsewhere, the concept of kin can be used to transform the principle of the common heritage of humankind, re-defining it as the common heritage of kin-kind.[80] While the existing legal principle has been framed in a way that seeks, in part, albeit questionably, to include a wider array of human interests in its focus on redistributing the plenty of environmental extraction in areas deemed to fall within the principle's remit, a queer framing of kin provides a far more radical conceptual

78 See, for instance, Tod Zoe, "Fish, Kin and Hope: Tending to Water Violations in *amiskwaciwâskahikan* and Treaty Six Territory," *Afterall: A Journal of Art, Context and Enquiry* 43, no. 1 (Spring 2017): 102–107; Darcey Lindberg, "Excerpts from Nêhiyaw Âskiy Wiyasiwêwina: Plains Cree Earth Law and Constitutional/Ecological Reconciliation," *Rooted* 1, no. 1 (2021): 10–16; Aaron Mills, "A Preliminary Sketch of Anishinaabe (a Species of Rooted) Constitutionalism," *Rooted* 1, no. 1 (2021): 2–7.

Kirsti Luke, CEO of Te Uru Taumatua (the organisation representing the Tūhoe *Iwi*) in the recognition of legal personality in New Zealand/Aetoera, likewise uses the term kinship to refer to human and nonhuman relations. See K. Luke, "Presentation at the United Nations Interactive Dialogue of the General Assembly on Harmony with Nature" (United Nations Headquarters, New York, Monday, April 23, 2018), as quoted in C. M. Kauffman, "Managing People for the Benefit of the Land: Practicing Earth Jurisprudence in Te Urewera, New Zealand," *ILSE: Interdisciplinary Studies in Literature and Environment* 27, no. 3 (Summer 2020): 6.

79 Donna J. Haraway, *Staying with the Trouble: Making Kin in the Chthulucene* (Durham: Duke University Press, 2016); See also, Jones, van Eijk and Heathcote, "The Common Heritage of Kin-Kind."

80 See Jones, van Eijk and Heathcote, "The Common Heritage of Kin-Kind."

basis for the principle. As noted above, the principle of the common heritage of humankind is deeply anthropocentric, viewing nature as a resource alone to be extracted. However, applying queer ideas of kinship to the principle works to challenge the idea of who the stakeholders of this heritage are, allowing for multiple interests to be conceived of as having a stake in this heritage, including differing human and nonhuman interests, thereby bringing environmental concerns to the fore of a principle that currently largely disregards them.[81]

In a similar vein, the field of human rights and the environment can arguably likewise be transformed by queer concepts of kinship. While rights under this paradigm are currently recognised primarily regarding human subjects, queering in this field may allow for the rights of nonhuman subjects also to be recognised. Of course, this is by no means a new suggestion – as the IACtHR example above shows – but it is also exemplified by decades of discussions on animal rights[82] and by recent discussions on the recognition of the rights of nature.[83] However, several issues are raised by seeking to recognise nonhuman rights, including issues of representation and the need for humans to represent nonhuman subjects at law, meaning that human power dynamics and ideologies will and are inherently coming into play during the enforcement of the rights of nature.[84] Furthermore, rights in international law come with their own liberal, colonial, gendered and neoliberal baggage through their application in international human rights law,[85] a legacy that will no doubt limit the radical potential of nonhuman rights if recognised in international law, too.[86]

Returning to queer theory, queer approaches have long been sceptical of the ability of rights paradigms to foster radical social change. Aeyal Gross, for

81 See Jones, van Eijk and Heathcote, "The Common Heritage of Kin-Kind."

82 Iyan Offor, *Global Animal Law from the Margins: International Trade in Animals and Their Bodies* (Abingdon and New York: Routledge, 2023); Maneesha Deckha, "Supplanting Anthropocentric Legalities: Can the Rule of Law Tolerate Intensive Animal Agriculture?," in *International Law and Posthuman Theory*, eds. Matilda Arvidsson and Emily Jones (Abingdon and New York: Routledge, 2023).

83 As of 2022, rights of nature provisions existed in at least 24 countries. See Craig Kauffman, "Global Patterns and Trends in Rights of Nature Legal Provisions: Insights from the Eco Jurisprudence Monitor," in *More Than Human Rights*, ed. César Rodríguez-Garavito (NYU MOTH Project, 2024).

84 See Jones, "Posthuman International Law and the Rights of Nature," 76–101.

85 See Ratna Kapur, *Gender, Alterity and Human Rights: Freedom in a Fishbowl* (Cheltenham: Edward Elgar Publishing, 2020).

86 Emily Jones, "Can the Rights of Nature Transform the Way Rights Are Conceptualized in International Law?," in *More Than Human Rights*, ed. César Rodríguez-Garavito (NYU MOTH Project, 2024). For a wider discussion of the risks of the rights of nature project see Jérémie Gilbert et al., "The Rights of Nature as a Legal Response to the Global Environmental Crisis? A Critical Review of International Law's 'Greening' Agenda," in *Netherlands Yearbook of International Law 2021*, eds. Daniëlla Dam-de Jong and Fabian Amtenbrink (Hague: T.M.C. Asser Press, 2023); Petersmann, "In the Break," 1–25.

example, argues that LGBT+ rights projects have worked, in many instances, to ensure the incorporation of LGBT+ people into state structures of power, noting the way this incorporation has been used to bolster state power concerningly.[87] This has led Ratna Kapur to argue that queer interactions with human rights paradigms have taken the radicality out of the queer project, calling instead for a queer envisaging of freedom beyond rights.[88] Indeed, queer theory comes from a long history of anti-assimilationist politics, having been created, in part, to reject projects framed around equal rights explicitly.[89] In short, given the liberal, colonial, gendered and neoliberal roots of the rights project and its predominant focus on formal equality, it seems that recognising nonhuman rights may, to some extent, challenge anthropocentrism (though only to some extent because, as noted, such paradigms still require humans to represent nature), but it may not necessarily provide the kind of transformative change that a queer approach to the nonhuman seeks. After all, rights are only recognised once they have been violated, meaning that more everyday forms of environmental destruction that may not meet a rights threshold, forms of environmental destruction that Rob Nixon has coined 'slow violence',[90] will not be captured by such projects. This operates to normalise this everyday form of destruction by focusing attention on the exceptional.[91] Furthermore, rights paradigms have long struggled to properly account for the wider inequalities which often lead to rights violations, such as the neoliberal normalisation of environmental destruction in a case on, for example, the right to a healthy environment. While the IACtHR has made attempts to think more broadly about the structures of inequality that impact such cases, as most famously exemplified by the *Cotton Fields* judgment, where the court sought to understand and provide transformative reparations to tackle the patriarchal structures that had

87 Aeyal Gross, "Gay Governance: A Queer Critique," in *Governance Feminism: Notes from the Field*, eds. Janet Halley et al. (Minneapolis: University of Minnesota, 2019), 344–374; Aeyal Gross, "Homoglobalism: The Emergence of Global Gay Governance," in *Queering International Law: Possibilities, Alliances, Complicities, Risks*, ed. Dianne Otto (Abingdon and New York: Routledge, 2018), 148–170. See also Dean Spade, "Under the Cover of Gay Rights," *New York University Review of Law and Social Change* 37, no. 1 (2013): 79–100; Jasbir K. Puar, *Terrorist Assemblages: Homonationalism in Queer Times* (Durham: Duke University Press, 2017).

88 Ratna Kapur, "The (Im)Possibility of Queering International Human Rights Law," in *Queering International Law: Possibilities, Alliances, Complicities, Risks*, ed. Dianne Otto (Abingdon and New York: Routledge, 2018).

89 See, for instance, Dean Spade, *Normal Life: Administrative Violence, Critical Trans Politics and the Limits of Law* (Durham: Duke University Press, 2015).

90 Rob Nixon, *Slow Violence and the Environmentalism of the Poor* (Cambridge, MA: Harvard University Press, 2011). See also, Cusato, *The Ecology of War and Peace*.

91 For a discussion of this phenomenon through the example of ecocide, see Eliana Cusato and Emily Jones, "The 'Imbroglio' of Ecocide: A Political Economic Analysis of the International Criminalisation of Ecological Destruction," *Leiden Journal of International Law* 37, no.1 (2024): 42-61.

fostered an environment in which femicide has become commonplace,[92] these attempts have been few and far between and compliance has been weak.[93]

More hope may be found, however, when seeking to queer other norms in international environmental law. Re-defining the subject as one that embraces both human and nonhuman kin may also allow for the embrace and a re-evaluation of human relationships beyond those between parent and child towards a politics of being-with. While the idea of protecting future generations suggests a sense that we need to protect 'our' children, the interests of future generations of kin allow the moral responsibility to be shifted towards all kinds of kin, human and nonhuman alike. In this model, humans may not be the future at all. Rather, responsibilities are created towards all future subjects, from humans to bacteria, plants to birds, whales to rocks. This notion of the subject is one that is not tethered to heteronormative reproductive politics as, after all, many of these subjects are created through other processes: rocks may be created by melting or cooling and bacteria reproduce through various means, including binary fission – where a cell grows to double its size and splits in two. Furthermore, as evolutionary biologist Joan Roughgarden argues, most biologists view nature through a heteronormative paradigm, meaning they fail to see multiple forms of queer biodiversity, from non-monogamous birds to homosexual lizards to hermaphroditic hyenas.[94] These future generations defy gender and heteronormative models of reproduction and thought, fostering a queer basis to reconstruct international environmental law's subject across human-nonhuman connections.

5. Conclusion

In this chapter, I have argued that international environmental law is based upon anthropocentric values, working to protect elite human interests over those of nonhuman animals and the environment itself. Furthermore, through an examination of calls in international environmental law to protect the environment for the sake of future generations, I argued that the law upholds heteronormative values, centring human reproductive futurity.

Following this analysis, I examined how queer theories of the nonhuman, which challenge human hierarchies over the nonhuman, read alongside queer concepts of kinship, which call for kinship to be understood beyond the heteronormative family, may be used to queer international environmental law.

92 Preliminary Objection, Merits, Reparations and Costs, Judgment, *González et al. v Mexico*, No. 205, Inter-Am. Ct. H.R. (Ser. C) (16 November 2009).

93 *Resolución de la Corte Interamericana de Derechos Humanos: Caso González y Otras ("Campo Algodonero") Vs Mexico, Supervisión de Cumplimiento de Sentencia*, Supervisión de Cumplimiento de Sentencia, Inter-Am. Ct. H.R. 12 May 2013.

94 Joan Roughgarden, *Evolution's Rainbow: Diversity, Gender, and Sexuality in Nature and People* (Berkely, Los Angels and London: University of California, 2013).

Overall, I argued that a queer notion of kinship, one that centres multiple human-nonhuman connections, may be used to queer international environmental law. To exemplify this point, I provided a brief analysis of what this queer notion of kinship may mean as applied to three areas of international environmental law: the principle of the common heritage of humankind, the fields of human rights and the environment and the principle of the need to protect the environment for the sake of future generations.

While I found some success in being able to 'queer' the concepts of future generations and common heritage, I found less success when seeking to queer the notion of rights. Rights have long been critiqued by queer, feminist and postcolonial thinkers, noting the limited freedom that rights promise and the assimilationist politics of formal equality that underlies dominant accounts of rights, such a politics sitting inherently in tension with a queer politics of anti-assimilation.

Furthermore, and in that vein, it is worth noting that a queer model of kinship cannot be applied with such ease to all areas of international environmental law. In the process of deciding which existing principles in international environmental law I would seek to queer, I faced some serious obstacles. For example, I initially began by thinking about what a queer idea of sustainable development might be before coming to the conclusion that the principle is so deeply embedded in anthropocentric and extractivist ideas that it cannot be queered.[95]

This tension is, of course, one that finds itself at the heart of the queer international legal project, that is, the tension between seeking to radically queer international law while being tethered to the normative framework that is international law. After all, as Vanja Hamzić has argued, law as we know it *is* violence. This leaves us with the question: can the law ever really be queered?[96] Each of the authors in these two volumes comes to terms with this dilemma in their own way. In this chapter, I have sought to understand whether and how international environmental law may be queered. While I have put forward some tentative proposals, there are clearly many tensions that have yet to be worked through in more detail if this project is to be pursued further, and it is evident that not all elements or areas of international environmental law *can* be queered. After all, if queerness is, as Muñoz argues, 'the thing that lets us feel that this world is not enough, that indeed something is missing',[97] seeking merely to transform the not-enough cannot ever be enough. Entirely new imaginaries may be needed, ideas that go well beyond the law and the global order as we know it.

95 With thanks to Julia Dehm at the 2022 Queering International Law 2.0 workshop in Melbourne for triggering this thought process.

96 Vanja Hamzić, "International Law as Violence: Competing Absences of the Other," in *Queering International Law: Possibilities, Alliances, Complicities, Risks*, ed. Dianne Otto (Abingdon and New York: Routledge, 2018).

97 Muñoz, *Cruising Utopia: The Then and There of Queer Futurity*, 1.

Chapter 3

Oceans versus Ghost Fleets

Gina Heathcote

1. Introduction

In this chapter, I consider the ocean as a queer subject exposing the intertwined production of heteronormativity, military-capital, and racialised knowledge histories central to international law. Through exploring alternative legal encounters with the ocean, the chapter opens toward the possibility of queer subjectivities that shift beyond the human or the state. Following scholarship in the hydrohumanities and critical ocean studies,[1] I accept the ocean as agential and consider it as resolutely queer in its nonlinear temporality and fluid resistance/existence. I also draw on the longer encounter of Indigenous and Oceania/Pacific traditions of knowing the sea differently.[2] I contrast Oceania knowledge with the regulation of automated naval vessels and maritime security, which reproduce heteronormative statehood in the regulation of the ocean and oceanic encounters. At the same time,

1 Kim De Wolff, Rina C. Faletti and Igancio López-Calvo, *Hydrohumanities: Water Discourses and Environmental Futures* (Oakland, CA: University of California Press, 2022); Hester Blum, "Introduction: Oceanic Studies," *Atlantic Studies* 10, no. 2 (2013): 151–155; Irus Braverman and Elizabeth R. Johnson, *Blue Legalities: The Life and Laws of the Sea* (Durham: Duke University Press, 2020); Elizabeth DeLoughrey, "Toward a Critical Ocean Studies for the Anthropocene," *English Language Notes* 57, no. 1 (2019): 21–36; Philip Steinberg and Kimberley Peters, "Wet Ontologies, Fluid Spaces: Giving Depth to Volume Through Oceanic Thinking," *Environment and Planning D: Society and Space* 33, no. 2 (2015): 247–264.

2 De Wolff et al., *Hydrohumanities*; Epeli Hau'ofa, *We Are the Ocean: Selected Works* (Honolulu: University of Hawai'i Press, 2008). Throughout the text, I move between the names 'Pacific' and 'Oceania'. When drawing on Western and foreign perspectives, I use the name 'Pacific' for the region; when drawing on regional knowledges, I use the preferred local name of 'Oceania' and, in a few places in this chapter, I draw on decolonising work that uses the term 'Pasifika'. I find the ambiguity of terms expressive of the tensions between global and international assumptions and local knowledge, which are dynamic and, at times, contested. In the final section, I follow Matapo and Brice's use of the term 'Pasifika', see Jacoba Matapo and Tim Brice, "The Art of Wayfinding: Pasifika Success," *MAI Journal: A New Zealand Journal of Indigenous Scholarship* 9, no. 1 (2020): 26–37.

DOI: 10.4324/9781032645339-4

as artificial intelligence and automated objects are deployed into the Pacific as components of US maritime security, and thus potential legal subjects, I juxtapose the ocean with these technologies to explore non-human encounters with 'humans-out-of-the-loop' technologies (autonomous technological systems that do not rely on human input). I argue that the queer ocean affords important apertures for reimagining legal subjectivity and, ultimately, international law.

In thinking with non-Western legal traditions, I reference the writing of Marshallese artist, activist, and poet Kathy Jetñil-Kijiner to question knowledge frames, temporalities, and the embodied military realities across human and non-human encounters in the ocean.[3] In parallel, I examine the Marshallese rimeto, or wave-riders, whose knowledge of the ocean frames an alternative encounter with ocean agency.[4] Through Oceania knowledges, I embrace legal forms that are not constrained by the Enlightenment fetishising of heteronormative man as the template for subjectivity or the trajectories of modernity that are underpinned by the excesses of military capital, racialised, extractive, and persistent.[5] I use the queer method of dwelling within nonlinear temporalities,[6] overlaying three Oceania encounters – the 'discovery' of the Pacific, nuclear testing in the Pacific, and the deployment of the US Ghost Fleet into the region – to examine the reproduction of a specific mode of legal regulation and maritime security, despite the persistence/existence of alternative, resistant modes that refuse the violence of maritime security produced and reproduced via automated maritime vessels.

The chapter unfolds over five sections: the first, a discussion of queer legal methods; the second, an account of the resonance of queer legal methods with critical ocean studies and the hydrohumanities; the third, an analysis of the legal repetitions produced in the deployment and development of the US Ghost Fleet and other automated maritime objects; the fourth, a non-expert thinking with rimeto, or wave riders; and the final, fifth and concluding section, a reflection on legal imaginaries that engage human-non-human encounters on the ocean, queer law, and legal subjectivity. In examining the development of naval vessels with the potential for humans-out-of-the-loop, I demonstrate how civilising narratives join Cold War repetitions that are replete with the Othering of non-Western legal traditions and the privileging of Empire and that persist within international law. At the same time, I note

3 Kathy Jetñil-Kijiner and Aka Niviâna, *Rise: From One Island to Another*, 2018, accessed April 25, 2024, https://350.org/rise-from-one-island-to-another/#poem.

4 Joseph H. Genz, *Breaking the Shell: Voyaging from Nuclear Refugees to People of the Sea in the Marshall Islands* (Hawai'i: University of Hawai'i Press, 2019).

5 Kathryn Yusof, *A Billion Black Anthropocenes or None* (Minneapolis: University of Minnesota Press, 2019).

6 Rahul Rao, *Out of Time: The Queer Possibilities of Postcoloniality* (Oxford and New York: Oxford University Press, 2020), 21–30.

the repetition of Cold War narratives of threat and deterrence to justify ongoing maritime surveillance and violence. I also demonstrate how the doctrine of freedom of the seas interlocks with collective security law and the law of armed conflict to provide licence for military capital to pursue its violence at sea and repeat the racialised history of the ocean.[7] I write to complicate these legal and military accounts through the introduction of scholarship from the Pacific, renamed and understood by Hua'ofa as Oceania,[8] to expose racialised, capitalist, and military traditions as central to international law, legal subjectivity, and the heteronormativity of international law.

I argue that the queer ocean undoes the temporal linearity of military masculinities, which rely upon repetitions of military forms that imagine a silent ocean, and unheard Oceanic accounts, to produce logics of violence and extraction. I consider what it means to think beyond the existing appropriation of non-human forms for violent ends to articulate queer posthuman feminism grounded in the ocean and sand justice of Oceania.[9] In addressing the queer ocean, humans-out-of-the-loop technologies produce an unexpected, additional, queer reading as the constraint in the development of automated maritime technologies is recognised as the ocean itself: inhibiting communications, unravelling geospatial co-ordinates, and holder of temporal encounters that challenge simple accounts of linear progress.[10] As Ghost Ships and other automated objects become the object of maritime security desires, humans-out-of-the-loop technology becomes a means to see and know the ocean as agential, queer: an ocean that challenges the persistence of militarised, human violence and the persistent heteronormative desire of conquest and ownership. Subsequently, an alternative ocean technology emerges in the navigational histories of the 'rimeto', translated as 'person of the ocean', passed down through the Marshallese community, along with stick charts, recording a knowledge of the ocean that 'provides information about land locations and thus affords navigational guidance'[11] through an intimate, rather than extractive, human-ocean encounter.

7 Mikki Stelder, "The Colonial Difference in Hugo Grotius: Rational Man, Slavery and Indigenous Dispossession," *Postcolonial Studies* 25, no. 4 (2022): 564–583.

8 Epeli Hau'ofa, *We Are the Ocean: Selected Works* (Honolulu: University of Hawai'i Press, 2008).

9 Emily Jones, *Feminist Theory and International Law: Posthuman Perspectives* (Abingdon: Routledge, 2023).

10 Sanur Sharma, "Global Development in Sea-based Unmanned Crafts," *Journal of Defense Studies* 16, no. 4 (2022): 21–50. See also Raul Pedrozo, "Advent of a New Era in Naval Warfare: Autonomous and Unmanned Systems," in *Autonomous Vessels in Maritime Affairs: Law and Governance Implications*, eds. Tafsir Matin Johansson, Jonaton Echebarria Fernándo, Dimitrios Dalaklis, Aspasia Pastra and Jon A. Skinner (Cham, Switzerland: Palgrave Macmillan, 2023), 63–80, 66.

11 Genz, *Breaking the Shell*; see also "Polynesian Wayfinding: Modern Methods and Techniques of Non-Instrument Navigation," *Polynesian Voyaging Society Hōkūle'a*, accessed April 11, 2024, https://hokulea.com/polynesian-wayfinding/.

2. Queer

In this section, I provide an exploration of queer theory as a method underpinning my research. I regard queer theory as a space of curiosity,[12] as unsettling normativities,[13] and as intersectional,[14] drawing patterns toward 'disruption, creativity, and hope'.[15] I think with Holzer et al., who find that what 'queer methods have in common' is an ability 'to re-orientate not only the subjects and objects of scientific inquiry, but also their author(s) as well as the reader(s)'.[16] I propose the ocean as queer and examine alternative methods for encountering law, the ocean, and global governance.

In turning to the ocean and exploring ocean subjectivity, queer methods work to disrupt rather than direct, reorientating expectations. It then follows that queer methods 'inherently oppose the assumption that methods are pre-discursive apparatuses that allow access to universally true knowledge'.[17] A poem, a military agenda, silk cloth, the nuclear bomb, and oceanic navigators sojourn throughout the text, speaking to – and with – the ocean, or oceans (?), undefined, multiple, singular, in singularity, fluid, sandy, dynamic, queer. I think with a friend, mentor, and international lawyer, Dianne Otto, who provokes us to step (swim? dwell?) 'outside the normal presumption of heterosexuality'.[18] This chapter follows the thread of asking about the role of heteronormative ordering in dominant law and governance structures, as Otto elaborates:

> Through a queer lens, heterosexuality emerges as the basic model for all dominant systems of social relations it provides some of the building blocks for international law's conception of "order." Understood as the elemental, natural, "normal" form of human association, heterosexuality not only shapes how we think of "normal" interpersonal and familial relationships, but is also the presumed basis for all forms of "normal" community, including that encompassed by the "normal" nation-state, international law's primary subject.[19]

12 Dianne Otto, "'Taking a Break' from 'Normal': Thinking Queer in the Context of International Law," *Proceedings of the Annual Meeting: American Society of International Law* 101 (March 28–31, 2007): 119–122.
13 Odette Mazel, "Queer Jurisprudence: Reparative Practice in International Law," *AJIL Unbound* 116 (2022): 10–15.
14 Rao, *Out of Time*.
15 Mazel, "Queer Jurisprudence."
16 Lena Holzer, Bérénice K. Schramm, Juliana Santos de Carvalho and Manon Beury, "An Introduction to International Law Dis/oriented: Sparking Queer Futures in International Law," *Australian Feminist Law Journal* 49, no. 1 (2023): 1–15, 2, 6.
17 Holzer et al., "An Introduction to International Law Dis/oriented," 2, 6.
18 Otto, "Taking a Break," 120.
19 Otto, "Taking a Break," 120.

Across the chapter, I examine how heteronormativity, and cis-normativity, infiltrate and shape legal subjectivity and international ordering at sea, as on land, embracing queer thinking that takes a 'conscious concern with pleasure, thereby "taking a break" from the politics of heteronormative injury, and imagines human sexuality as much more diverse and shifting than the dualism of heterosexuality and homosexuality implies'.[20]

Should pleasure be remembered or rethought as mere folly, this chapter thinks with Rao's articulation of the ever-present spectre of homocapitalism through turning away from dominant epistemologies within international legal traditions. The chapter then pauses, splashes, immerses, floats, and learns – tentatively, slowly – with confusion and likely miscomprehension, as well as limited vocabulary, with Oceanic knowledge, to rethink human-non-human relations and perceptions of the gender binary and sexuality, hetero- and cis-normativity.[21] I remember an encounter with the art of Yuwi artist Léuli Eshrāghi at a gallery in Meanjin (renamed Brisbane by white settlers) described as 'the "dawn" of a series of siapo viliata (animated silk cloths), offering "recent future" feelings from 2025 on faiga fa'akolonē (colonial impacts) in the Great Ocean region'.[22] The silk cloths shiver and float, mesmerising me. The art speaks to sexuality alongside stories of human-ocean relations in the work TAFA (((O))) ATA (SINA LOA) (2020/22), and the accompanying animation, TAFA (((O))) ATA, described on the artist's website as follows:

> This work is part of Eshrāghi's wider focus on recentering the Indigenous gender spectrum of fa'afafine-fa'atama in kinship structures and representing Sāmoan visual cultures by meditating on online access to the oldest bark cloths held in colonial collections. These include siapo mamanu (hand painted bark cloths) collected by the British Navy and donated between 1700–1783 to the University of Glasgow and 1837–41 to the British Museum. Combining animated linework highlighting three of these bark cloths and a poem on the colonial ruptures between cyclical and linear temporality, TAFA (((O))) ATA is a way of haunting colonial museums and knowledge systems with the affirmation of continuing Indigenous pleasures, temporalities and ceremonial-political structures.[23]

Eshrāghi's haunting of the colonial museum inspires my inquiry into the international law of the sea, challenging mainstream legal representations of

20 Otto, "Taking a Break," 120.
21 Rao, *Out of Time.*
22 "QAGOMA," *Queensland Art Gallery Board of Trustees*, accessed April 11, 2024, qagoma.qld.gov.au.
23 Léuli Eshrāghi, *TAFA (((O))) ATA (SINA LOA)*, 2022, digital print on silk, Queensland Art Gallery: Gallery of Modern Art, Brisbane, http://leulieshraghi.art/siapoviliata.

the ocean as free, unencumbered, neutral, and available, without agency and distinctly not human, not territory, not owned, and yet permitting repetitions of imperial violence: including, always, militarised projections of strength and extractive frames that expel/contain/deposit harmful waste in the name of security. I find myself asking (myself) what I mean by queer methods, unsettling me and asking me to know that which is disorderly, disorientated, and resistant[24] as equally living, knowable, and agential.

With curiosity, I read queer theory to embrace spaces of resistance and liberation that approach legal knowledge and legal subjectivity outside of the frames of liberal humanism, addressing queer lives through an intersectional understanding of systems and frames that reinforce and consolidate one another. I am in the Pacific – Oceania – but I remember Tinsley's account of the queer Atlantic:

> [W]hat happens when queer theories start with explicit formulations of racialized sexuality and sexualized race, rather than add them in after theories like performativity have already been elaborated? How does this change in point of departure change the tidal pattern of queer theory? How might it shift the field's dominant metaphors, decentering performativity's stages and unearthing other topoi?[25]

This cultivates in me a curiosity about the frames of law – not only 'to destabilize and deconstruct identity categories, but the systems based on those categories'.[26] While I regard these destabilising moves as commencing with sexuality, including a refusal of cis-gendering and heteronormativity, the co-constitutive nature of vectors of power leads me toward an intersectional recognition of how gender and sexuality are deeply invested in the production of race, ableism, class, caste, religion, and nationalism.[27] Strangeness before, and estrangement from the law, to dwell outside of the law's dominant frames of subjectivity, becomes a space for queer curiosity.[28] The persistence of the production of the state, and sovereignty, as a heteronormative and gendered matrix entreats an unruly journey toward what remains outside of that prism toward the ocean, in the ocean, across oceans, agential and outside of the heteronormative mainstream of international law; the international law of the sea; maritime security; the state. The ocean, as a legal entity/agent, refuses to belong, fit, or comply with the frames of normativity that exist within

24 Holzer et al., "An Introduction to International Law Dis/oriented."
25 Omise'eke Natasha Tinsley, "Black Atlantic, Queer Atlantic: Queer Imaginings of the Middle Passage," *GLQ: A Journal of Lesbian and Gay Studies* 14, no. 2–3 (2008): 191–215, 205.
26 Mazel, "Queer Jurisprudence."
27 Rao, *Out of Time*, 54.
28 Sara Ahmed, *Strange Encounters: Embodied Others in Post-Coloniality* (Abingdon: Routledge, 2000).

international law. Alternative legal structures, such as those within Oceania and Indigenous legal traditions, already offer oceanic subjectivity that is relational and integral to human experience with vastly different temporal arcs.

In shifting from queer lives to the/a queer ocean, I am conscious of the shift away from the political commitment to queer livelihoods at the centre of queer theory. Yet, I regard queer antinormativity as an aperture for seeing the 'shape-shifting quality of queerness' that is pivotal in demonstrating 'how gender and sexuality are co-constituted by a host of other categories including (but not only) nation, religion, race, class, and caste'.[29] I seek to embrace a productive space of antinormativity, of temporal dissonance, of both and neither, while navigating two significant adjunct concerns within queer scholarship. First, the question of futurity, which Rao describes as risking 'a refiguration of queer as model capitalist subject whose inclusion promises a future growth and economic dynamism' in contrast to queer temporalities, which acknowledge 'queer theory's determination to stand askew to the progressive march of time'.[30] Second, the tension between pleasure and curiosity as a queer method, on the one hand, and the enduring violence – its persistence and spaces of growth – through which global capital produces 'forms of material precarity in which homophobic moral panics flourish',[31] on the other. Queer futurity, understood through these frames (tensions), requires urgent legal strategies that do not dwell outside of the possible and yet which do not collapse back into dominant modes of law and governance. I propose a zooming out from the individual, beyond the state, to think with human-non-human encounters, following queer posthuman feminist thinkers to 'explore the multiple forms of interconnection between and across the inhuman or non-human categories, in a manner that avoids dialectical oppositions'.[32] Through this queer encounter with law, I explore the possibilities beyond the inevitability of the reproduction of the liberal – capital – military mode that underpins international law informed by, in Rao's frame, western modernity[33] or, as I have described here, Enlightenment man (and his predisposition for cis- and heteronormative ordering) through Oceanic encounters with the non-human ocean as queer Other.

3. Ocean

The ocean is not a random choice of queer subject. Critical ocean studies identify the fluid and unmoored nature of the ocean as more than a visual

29 Rao, *Out of Time*, 12.
30 Rao, *Out of Time*, 12, 2.
31 Rao, *Out of Time*, 25; See also Vanja Hamzić, "International Law as Violence: Competing Absences of the Other," in *Queering International Law: Possibilities, Alliances, Complicities, Risks*, ed. Dianne Otto (Abingdon and New York: Routledge, 2018).
32 Jones, *Feminist Theory and International Law*, 126.
33 Rao, *Out of Time*, 26.

or geographical frame, identifying systems of knowledge,[34] ways of being in the world, and temporal re-imaginings that are of significant value to a queer encounter within international law.[35] Blum articulates the potential of the sea, or ocean, as a focus of critical inquiry, describing it as:

> central not just as a theme or organizing metaphor with which to widen a landlocked critical prospect: in its geophysical, historical, and imaginative properties, the sea instead provides a new epistemology – a new dimension – for thinking about surfaces, depths, and the extra-terrestrial dimensions of planetary resources and relations.[36]

Further, drawing on Steinberg, Blum argues 'modes of oceanic thought are themselves predicated on relations whose unfixed, ungraspable contours are ever in multi-dimensional flux',[37] contending that 'in deriving from the fluidity of its object of study a constitutive position of unboundedness, drift, and solvency, oceanic studies does not heed the global political designations fundamental to transnational work'.[38] Critical ocean studies use the oceans' liminality and fluidity to unsettle political and legal hegemonies, while scholarship across the hydrohumanities identifies matter as agential – 'meaning that the matter itself is always queer, always surprising and fundamentally entangled'.[39] These encounters with ocean knowledge find much deeper resonance and expression in Oceania, where:

> Indigenous epistemologies from Oceania provide alternative conceptual frameworks that inform our critique of these notions of protection, security, and border waters themselves. As Indigenous epistemologies theorize and articulate, these externally constructed 'borders' are fluid and interconnected pathways – thus, the impacts of military pollution cannot be contained or controlled within a seemingly static area of the ocean.[40]

DeLoughrey analyses the 2016 RIMPAC (Rim of the Pacific) exercise and argues for 'a vigorous engagement with naval hydro-politics',[41] develop-

34 Stefan Helmreich, *A Book of Waves* (Durham and London: Duke University Press, 2023); Blum, "Introduction: Oceanic Studies."
35 DeLoughrey, "Toward a Critical Ocean Studies for the Anthropocene."
36 Blum, "Introduction: Oceanic Studies," 151.
37 Blum, "Introduction: Oceanic Studies," 151; Philip E. Steinberg, "Of Other Seas: Metaphors and Materialities in Maritime Regions," *Atlantic Studies* 10, no. 2 (2013): 156–169.
38 Blum, "Introduction: Oceanic Studies," 152.
39 Heather Davis, *Plastic Matter* (Durham: Duke University Press, 2022), 7.
40 Tiara R. Na'puti and Sylvia C. Frain, "Indigenous Environmental Perspectives: Challenging the Oceanic Security State," *Security Dialogue* 54, no. 2 (2023): 115–136, 130.
41 DeLoughrey, "Toward a Critical Ocean Studies for the Anthropocene," 31.

ing, as Na'puti and Frain do, a move beyond environmental humanities, hydrohumanities, or critical ocean studies, to think with, to decolonise, and to shift knowledge through knowing Oceania, diverse and complex, already knowing and living with the non-human. In an important issue of the journal *Intersections,* the nexus between constructions of gender and sexuality and the repetitions of militarism in Oceania are voiced through:

> multiple methodologies of approaching the complex gendered, social, political and cultural implications of Pacific Island militarisation, thereby demonstrating a cross-regional, multilingual and vibrant brand of Pacific Studies that is not tied to a single language or colonial origin (particularly Anglophone), nor caught in a binary between the 'Rim' and the 'Basin.' Turning to militarisation as a frame was vital for mapping alternative notions of the region that crossed and even contested various colonial, political and language histories as they have been articulated in Pacific Studies.[42]

Drawing these scholarships and thinkers together and writing as an international lawyer, I find the ocean as resolutely queer in its nonlinear temporality and fluid resistance, potentially addressing the risks of queer futures returning to Western heterocaptialist frames through a rethinking of legal subjectivity that is not premised on Western heteronormative masculinity, thus providing international law with global systems, of law and of oceans, that reconceive of a human-non-human subjectivity, conceptions of humanness, community, and kin. In contrast, global militaries and powerful maritime states deploy the posthuman military technology of the automated naval vessel via a matrix of deterrence through strength, heteronormative masculinity as military might, and gendered symbolism. I argue for a queer reading of the ocean that moves beyond binary thinking and which deploys the oceans' fluid, dynamic, and curious form as a means to unravel military-capital's stranglehold on legal relations. The chapter thus teases out the possibilities of queer method as a mechanism for rethinking encounters with the non-human, whether technologies or matter, to think with humans-out-of-the-loop technologies as existing in agential forms in other non-human entities, here the ocean, in a manner that need not reproduce heteronormative violence of the Anthropocene.

4. Ghost Fleets

In 2022, automated naval vessels, developed by the United States Department of Defense, held a significant role in the biennial RIMPAC multinational

42 Victor Bascara, Keith L. Camacho and Elizabeth DeLoughrey, "Gender and Sexual Politics of Pacific Island Militarisation," *Intersections: Gender and Sexuality in Asia and the Pacific* 37 (2015), para. 5.

maritime exercise.[43] Previously suspended in 2020 due to the global COVID-19 pandemic, the 2022 RIMPAC operations are described as 'a month of realistic, relevant combined operations training conducted in and around the Hawaiian Islands and Southern California'.[44] As a form of maritime war games, RIMPAC offers training and logistics development for allied forces in the Pacific. In July-August 2022, the states participating were Australia, Brunei, Canada, Chile, Colombia, Denmark, Ecuador, France, Germany, India, Indonesia, Israel, Japan, Malaysia, Mexico, Netherlands, New Zealand, Peru, the Republic of Korea, the Republic of the Philippines, Singapore, Sri Lanka, Thailand, Tonga, the United Kingdom and the United States. Larger studies of the RIMPAC project and, in particular, the continued use of Hawai'ian waters as maritime playgrounds are urgent and already have an expression in Hawai'ian scholarship.[45] In this chapter, I examine the presence, meaning, and consequences of automated maritime vessels at RIMPAC 2022 and, more broadly, in US maritime security policy.

Also known as the US Ghost Fleet, automated naval vessels form part of the current and future maritime security agenda of the United States, its allies, and – increasingly – other states with naval ambitions. In the two years it takes me to write (think, speak, discuss) this chapter, what was a largely US initiative now ripples into the naval futures of China, Iran, Australia, and beyond. The testing of new technologies in the Pacific during RIMPAC 2022 echoes past decisions by military powers to test nuclear technologies in the region. The earlier testing displaced the population of the Marshallese Islands and left behind the Runit Dome, or the tomb, comprising approximately 73,000 cubic metres of radioactive waste.[46] The Pacific Ocean traces the legacy of Englishman James Cook's expeditions 'discovering' the region, the nuclear fallout of testing contaminating water, humans, sand, and stones, and the routes sailed during the RIMPAC war games, again and again. In each of these arrivals, the sea of islands that form Oceania are not consulted,

43 DeLoughrey, "Toward a Critical Ocean Studies for the Anthropocene"; Craig Santos Perez, "From Understory: During RIMPAC 2014," *Hawai'i Review*, no. 81 (2013–2015): 32.

44 Commander, U.S. Third Fleet Public Affairs, "RIMPAC 2022 Concludes," *America's Navy*, August 3, 2022, www.navy.mil/Press-Office/News-Stories/Article/3118649/rimpac-2022-concludes/. See also Caitlin M. Kenney, "Robot Ships Debut at RIMPAC, Helping US Navy Sail Toward a Less-Crewed Future," *Defense One*, August 3, 2022, www.defenseone.com/technology/2022/08/robot-ships-debut-rimpac-helping-us-navy-sail-toward-less-crewed-future/375305/.

45 Kyle Kajihiro and Ty P. Kāwika Tengan, "The Future Is Koa," in *The Value of Hawai'i3: Hulihia, the Turning*, eds., Noelani Goodyear-Ka'ōpua, Craig Howes, Jonathan Kay Kamakawiwo'ole Osorio, Aiko Yamashiro, Paige Rasmussen and Craig Howes (Honolulu: University of Hawai'i Press and the Center for Biographical Research, 2020), 62–66.

46 Joy Lehuanani Enomoto, "Nuclear Hemorrhage: Enewetok Does Not Forget," *Native American and Indigenous Studies* 9, no. 2 (2022): 1–2; Aimee Bahng, "The Pacific Proving Grounds and the Proliferation of Settler Environmentalism," *Journal of Transnational American Studies* 11, no. 2 (2020).

imagined as tiny specks of land, with traditions un-modern, and of little use to those whose capital and militaries reinscribe Cook's maps of the Pacific.[47]

The US Ghost Fleet incorporates new modes of surveillance and violence into naval capabilities while reproducing old modes of discourse around security actors, deterrence, threat, and strength, alongside the production of the Pacific (for the US, this is not Oceania but the Pacific) as barely inhabited such that its human and non-human residents are not consulted or included in assessments of risk. The repetition of disregard for human and non-human residents of Oceania is striking in its similarities to the earlier period of nuclear testing, repeating, in turn, the worldview of European 'explorers' that came before that. Explorers/colonisers whose perception of the world dictated understanding of property, rights, and humanness that seemingly infiltrates international law without question. The US Ghost Fleet, and the changing US agenda with regard to its development and deployment of military technologies in the Pacific, traverses a different posthuman ocean to the possibility of queer oceanic knowledge. Across these temporalities, human and non-human lives in Oceania are reproduced as peripheral, silent, and unknowing, just as the ocean is perceived as, at best, akin to land territories: neutral, uninhabited, and flat. In contrast, Marshallese wave riders, or rimeto, use the visceral and visual knowledge of wave motion to navigate with the sea such that 'Marshallese piloting extends to long-distance voyages and that waves, which are always in motion, constitute the main environmental feature as seamarks or navigation signs'.[48] For rimeto, the sea, the ocean, literally speaks through the encounter of the human body with the motion of waves. I am interested in the queer legal relations enacted when human-non-human encounters are framed as integral to the experience of being in the world, the agential nature of oceans functions – and the unsettling international lawyers might experience as a result – as a prompt to accommodate, address, and to hear the ocean, or perhaps to think what it means to be human in the ocean, of the ocean, at times of ocean vulnerability.

Instead of ocean vulnerability, the Ghost Fleet is framed by the US as apprehending state maritime vulnerabilities. As Grome explains, 'the hope is to utilize the technologically-advanced Ghost Fleet to maintain and perpetuate peaceful relations through the demonstration of military superiority'.[49] The 2022 US Ghost Ship Fleet sent to RIMPAC consisted of four different automated maritime vessels, named by the US Department of Defense as Nomad,

47 Gina Heathcote, "Terraqueous Feminisms and the International Law of the Sea," in *International Law and Posthuman Theory*, eds. Matilda Arvidsson and Emily Jones (Abingdon: Routledge, 2024).

48 Genz, *Breaking the Shell*, 127.

49 Erich D. Grome, "Spectres of the Sea: The United States Navy's Autonomous Ghost Fleet, Its Capabilities and Impacts, and the Legal Ethical Issues That Surround," *Journal of Maritime Law and Commerce* 49, no. 1 (2018): 31–69, 34–35.

Ranger, Sea Hawk, and Sea Hunter, each with varied capabilities. The larger US Ghost Fleet project, initiated in 2019, was originally scheduled to lead to the production of ten vessels by 2024. However, shifting US agendas reduced the size of the fleet to four vessels. Undertaken by the Department of Defence Strategic Capabilities Office in partnership with the US Navy, the US Ghost Fleet project underscores how complex gendered and civilising narratives infiltrate maritime security. The articulation of a need for the Ghost Fleet to patrol the Pacific, extending out from US bases in the Marshallese Islands, as well as rhetoric around maritime threats from China and Russia, and, from 2022, the sheer joy in the deployment of the growing Ghost Fleet into the Pacific as part of RIMPAC 2022, illustrate the poverty of the international law of the sea to address changing modalities and technologies in maritime spaces, including the development of posthuman actors that cross between human and machine decision-making capacities. The vast naval and military reporting and analysis of the development of automated maritime vessels, as well as the role of machine learning and artificial intelligence, fails to discuss the legal dimensions of their development.[50] Similarly, there is an assumption that the law on collective security, as found in Chapter VII of the United Nations Charter,[51] is untouched by the development of new naval capabilities. In the Pacific Ocean, the combination of US access to vast Exclusive Economic Zones adjacent to US Pacific territories (including the Marshallese Islands) established via Article 5 of the United Nations Convention on the Law of the Sea (UNCLOS),[52] and the enshrining of the freedom of the High Seas in the same convention and as customary international law, permits the US to use the Pacific to test and manoeuvre new forms of maritime systems with relative impunity. The UNCLOS defines a warship in Article 29 as having to fulfil four criteria: that a ship must bear external marks distinguishing its nationality, be under the command of an officer of the appropriate state, be registered, and be – in the archaic language of the convention – 'manned' by a crew under the state's armed forces.[53] For an automated maritime warship, vessel, or drone, these requirements leave new technologies in a grey zone with respect to how they are governed under the law of the sea.[54] Similarly,

50 George Galdorisi and Sam J. Tangredi, *AI at War: How Big Data, Artificial Intelligence, and Machine Learning Are Changing Naval Warfare* (Annapolis, MD: Naval Institute Press, 2021).

51 Charter of the United Nations, 1 UNTS XVI (1945).

52 Convention on the Law of the Sea, 1833 UNTS 397 (November 16, 1994).

53 Bernard H. Oxman, "The Regime of Warships Under the United Nations Convention on the Law of the Sea," *Virginia Journal of International Law* 24, no. 4 (1984): 809.

54 Robert Veal, Michael Tsimplis and Andrew Serdy, "The Legal Status and Operation of Unmanned Maritime Vehicles," *Ocean Development & International Law* 50, no. 1 (2019): 23–48; Sabrina Hasan, "Analysing the Definition of 'Ship' to Facilitate Marine Autonomous Surface Ships as Ship Under the Law of the Sea," *Australian Journal of Maritime & Ocean Affairs* 15, no. 3 (2022): 268–283; S. Lindsay, "Sufficiency of Existing Legal Frameworks

legal inquiries into the legality of drones (airborne) under the law of armed conflict have largely concluded that the weapon system itself is not illegal, although their use is governed by existing laws of war and international humanitarian law. Furthermore, the laws of war do not address the development of military technologies and their impact on the communities where they are tested, while the doctrine of the freedom of the high seas means no permissions need to be obtained. In the Pacific Ocean, the detonation of nuclear weapons leads to the displacement of the Marshallese people, long-term health consequences, and, less well-known, the curtailment of specific ocean technologies, including the use of stick charts and the training of a new generation of rimeto. This ocean technology, where humans encounter the ocean as their guide, repeats the moments of loss and displacement – of people and knowledge – in the region, felt as climate change refugees, as nuclear refugees, and as peoples 'discovered' by Europeans. The Ghost Ships' navigation of the region, thus, arrives at a sea of islands that knows the ocean as agential, readable, and dynamic, even as Western European knowledge persists in displacing both people and understandings.

Existing legal regimes provide little restraint on the development and use of automated maritime vessels. The language of 'testing' has also been deployed strategically in the Pacific as a consolidation of strength through deterrence and with the continued articulation of China as lurking aggressively in the South China Sea. Bascara et al. identify 'the constitutive role for gender and sexuality for understanding notions such as empire, war, security, development, resistance and subalternity, made legible and meaningful through a critical engagement with militarisation in the Pacific'.[55] Maritime law, the law of the sea, and laws of war offer little insight into future – or current – regulation of automated maritime vessels, just as with nuclear testing in the prior century. This is, in part, because of the nature of the ocean itself, deemed a benign surface for maritime and naval activities, with the tiny island communities in the Pacific often envisaged as benefiting from the presence of larger military networks – either through discourses of protection or through assurances of increased trade in port towns.

for Addressing Maritime Security Challenges Surrounding Autonomous Vessels," *Australian Naval Review*, no. 2 (2020): 104–116; Anna Petrig, "Unmanned Offender and Enforcer Vessels and the Multi-Dimensional Concept of 'Ship' under the United Nations Convention on the Law of the Sea," in *The United Nations Convention on the Law of the Sea: A System of Regulation*, eds. Kristina Siig, Fenella Billing and Birgit Feldtmann (Abingdon: Routledge, 2021). The 2022 edition of the US Commander's Handbook empowers the US Chief of Naval Operations to designate USVs and UUVs as warships, acknowledging that a warship may be crewed remotely or by other means. See, for instance, Department of the Navy, Office of the Chief of Naval Operations, Headquarters, U.S. Marine Corps Department of Homeland Security and U.S. Coast Guard, *The Commander's Handbook on the Law of Naval Operations* (March 2022), Section 2.2.

55 Bascara et al., "Gender and Sexual Politics," para. 1.

Maritime war games, such as RIMPAC 2022, and military thinking gain new expression via the arrival of the US automated maritime fleet. In describing how automated maritime vessels are understood within military networks, including the changing agenda for the fleet's growth and use, Wilcox's account of human-non-human dependencies seems pertinent:

> The challenge that the cyborg or posthuman body poses is not the addition of new technological advances to an already-existing human body, but of a body that is always already formed through norms and relations to others, whether these others are human, technological or animal.[56]

Rather than only encountering the international legal regime as satisfactory in being able to adapt to new technologies, such as automated maritime vessels, or requiring new tools that maintain the *status quo* of legal relations, maritime posthuman technologies might be analysed through the lens of legal knowledge drawn from outside of dominant and mainstream contemporary legal relations. In Oceania, the framing of ocean agency and subjectivity, produced through a non-hierarchal account of human and non-human encounters, requires processes that address the strangeness of the Other as well as recognition of how the inhuman and the non-human are constructed as central to humanist traditions.

The military manoeuvres in the Pacific during RIMPAC 2022, understood within naval communities as capacity building and technology testing grounds, demonstrate a further account of queer more-than-human oceans, where the ocean presents and arrives as a troubling additional actor intertwined in military, economic, and human decision-making. The absence of international legal responses to automated technologies on the ocean, across collective security and the law of the sea, replicates a perception of the ocean, informed by the expansion of Empire and repeated during the Cold War, as a flat and neutral space of encounter, largely uninhabited, and unaffected by human actions. This is an ocean that law constructs as beyond the state and thus permitting maritime, military, and extractive behaviour without constraint while furthering heteronormative, racialised, and gendered laws that are significant in their contribution to environmental violence, alongside a forgetting and maligning of non-Western traditions, while functioning as intergenerational sites of injury to island communities and centring of violence as the status quo of international law.[57]

In January 2022, there was a curious shift away from the Ghost Fleet project by the US Strategic Capabilities Office when the existing four automated

56 L. Wilcox, "Drones, Swarms and Becoming-Insect: Feminist Utopias and Posthuman Politics," *Feminist Review* 116, no. 1 (2017): 25–45, 27.

57 Stelder, "The Colonial Difference."

marine vessels were gifted to the US Navy, and the ambitions for a larger Ghost Fleet halted. This shifting US agenda suggests the ocean curtailed the original Ghost Fleet project: ocean unpredictability, extreme weather conditions, and an oceanic refusal to be simply a surface for the deployment of automated maritime vessels to travel over, signals a different sort of posthuman encounter where technology and ocean undermine the human. While changing US Ghost Fleet agendas mask a series of different influences on US naval policy, including changes in political and military leadership, changing sites of military violence and threat, economic agendas, and a fast-changing pace of technological development, there are some constants. First, the interplay of a need for testing grounds (or seas) and deterrence as strength underscores how agendas and communications around the Ghost Fleet are given traction, regardless of whether they articulate a retraction or an expansion of automated systems. Second, the international law of the sea is not seriously regarded as a hindrance to the use of new technologies in multinational maritime exercises, such as RIMPAC, or in naval warfare. The consequence is spaces of contestation in the law are ignored through an assumption of consensus and licence for states to embark on maritime agendas without significant consultation with the island, coastal, and land communities directly affected and without reflection on adjunct regimes that impact the ocean, including climate change law. Third, the persistence of civilising narratives and the identification of rogue states as creating the need for increased capacity for violence via technology deploys well-known tropes requiring the language of suspicion, mistrust, and dishonesty that often ignore legal regimes and invoke discourses of morality that are fused with gendered, queer, and racialised stereotypes to be given meaning.

5. Rimeto

I want to examine the possibility of the ocean as providing 'new understandings of mapping and representing; living and knowing'[58] to consciously deploy queer methods and offer oceanic legal encounters with the capacity to reimagine legal possibilities and legal subjectivities. Steinberg and Peters write:

> The ocean, as we have argued – through its material reformation, mobile churning, and nonlinear temporality – creates the need for new understandings of mapping and representing; living and knowing; Wet ontologies, fluid spaces, governing and resisting. Like the ocean itself, maritime subjects and objects can move across, fold into, and emerge out of water in unrecognised and unanticipated ways.[59]

58 Steinberg and Peters, "Wet Ontologies," 260.
59 Steinberg and Peters, "Wet Ontologies," 260.

The synergy between queer theories and critical ocean studies, as well as the hydrohumanities, undoes the dominance of Enlightenment traditions and, in particular, their preoccupation with property, capital, and violence, inviting alternative legal traditions into international legal vocabularies.[60] The unsettling of temporal and fixed encounters, of progress narratives, and of security through violence has resonance with queer approaches to international law[61] and with critical ocean studies that encounter the ocean through a postcolonial and posthuman concern for the non-human outside the logics of settler-colonialism.[62] In this section, I enlarge my discussion of Oceania knowledges and begin to bring the chapter to a close with an account of rimeto – wave riders – in the Marshallese Islands. However, this is preceded by a number of reflections on the potential limitations and frustrations with the approach I have taken in this chapter.

Although my focus on the queer ocean has drawn in scholarship and knowledge of the Oceania region, my approach has not, *per se*, centred queer lives in Oceania. In speaking of the ocean as queer and in drawing on indigenous and island knowledge, it is not my intention to imagine a space free of the persistent discrimination and harm directed at LGBTQI+ communities and individuals. I have highlighted Eshrāghi's art to prompt further engagement with the multifaceted experiences of gender and sexuality in Oceania, otherwise outside of the scope of my study, while simultaneously inscribing the necessity of decolonised accounts of law that refuse dominant frames of non-normative sexualities and which recognise and name the gender binary so central to both Western and international legal traditions. The possibility of law decolonised functions as a sub-theme, perhaps an assumption, throughout the chapter underpinning my understanding of queer feminist posthuman thinking. Kapur and Tamale develop legal pluralism within international law while addressing and naming the specificity of legal liberalisms. Kapur's critique of legal liberalism articulates its 'proven inability to be "open to", to "engage with" and to "learn from" the "Other", whomever or whatever that "Other" might be', opening her own text to diverse accounts of freedom beyond the liberal imaginary.[63] In a complementary yet distinctly different encounter with law and Pan-African knowledges, Tamale frames a decolonial ideology that:

> must be anti-imperialist, anti-patriarchal and anti-militarist. It must jealously safeguard the interests of those who suffer from intersectional

60 Heathcote, "Terraqueous Feminisms."
61 Rao, *Out of Time*; Hamzić, "International Law as Violence"; Otto, "Taking a Break."
62 Steinberg, "Of Other Seas"; Blum, "Introduction; Oceanic Studies"; Helmreich, *A Book of Waves*.
63 Ratna Kapur, *Gender, Alterity and Human Rights: Freedom in a Fishbowl* (Cheltenham: Edward Elgar Publishing, 2018), 47; Sylvia Tamale, *Decolonisation and Afro-Feminism* (Toronto: Daraja Press, 2020).

> oppression on the basis of their gender, social status, ethnic and cultural origin, sexuality, disability, age and other grounds.[64]

Oceania's plural knowledges of gender, sexuality, law, humans, and the non-human offer important, often overlooked, accounts of living and being in the world with both global and local understandings. While they inform my understanding of queer ocean subjectivity, there is much more to know, and, following Na'puti and Frain, I acknowledge the diversity of how 'Indigenous oceanic perspectives theorize water in relation to land, arguing that place is archipe-lagic, fluid, dynamic, and moving'.[65]

The urgency of Oceania and its knowledge of, in Jetñil-Kijiner and Niviâna's words, land and sea justice is made visible as climate change threatens to unravel Oceania knowledges further, repeating the dispossession already produced through colonialism, occupation, military manoeuvres, and nuclear testing.[66] The Runit Dome, holding the nuclear fallout, alongside island homes and shorelines, traces rising sea levels that threaten the security of humans and non-humans globally. As such, my analysis is not only an analytical exercise delighting in the metaphors of fluidity and waves and its resonance with non-binary and non-normative sexuality and gender. Rather I am alert to the confluence of settler colonial, imperialist, Anthropocene, and discursive violences that interlock to displace Oceania as home and as a site of knowledge, just as they displace queer lives within the heteronormative and cis-normative ordering of law.[67] In Oceania, ways of knowing embrace how:

> the ocean is understood as a pathway connecting islands, rather than a divider separating landscapes or regions. Such ideas are foundational to Indigenous oceanic knowledge systems and expansive spatial geographies that conceptualize space in more holistic, relational, and archipelagic ways not exclusively tied to land.[68]

The disappearance of small islands threatened by rising sea levels and the violence wrought by climate change is intimately connected to the possibility of a queer ocean undoing how legal relations perceive the relationship between states, humans, and the environment. The displacement of knowledge traditions during colonial expansion, the displacement and disfigurement during nuclear testing, and the displacement of humans and the destruction of the environment and non-human actors due to climate change provide cycles of

64 Tamale, *Decolonisation and Afro-feminism*, 382.
65 Na'puti and Frain, "Indigenous Environmental Perspectives," 118.
66 Jetñil-Kijiner and Niviâna, *Rise*.
67 Steinberg, "Of Other Seas."
68 Na'puti and Frain, "Indigenous Environmental Perspectives," 119.

memory and repetitions of violence. The ocean as a legal subject can only emerge within Western legal traditions through a queer posthuman encounter that understands these multiple repetitions of Othering of humans and non-humans, even as the non-international legal ways within Oceania provide ways of knowing the ocean that also displace the hierarchies central to Enlightenment and dominant legal traditions.

Encountering the ocean as a subject returns the chapter to Oceania scholarship and the remembering of queer ways of being and knowing the ocean, as within the human rather than as Other, and alternative legal traditions that refuse the hoisting of humanity as the template for legal subjectivity. The queer ocean thus undermines the attempts at regulating, harnessing, owning, or instrumentalising the ocean in maritime war games, deterrence projects, and human violence.[69] In examining automated maritime manoeuvres, I argue for the ocean as subject, unspeaking, and yet reclaiming, returning, undoing the excesses of human military-capital and, perhaps, better understood through the subsuming of human identities into human-non-human traditions, such as those expressed and understood by Oceania thinkers. I draw on the rimeto, or wave riders, in the Marshallese Islands whose challenge to climate change and localised nuclear histories, beyond fixations with baselines and extractive encounters at sea, offer a queer ocean.[70] This draws together with Jetñil-Kijiner's activism on alternative Oceanic figurations that disrupt gender binaries and human-nature hierarchies to address climate change, violence, and planetary survival.[71]

Genz narrates their encounter with alternative ocean technologies in the Marshallese Islands and records the dislocation of knowledge after the thermonuclear tests in 1954, and the further displacement of the Marshallese from Rongelap in 1985 to evocatively evidence the relationship between humans and the ocean, and the value of technologies that work with the ocean. The displaced knowledges of the Marshallese Islanders are complemented by the complex, varied navigational systems from Hawai'i to Kiribati, demonstrating how these technologies provide a way of knowing the ocean.[72] Genz documents the attempts to revive the knowledge lost due to displacement after the nuclear testing removed communities from Bikini and Rongelap Atolls. While Bikini Atoll was left uninhabitable, 'the community returned to Rongelap three years later, being informed by scientists that the land and its resources were safe'.[73] Radiation-related sickness had the subsequent effect

69 Tinsley, "Black Atlantic, Queer Atlantic."

70 J. H. Genz, "Resolving Ambivalence in Marshallese Navigation: Relearning, Reinterpreting, and Reviving the "Stick Chart" Wave Models," *Structure and Dynamics* 9, no. 1 (2016).

71 Jaimey Hamilton Faris, "Ocean Weaves: Reconfigurations of Climate Justice in Oceania," *Feminist Review* 130, no. 1 (2022): 5–25.

72 Genz, *Breaking the Shell*, 128.

73 Genz, *Breaking the Shell*, 2.

of either displacing or causing severe illness to the Rongalese and, as Genz documents, ending the traditional training of wave riders, the rimeto, as well as knowledge of stick charts and their use as a navigational tool.[74]

The navigational skills of Marshallese rimeto sit within the context of diverse navigational techniques across the region, including Hawai'ian star compasses and systems which 'read' wind and weather to chart journeys at sea.[75] The knowledge passed down through Marshallese communities has the separate, distinct characteristic of relying on embodied responses to waves, as well as stick charts, which are used on land to teach future rimeto how to read oceanic conditions and direction.[76] The gaps in rimeto knowledge today are linked to the upheaval on the islands after nuclear testing; Huffer records Lijon Ekinlang's partial knowledge, which she reported to Huffer such that she:

> might have become a navigator and could have passed her navigation test when she was young but was prevented from doing so by her father's death and then by a move away from Rongelap.[77]

In Genz's research, the specific nature of oral histories passed to some but not all, as well as the recognition of rival rimeto methods – closely guarded – inhibited his attempts to study the capacity of rimeto to navigate, although drawing together these partial knowledges has shown how both stick charts and the capacity to read, or listen, to changes in the ocean produce legitimate methods for travelling in Oceania. This is further reinforced by the wider research across the region that sees sophisticated methods of navigation crucial to the establishment of settlements over 2,000 years ago and which, possibly, informed the understanding of Cook's Tahitian companion – and navigator – Tupaia.[78] Across Oceania, both stick and shell charts provide what Genz describes as 'sensory sources of information about the oceanic environment',[79] which require an integrated human encounter with the non-human that is premised on knowledge derived from the ocean.

In their research on decolonising Pasifika education, Mapato and Brice identify stick and shell charts, as well as techniques of wayfinding on the ocean, as key to shifting from Western knowledge forms toward onto-epistemologies,[80]

74 Genz, "Resolving Ambivalence."

75 "Polynesian Wayfinding: Modern Methods and Techniques of Non-Instrument Navigation," *Polynesian Voyaging Society Hōkūle'a*, accessed April 11, 2024, https://hokulea.com/polynesian-wayfinding/.

76 See, for instance, "The Vaka Taumako Project of Pacific Traditions Society," *Vaka Taumako Project*, accessed April 12, 2024, www.vaka.org.

77 Elise Huffer, "Women and Navigation: Does Exception confirm the Rule?" *International Journal of Maritime History* 20, no. 2 (2008): 265.

78 Heathcote, "Terraqueous Feminisms."

79 Genz, "Resolving Ambivalence."

80 Matapo and Brice, "The Art of Wayfinding: Pasifika Success."

in a way that resonates with Genz's description of the work of rimeto as deploying 'oceanic systems of navigation [that] involve a process of combining cognitive information in memory with active sensory sources of information about the oceanic environment'.[81] This is more than a description of a way of navigating between islands, as Maputo and Brice describe:

> Onto-epistemology brings together ontology of being and nature of knowledge, bridging a divide between dualisms of mind over matter (such as Cartesian dualism) and contest the dominant human subject position presented in the "great chain of being" (a presumption that separates the human subject from cosmos and cosmology).[82]

Wayfinding, rimeto, and stick and shell charts open an aperture to modes of thinking and being with the non-human that is not premised on forms of human exceptionalism – that is, the forms of thinking and doing that have limited, but not destroyed, these Oceanic knowledges for the past two hundred years following Cook's 'discovery' of Pacific islands. The embedded human experience of the rimeto, a person of the ocean, attuned to the subtle changes of the ocean, invites a queer imagining of the international legal order that might traverse these temporalities and allow us to know the ocean in queer ways and as queer.

Throughout military and state agendas the ocean is always framed as an empty space, distinct from human lives – which are assumed to happen on land. Embedded in this component of US Ghost Fleet rhetoric is a refusal to know the ocean differently. In examining and drawing out a tiny sample of the rich Oceanic methods of encountering, being, and knowing with the ocean, it is possible to begin to understand how Western Enlightenment and histories of humanism displaced important and sophisticated knowledge structures in Oceania, as elsewhere. At the same time, the articulation of human-ocean encounters in Oceania speaks to the cutting-edge of climate change agendas and offers ways to be with the ocean that recognise Anthropocene violence and the complicity of Western sovereignty, military-capital, and international legal structures in the perpetuation of planetary harms.

6. Humans-out-of-the-loop

In Jetñil-Kijiner's art and poetry, the ocean emerges as a subject, reflecting island epistemologies that befuddle the specificity of international law, arguing, 'We will choose to be rooted in this reef forever'.[83] In the story of the two sisters in Jetñil-Kijiner's exchange with Greenland poet Aka Niviâna, *Rise from One*

81 Genz, "Resolving Ambivalence," 10.
82 Matapo and Brice, "The Art of Wayfinding: Pasifika Success," 27.
83 Jetñil-Kijiner and Niviâna, *Rise*.

Island to Another, and in Marshallese lore, the sisters represent stone and land in the ocean and a 'lesson in permanence'.[84] These are stones that also endure the toxicity of nuclear testing, staying as islanders were displaced and as they return. The violence wrought onto the Marshallese Islanders through nuclear testing forms the impetus for climate change activism in Oceania in a way that centres a shift away from 'the patriarchal structures of introduced parliamentary democracy imbricated with colonial-settler ties and logics'.[85] I have argued through this chapter that as queer as it might sound to international lawyers schooled in seeing knowledge that emphasises human dislocation from nature, Oceania's knowledge and technologies of navigation produce a queer ocean, agential and relational, that resonates with and expands the work of scholars writing in the hydrohumanities and critical ocean studies.

Queer oceans belittle the capitalist desires of military expansion, war games, and racialised violence that have long framed non-Oceanic navigation of the sea of islands. As navies embark on a race to own more automated vessels to circumnavigate oceans with humans safely onshore, the ocean is reproduced as unknown, not-human, fluid, chaotic, unremarkable, a surface to be traversed. Human experiences are imagined as distinct and disconnected from the ocean. In contrast, the queer ocean is an ocean where human-non-human encounters occur with the knowledge that each is in the other, such that the dynamic flow of water is the dynamic flow of humans, leaky, spilling, a million specs of organisms too small to know, and the messy lives of humans are imbricated in the oceanic ripples, of changing tides, and shifting sands. The nanoparticles in the ocean are in the fish, in humans, and are interconnected. I dream of water. I am seasick. Fluid lives disconnect me from landed, propertied configurations of subjectivity that dictate who gets to be human, gendered, racialised, heteronormative, ableist, sinking.

Human-out-of-the-loop technologies are ultimately curtailed by the same ocean features, which disrupt communications and destabilise the unmanned fleet. The ocean evokes a different kind of human-out-of-the-loop as human desire for new technologies and deterrents is undermined by the ocean. In contrast:

> Ancient navigational practices rely on the moon, stars, sun, water currents, wave patterns, smells of the air, and even cloud formations – it is an Indigenous knowledge form that orients ocean spaces as interconnected experiential pathways. Seafaring also requires deep knowledge of place-based ecologies and environments such as the reefs, wind currents, sea swells, whales, and shoals.[86]

84 Jetñil-Kijiner and Niviâna, *Rise*.
85 Hamilton Faris, "Ocean Weaves," 11.
86 Na'puti and Frain, "Indigenous Environmental Perspectives."

Chapter 4

On Straightening and Subversion

A Queer Feminist Exploration of International Space Law and Politics

Claerwen O'Hara and Cris van Eijk[1]

1. Introduction

Outer space holds radical imaginative potential. It provides an outside, an alternative to this world, through which critical thought and resistance can emerge.[2] Outer space is vast and infinitely diverse. It is queer. Through its boundless possibilities, outer space can disrupt human regimes of normativity and make earthly hierarchies seem small, strange, and irrelevant. It can help us to find 'cracks in the imagery of a present that is often not nearly as hegemonic as thought',[3] providing 'imaginal breaks' that render other ways of doing and being thinkable.

The capacity of outer space to inspire in us a belief that things could be different can be seen in the role it has played in anticolonial and revolutionary movements. In the early-1960s, in Kenya, outer space became a metaphor for a better future, leading the Kenyan National Assembly to link their struggle for independence with the 'space age'.[4] In the mid-1960s, science teacher and member of the Zambian resistance movement, Edward Mukuka Nkoloso, went even further, wishing to blast Zambia into independence with the launch of a Zambian-made rocket into space.[5]

1 We would like to thank Tamsin Phillipa Paige and the peer reviewer for their detailed and insightful feedback on this chapter. An earlier version of this chapter was presented at the Law, Literature and Humanities Association of Australasia Conference in Meanjin (Brisbane) in December 2023 as part of the Australian Feminist Law Journal's stream, 'Feminist legal scholarship to reimagine the world: A celebration'. This chapter was partly written on the lands of the Wurundjeri people of the Kulin nation, whose sovereignty was never ceded, and we pay our respect to their elders, past and present.

2 Stevphen Shukaitis, "Space Is the (Non)Place: Martians, Marxists, and the Outer Space of the Radical Imagination," *The Sociological Review* 57, no. 1 (2009): 99.

3 Shukaitis, "Space Is the (Non)Place," 111. See also Treviño's concept of 'Cosmic Hope' in Natalie Treviño, "The Cosmos Is Not Finished" (PhD, London, Canada, Western University, 2020), 19.

4 Kenya Legislative Council (Committee on Ways & Means) 30 May 1961, vol. 87, col 600.

5 "Zambia's Forgotten Space Program," *Lusaka Times*, January 28, 2011, www.lusakatimes.com/2011/01/28/space-program/.

DOI: 10.4324/9781032645339-5

Closer to the present, in the mid-2010s, the phrase 'Fully Automated Luxury Gay Space Communism' became Internet shorthand for leftist utopian thinking, inspiring a suite of playful memes of rainbow astronauts and planets and helping to foster new online communities.[6] This phrase is based on Aaron Bastani's idea of 'Fully Automated Luxury Communism', which holds that technology can be used to create a post-scarcity, post-work economy of widespread prosperity.[7] 'Gay' and 'space' were added later; the former to 'queer' this new utopia, the latter, because, according to one of its proponents, 'space is fucking cool'.[8] In all of these examples, we see outer space functioning as a stimulus for the imagination, inspiring different groups to pursue alternative ways of doing and being.

Despite the radical imaginative potential of outer space, the imaginary underlying international space law is strikingly limited. There are five core United Nations (UN) treaties specifically focused on outer space: the Outer Space Treaty (OST) (1967),[9] the Rescue Agreement (1967),[10] the Liability Convention (1971),[11] the Registration Convention (1975),[12] and the Moon Agreement (1979)[13] – although some of these are more subscribed than others.[14] Broadly, these treaties extend international law into outer space; declare that outer space, the Moon, and celestial bodies must be used 'exclusively for peaceful purposes' and are not subject to national appropriation; and provide that the exploration and use of outer space should be carried on for the benefit and in the interests of 'all mankind'. At first blush, these

6 Tchefuncte Bonaparte, "Fully Automated Luxury Gay Space Communism," *Know Your Meme* (blog), 2017, https://knowyourmeme.com/memes/cultures/fully-automated-luxury-gay-space-communism.

7 Aaron Bastani, *Fully Automated Luxury Communism: A Manifesto* (London: Verso, 2019).

8 Quoted in Annie Lowrey, "Give Us Fully Automated Luxury Communism," *The Atlantic*, June 20, 2019, www.theatlantic.com/ideas/archive/2019/06/give-us-fully-automated-luxury-communism/592099/.

9 Treaty on Principles Governing the Activities of States in the Exploration and Use of Outer Space, including the Moon and Other Celestial Bodies, 610 UNTS 205 (January 27, 1967) ('OST'). The OST entered into force in October 1967.

10 Agreement on the Rescue of Astronauts, the Return of Astronauts and the Return of Objects Launched into Outer Space, 672 UNTS 119 (December 19, 1967) ('Rescue Agreement'). The Rescue Agreement entered into force in December 1968.

11 Convention on International Liability for Damage Caused by Space Objects, 961 UNTS 187 (November 29, 1971) ('Liability Convention'). This Liability Convention entered into force in September 1972.

12 Convention on Registration of Objects Launched into Outer Space, 1023 UNTS 15 (January 14, 1975) ('Registration Convention'). The Registration Convention entered into force in September 1976.

13 Agreement Governing the Activities of States on the Moon and Other Celestial Bodies, 1363 UNTS 3 (December 5, 1979) ('Moon Agreement'). The Moon Agreement entered into force in July 1984.

14 For example, as of April 2024, the OST has 115 parties, whereas the Moon Agreement currently only has 17 parties.

treaties' emphasis on peace and collectivity may seem idealistic, even radical. But upon closer inspection, we find they are structured by logics of gender, militarisation, and commodification. As such, far from undoing earthly power relations and regimes of normativity, international space law may be seen as an outward projection of them.

In this chapter, we explore international space law and politics through the lens of queer and feminist theory. Drawing on Sara Ahmed's work on queer phenomenology, we argue the projection of dominant imaginaries onto outer space can be seen as an exercise in 'straightening', aimed at bringing the radical and disorienting queer effects of space into line with earthly power relations. However, engaging with Judith Butler's account of the subversive function of drag, we contend that the 'spectacular' nature of this exercise can also help to reveal power relations on Earth, opening up opportunities for contesting them.

This chapter begins with an account of how international space law has helped to configure the celestial regions as the domain of White,[15] heterosexual masculinity (Section 2). It then turns to a critique of the militarised and extractive imaginaries underpinning the outer space treaties, showing how these, too, display a heteronormative and patriarchal orientation (Section 3). Following this, we theorise these gendered, militarised, and extractive imaginaries through the work of queer feminist scholars Sara Ahmed and Judith Butler (Section 4). Section 5 concludes.

2. Gender, Sexuality, and the Notion of 'Mankind'

Perhaps the most evident critique of international space law from a queer feminist perspective is that the language of the space treaties is gendered.[16] Article I of the English version of the OST declares 'the exploration and use of outer space, including the Moon and other celestial bodies . . . the province of all *mankind*'.[17] Similarly, the Moon Agreement states that the 'exploration and use of the Moon shall be the province of all *mankind*'[18] and establishes that the 'moon and its natural resources are the common heritage of *mankind*'.[19] The cumulative regime is, therefore, one where 'mankind' stands as the collective beneficiary of any human activities in outer space. In

15 Following Matiangai Sirleaf, "Rendering Whiteness Visible," *American Journal of International Law* 117, no. 3 (July 2023): 484–487, we capitalise the 'W' on White to render Whiteness discernible.

16 Cassandra Steer, "The Province of All Humankind: A Feminist Analysis of Space Law," in *Commercial and Military Uses of Outer Space*, eds. Melissa de Zwart and Stacey Henderson (Singapore: Springer, 2021), 169–188.

17 OST, Article 1 [emphasis added].

18 Moon Agreement, Article 4(1) [emphasis added].

19 Moon Agreement, Article 11(1) [emphasis added].

addition, the OST and its non-binding predecessor, the Declaration of Legal Principles Governing the Activities of States in the Exploration and Use of Outer Space (1963) (Principles Declaration), include identical language designating astronauts as 'envoys of *mankind* in outer space'.[20]

Today, this gendered language is often treated as an inconsequential relic of the past, and international lawyers tend to re-read the term 'mankind' in the outer space treaties as 'humankind', in the same tenor as they 'read out' the reference to 'civilised nations' from Article 38 of the Statute of the International Court of Justice.[21] But even if the gendered nature of this term has been ignored, its legal meaning and significance have not been. International legal scholars have long argued over whether the reference to 'mankind' in the OST established a new, collective subject of international law[22] or whether the phrase 'province of mankind' is 'merely an idealistic and declaratory statement intended to negate any possible exercise of sovereignty or appropriation'.[23] Legal scholars discussing the former have also pored over the content and scope of the term 'mankind'. Does it include '(a) all states; (b) all states, particularly developing states; (c) all nations; (d) all living human beings; or (e) all human beings, present, and future'?[24] Does it mean 'a social and legal system with the individual at the center, or . . . a common interest of peoples, states or groups of states, or . . . a politically – ideologically oriented composite body'?[25]

In the context of all this questioning, it seems remiss not to query also the extent to which the notion of 'mankind' in international space law has been shaped by gendered (as well as sexual, racial, and class-based) relations. After all, as Cassandra Steer argues, the term 'mankind' certainly reflects the

20 OST, Article V, adopted verbatim form UNGA Res 1962 (XVIII), UN Doc A/RES/1962 (XVIII) (December 13, 1963) ('Principles Declaration'), para. 9 [emphasis added].

21 Ntina Tzouvala, *Capitalism as Civilisation: A History of International Law* (Cambridge: Cambridge University Press, 2020), 7–8.

22 See, for example, Aldo Armando Cocca, "General Principles for the Utilization of Outer Space: Determination of the Meaning of the Expression Res Communes Humanitatis in Space Law," in *Proceedings on the Law of Outer Space*, vol. 6 (Proceedings on the Law of Outer Space, Paris, 1964), 1–6; Ernst Fasan, "The Meaning of the Term Mankind in Space Legal Language," *Journal of Space Law* 2, no. 2 (1974): 125–132; Andrew James Simon-Butler, "Bifurcated Sovereignty and the Territorial Conception of the Province of All Mankind," *Journal of Space Law* 43, no. 1 (2019): 1–59.

23 Ricky J. Lee, *Law and Regulation of Commercial Mining of Minerals in Outer Space* (Dordrecht: Springer, 2012), 217. See also Egypt's attempt to explicate the term during OST negotiations: United Arab Republic, 'Working Paper No. 8' (22 Jul 1966) UN DOC A/AC.105/35, 6.

24 David Tan, "Towards a New Regime for the Protection of Outer Space as the Province of All Mankind," *Yale Journal of International Law* 25 (2000): 162, fn 79.

25 Adrian Bueckling, "The Strategy of Semantics and the Mankind Provisions of the Space Treaty," *Journal of Space Law* 7, no. 1 (1979): 19.

gendered reality of the OST's historical context.[26] Accordingly, in the following sub-section, we outline the gendered history of space lawmaking and spacefaring. We then consider how this history has both shaped and been shaped by the references to 'mankind' in the outer space treaties.

2.1 *The Gendered and Sexual History of Human Encounters with Outer Space*

The outer space treaties have a gendered history. Though dozens of women contributed to making the space treaties,[27] the pace, process, and products were decided by a relatively small group of powerful men. Likewise, the history of space flight is gendered. For the first few decades of the US space program, for example, the astronauts that it sent into outer space could only be men due to the requirement that one had to be a military test pilot.[28] This requirement was disingenuously treated as a matter of merit rather than exclusion. 'When we find (a woman or) Negro with the right qualifications, they'll be selected', said Gemini astronaut Gordon Cooper to a Nigerian crowd in 1965. 'Presently no Negroes (or women) have been found to be anywhere near qualified'.[29]

Further, gender mattered to those states active in space at the time the outer space treaties were drafted. In the 1950s and 1960s, for example, NASA went out of its way 'to publicize its strong, healthy astronauts as representing the epitome of [White, American] masculinity'.[30] In 1959, NASA gave *Life* magazine exclusive access to a feature on the personal lives of its astronauts, which included repeated praise of their strong, healthy physiques.[31] *Life* ran headlines such as 'Making of a Brave Man' (1962) and stories about the astronauts' exercise regimes, including photos of them doing push-ups and a description of one doing sprints around the block with his wife on his back.[32] The magazine also routinely compared NASA's astronauts to colonisers of the 'US West' in the nineteenth century, describing them as 'pioneers' and outer space as a 'frontier'.[33] Historian Neil Maher argues NASA's astronauts were seen as an antidote to a perceived crisis of American masculinity in the

26 Steer, "The Province of All Humankind."
27 Including Joyce Gutteridge (UK), Agda Rössel (Sweden), Elisa Aguirre (Mexico), Margaret Chase Smith (US), and Kwen Chen (UN Secretariat).
28 Steer, "The Province of All Humankind," 175.
29 "Gemini 5 Astronauts Visit Kenya, Nigeria," *Afro-American (1893-)*, October 2, 1965.
30 Neil Maher, *Apollo in the Age of Aquarius* (Cambridge, MA: Harvard University Press, 2017), 145.
31 Maher, *Apollo in the Age of Aquarius*, 145. See also Dario Llinares, *The Astronaut: Cultural Mythology and Idealised Masculinity* (Newcastle: Cambridge Scholars Publishing, 2011), 19–60.
32 Maher, *Apollo in the Age of Aquarius*, 145.
33 Llinares, *The Astronaut: Cultural Mythology and Idealised Masculinity*, 47.

late 1950s and early 1960s – or, in the words of US President John F. Kennedy, the country's 'growing softness'.[34]

Sexuality also mattered to NASA. In addition to promoting its astronauts' masculinity, the space agency made efforts to put their heterosexuality on display by ensuring the public became well acquainted with the astronauts' wives. The 1959 *Life* issues, for example, featured two consecutive covers – one depicting the astronauts, the other their wives. In the latter, the astronauts' wives were constructed as 'demure, passive, domestically bound', in contrast to the astronauts, who were presented as heroes embarking on an 'epochal mission'.[35] In Sage's account, NASA's careful crafting of these relationships through binary performances of gender reflects what Judith Butler calls the 'heterosexual matrix'[36] – that is, the way the '[t]he institution of compulsory and naturalized heterosexuality requires and regulates gender as a binary relation in which the masculine term is differentiated from the feminine term, and this differentiation is accomplished through the practices of heterosexual desire'.[37]

In addition, NASA actively sought to exclude queer people from the agency, perceiving non-normative sexuality to be a weakness. An example is the 1963 firing of NASA budget analyst Clifford Norton for 'immoral conduct'.[38] Norton was arrested by DC Police's Morals Division at 2 a.m. for 'speeding', though he had not. Norton was interrogated about his sexuality for two hours while Morals Officers waited for NASA's Security Chief Bart Fugler to arrive. Fugler observed the last twenty minutes of the interview without Norton knowing,[39] then took Norton to a NASA building and questioned him for four more hours, coercing Norton to disclose intimate details about his sexual life – though none of the acts in question had occurred at work.[40] The prior arrangement between the police Morals Division and NASA Security implies a covert system that worked to excise queer people from NASA. Indeed, firing queer NASA employees was broadly considered 'a custom within the agency' at the time, '[b]ecause of the potential for

34 Quoted in Maher, *Apollo in the Age of Aquarius*, 147.

35 Quoted in Daniel Sage, "Giant Leaps and Forgotten Steps: NASA and the Performance of Gender," *The Sociological Review* 57, no. 1 (2009): 148.

36 Sage, "Giant Leaps".

37 Judith Butler, *Gender Trouble: Feminism and the Subversion of Identity* (London and New York: Routledge, 1990), 30.

38 In relation to this story, we are grateful to the extensive research and advocacy of Chanda Prescod-Weinstein, Lucianne Walkowicz, Sarah Tuttle, and Brian Nord, who have expanded historical understanding and fought to make it matter. See Chanda Prescod-Weinstein et al., "The James Webb Space Telescope Needs to Be Renamed," *Scientific American*, March 1, 2021, www.scientificamerican.com/article/nasa-needs-to-rename-the-james-webb-space-telescope/l.

39 *Norton v Macy*, 417 F.2d 1161 (D.C. Cir. 1969).

40 *Norton v Macy*.

blackmail' and because it could 'be evidence of an unstable personality'.[41] This hostility towards queer sexuality was still extant decades later when NASA began to feature women in prominent roles. Sally Ride, who became the first American woman in space in 1983, did not publicise her 27-year relationship with a woman; the public only learned about her spouse after she died. Ride's decision has been attributed, in part, to a sense that revealing her queer relationship would have been a 'career-wrecker'.[42]

It was not only the US that curated the gendered and sexual representations of its astronauts. Soviet space program authorities also fashioned Yuri Gagarin, the Soviet cosmonaut who became the first human in space in 1961, into 'a model socialist man for the gaze of audiences at home and aboard'.[43] In this role, Gagarin was presented as both a 'family man' and a 'desirable (hetero)sexual commodity'.[44] He would move between uttering flirtatious lines in press conferences and appearing in documentary films where 'Gagarin sunbathed, threw stones into the surf, swam and went rowing (all without his shirt) while . . . [his wife] sat on the beach, happily watching him and rocking a baby carriage'.[45]

The Soviet Union broke with this masculine script in 1963 when cosmonaut Valentina Vladimirovna Tereshkova became the first woman in space. However, Tereshkova was still shaped by a gendered discourse, often being described as a 'daughter' or 'girl' of the Soviet Union when no such familial language was extended to the Soviet men who went into space. On her first day in flight, for example, Tereshkova received a radio call from then-Premier of the Soviet Union, Nikita Khrushchev, in which he said, 'People are calling you "Seagull." Allow me to call you simply Valya, Valentina. I am very happy and as proud as a father . . . [of] our girl (devushka), a girl from the Soviet Union'.[46] Sylvester argues that this rhetoric reflected 'the masculine inflected' Communist state, as well as 'the "feminine" emotional landscapes of the homeland',[47] helping to reinforce both Soviet ideology and patriarchal gender relations.[48]

41 *Norton v Macy*, 1166–1167.
42 Natalie Wolchover, "Why Aren't There Any Openly Gay Astronauts?" *Space.Com*, July 25, 2012, www.space.com/16735-gay-astronauts-sally-ride.html.
43 Erica Fraser, "Yuri Gagarin and Celebrity Masculinity in Soviet Culture," in *Gender, Sexuality, and the Cold War*, ed. Philip E. Muehlenbeck (Nashville: Vanderbilt University Press, 2017), 275.
44 Fraser, "Yuri Gagarin and Celebrity Masculinity," 276.
45 Fraser, "Yuri Gagarin and Celebrity Masculinity," 278–279.
46 Quoted in Roshanna Sylvester, "'You Are Our Pride and Our Glory!' Emotions, Generation, and the Legacy of Revolution in Women's Letters to Valentina Tereshkova," *The Russian Review* 78, no. 3 (2019): 398.
47 Sylvester, "'You Are Our Pride and Our Glory!'," 399.
48 Shayler David and Ian Moule, *Women in Space – Following Valentina* (London: Springer, 2005).

2.2 *The Gendered Figure of the Astronaut and International Space Law*

In our argument, the gendered projects surrounding the early US and Soviet space programs came to exist in a co-constitutive relationship with international space law and, in particular, its references to 'mankind'. First, by designating astronauts as the 'envoys of mankind', the Principles Declaration and OST gave the US and Soviet Union an international platform upon which the gendered representations of their astronauts could be performed. Even before these documents were drafted, US astronauts and Soviet cosmonauts occupied semi-diplomatic roles. In 1961, for example, Soviet cosmonaut Yuri Gagarin met with Indian President Jawaharlal Nehru and breakfasted with Queen Elizabeth II at Buckingham Palace.[49] The US astronauts made similar diplomatic visits. In 1965, NASA's Gemini 5 astronauts, L. Gordon Cooper and Charles Conrad, Jr, went on a world tour with their wives, visiting Greece, France, Kenya, and Nigeria, amongst other states.[50] Astronauts and cosmonauts also visited the UN. On separate occasions in 1962, for example, Secretary General U Thant invited American astronaut John Glenn, Jr and Soviet cosmonaut Gherman Titov to the UN Headquarters in New York to meet with members of the UN Committee on the Peaceful Uses of Outer Space (UNCOPUOS).[51]

In arranging these visits and accepting these UN invitations, Washington and Moscow no doubt wished to promote the superiority of their respective states and ideologies. In this pursuit, the gendered construction of the astro/cosmonauts was considered important. As Fraser writes on the Soviet space program, 'Gagarin and his masculine persona were dispatched around the world to rebrand the Soviet Union . . . as a modern, technologically sophisticated state where young, handsome men like Gagarin were building communism and flourishing in the comfortable life it provided'.[52] But affording the astro/cosmonauts diplomatic roles also provided the US and Soviet Union with a way to *universalise* their particular vision – of the state, of space, and of international governance more broadly.[53] After all, the fact that these men had exited the Earth gave them a universal appeal; now, they were seen not

49 Fraser, "Yuri Gagarin and Celebrity Masculinity," 282.

50 John Pomfretspecial, "Cooper and Conrad to Visit 6 Nations on Goodwill Tour; Astronauts to Go on Goodwill Tour," *New York Times*, September 12, 1965, www.nytimes.com/1965/09/12/archives/cooper-and-conrad-to-visit-6-nations-on-goodwill-tour-astronauts-to.html.

51 On John Glenn's visit, see "Glenn UN visit" (March 2, 1962) UNA S-0864-0001-02-00001; on Titov's visit, see "Cosmonaut Titov soiree" (April 26, 1962) S-0864-0001-01-00001.

52 Fraser, "Yuri Gagarin and Celebrity Masculinity," 280–281.

53 This objective of universalising each state's vision not only characterised the first decade of space lawmaking, see, e.g., Cristian van Eijk, "Unstealing the Sky: Third World Equity in the Orbital Commons," *Air and Space Law* 47, no. 1 (2022): 25–44. It can also be seen in basic language pertaining to outer space – consider the political choice between 'astronaut' and 'cosmonaut', for example.

just as representatives of the US or Soviet Union but of the world. This can be seen in a 1962 speech by Indian Representative C.S. Jha to UNCOPUOS, in which he said, '[t]he achievements of Gagarin, Titov and Glenn are thought of, not in terms of their particular nationalities, but as symbols of the universal man'.[54]

With the adoption of the Principles Declaration and the OST, the language of 'envoys of mankind' lent further legitimacy to the idea of 'astronaut-diplomats', as well as to the visions of universality that had begun to surround them. According to this language, the astronauts were not simply domestic military personnel going on space flights and traveling around the world upon their return. They now enjoyed the status of international 'envoys', at least when in outer space. The practical effect of this status was to ensure states would render astronauts 'all possible assistance in the event of accident, distress, or emergency landing on the territory of another State Party or on the high seas'.[55] However, the notion that astronauts were 'envoys of mankind' also took on a wider symbolic meaning.[56] This can be seen in public requests to the UN that the Apollo 11 astronauts plant a UN flag on the Moon in 1969,[57] as well as expressions of disappointment when they did not,[58] indicating many considered the mission to have an international quality. It can also be seen in the fact that the Apollo 11 astronauts nevertheless left a plaque on the Moon, inscribed with the words: 'we came in peace for all mankind'.[59] As a result of this wider symbolic meaning, the status of 'envoy' in the Principles Declaration and OST helped to give an international platform to the gendered figure of the astronaut, ensuring their idealised White, heterosexual masculinity would be consumed not just by domestic audiences, but audiences the world over.

Second, by simultaneously giving the astronauts the status of 'envoys of *mankind*' and declaring outer space to be the 'province of all *mankind*', the OST allowed the gendered figure of the astronaut to give visual form to the collective entity to whom the freedoms and benefits of outer space were supposed to belong. After all, astronauts were now not only the ones accessing

54 C.S. Jha, Speech to UNCOPUOS (March 20, 1962) Foreign Affairs Records vol 8(3), 68.

55 OST, Article V.

56 Sreejith, "The Fallen Envoy," 133.

57 See, e.g., Mr Jares Kunetka, Lieut. Dennis Boyles, USAF and Lieut. Miguel Berumen, USAF, Letter to UN Secretary General U Thant, July 10, 1969; United Nations Association of Los Angeles, Letter to UN Secretary General U Thant, July 14, 1969. These letters are contained in Astronaut visit logistics (5:9:1969) S-0864-0012-25-00001.

58 See, e.g., Professor Walter Laves, Letter to UN Secretary General U Thant (July 31, 1969) in Astronaut visit logistics (5:9:1969) S-0864-0012-25-00001.

59 UN News, "First Men on the Moon 'Came in Peace' to UN Headquarters 'for All Mankind'," July 19, 2019, https://news.un.org/en/story/2019/07/1042921.

outer space; they were also the designated representatives of a 'mankind' who could claim outer space as their 'province' – giving colour and meaning to that collective entity. The blending of the gendered image of the astronaut and ideas about 'mankind's romantic collective'[60] was also facilitated by the astronauts themselves. For example, Neil Armstrong chose to speak of 'one small step for man, one giant leap for mankind' on the Moon in 1969. In this instantly famous phrase, the idea of a collective 'mankind' as the beneficiary of space exploration was again linked to the image of a particular man – one who embodied idealised American gender standards. As such, even if we now read the term 'mankind' as 'humankind' in the Principles Declaration and OST, the collective entity it ushered into existence was infused with a gendered imaginary, helping to configure the celestial regions as the domain of White, heterosexual masculinity.

In our view, this gendered configuration helped to pave the way for today's 'Space Billionaire' phenomenon. Beginning in the early 2000s, and especially since 2015, wealthy White male entrepreneurs like Elon Musk, Jeff Bezos, and Richard Branson have become dominant actors in the space sector. Musk's SpaceX operates 55% of all active satellites at the time of writing.[61] NASA has awarded contracts to SpaceX and Blue Origin, among other companies, to launch the Artemis missions to the Moon, resupply the International Space Station, and build new space suits for future astronauts. Even more visibly, in 2021, Jeff Bezos and Richard Branson launched themselves into space. This triggered a flurry of media and academic articles debating whether they now enjoyed the status of 'astronauts'.[62] Arguably, Bezos and Branson's desire to take part in their own space programs, and the public interest in whether they qualified as 'astronauts' as a result, was shaped by the gendered construction of the early astronauts and their legal status as 'envoys of mankind'.[63] By entering outer space, these men could not only demonstrate their own masculinity and buy into the prestige of spacefaring

60 Sreejith, "The Fallen Envoy," 130.

61 Based on data from T.S. Kelso, "CelesTrak," *CelesTrak*, August 24, 2023, https://celestrak.com/.

62 See, for example, Kenneth Chang, "Is Jeff Bezos Really an Astronaut?," *New York Times*, July 26, 2021, www.nytimes.com/2021/07/26/science/jeff-bezos-astronaut-definition.html; "Jeff Bezos and Sir Richard Branson May Not Be Astronauts, US Says," *BBC News*, July 23, 2021, www.bbc.com/news/world-us-canada-57950149; Ben Turner, "Jeff Bezos Went to the Edge of Space. Does That Make Him an Astronaut?," *Live Science*, July 21, 2021, www.livescience.com/is-bezos-an-astronaut.html; Leah Crane, "Who Gets to Be an Astronaut?," *New Scientist* 251, no. 3345 (2021): 16. See also Vijay Kumar, S. R. Subramanian and K. D. Raju, "Viewpoint Research 'Envoys of Mankind' in the Era of Commercial Human Spaceflight," *Astropolitics: The International Journal of Space Politics & Policy* 18, no. 2 (2020): 144–157.

63 On the connection between the Space Billionaires and this legal status, see, e.g., Ceridwen Dovey, "Elon Musk and the Failure of Our Imagination in Space," *New Yorker*, June 14, 2018, www.newyorker.com/books/under-review/elon-musk-and-the-failure-of-our-imagination-in-space;

but also claim to represent collective interests in the process. This has helped to obfuscate the profit-driven nature of their activities over the long term. Further, by becoming the dominant actors of contemporary space activity, the Space Billionaires have been able to mould the collective notion of 'mankind' in their own image, just as the Cold War astronauts had before them. But where the last century had a militarised, masculine vision of a spacefaring humanity, ours has become a capitalist, masculine one instead.[64]

3. Imaginaries of Militarisation and Commodification

In addition to giving rise to narrow ideas about who can access and benefit from the celestial regions, international space law has helped to project violent and extractive imaginaries onto outer space. Matt Craven argues that while a surface reading of international space law tells a story of a regime grounded in the principles of peace and collectivity, an Althusserian 'symptomatic reading' of the treaty regime's constitutive silences reveals an international legal framework built around the dual rationalities of militarisation and commodification.[65] In this section, we explain how, like the notion of 'mankind', these rationalities reflect a heteronormative and patriarchal orientation.

3.1 The Militarised Imaginary Underpinning International Space Law

Let us begin with militarisation. As Craven points out, the outer space treaty regime conceives of the idea of peace in outer space through its opposition to war.[66] In the OST, for example, peace is based around the *non-establishment* of 'military bases, installations and fortifications, the testing of any type of weapons and the conduct of military manoeuvres on celestial bodies' and the *non-placement* of 'objects carrying nuclear weapons or any other kinds of weapons of mass destruction' into orbit,[67] rather than around positive ideas of solidarity or cooperation. In this way, the OST's understanding of 'peace'

'The elevated status of astronauts is not only cultural but legal . . . In Article V of the Outer Space Treaty, astronauts are defined as "envoys of mankind."'

64 In 2018, Elon Musk launched a red sports car into space, described by some as 'a symbol of elite wealth and masculinity', see Alice Gorman, "A Sports Car and a Glitter Ball Are Now in Space – What Does That Say about Us as Humans?" *The Conversation*, February7,2018,https://theconversation.com/a-sports-car-and-a-glitter-ball-are-now-in-space-what-does-that-say-about-us-as-humans-91156.

65 Matt Craven, "'Other Spaces': Constructing the Legal Architecture of a Cold War Commons and the Scientific-Technical Imaginary of Outer Space," *European Journal of International Law* 30, no. 2 (2019): 547–572.

66 Craven, "Other Spaces," 556.

67 OST, Article IV.

is limited to what queer feminist legal scholar Dianne Otto describes as 'the absence of armed conflict'.[68] This idea of 'peace' is similar to that found in the UN Charter, where peace is coupled with references to 'security' and envisaged as something to be enforced by the military strength of certain powers.[69] In Otto's account, this negative model of peace is based on masculinist assumptions 'about the inevitability of aggression in international society, driven by self-interest, and the need for military strength to constrain such violence or act as a deterrent'.[70] A queer feminist vision of peace, by contrast, would be more substantive in nature, emphasising 'social embeddedness and interconnectedness'.[71] Extending this insight to international space law, the OST's adoption of the UN Charter's negative vision of peace appears to be an outward projection of the idea of humanity as inherently aggressive. In the celestial regions, as on Earth, humans are construed as a warlike people.

According to Otto, international law's negative conception of peace has the effect of concealing forms of human suffering and environmental destruction that does not constitute 'war'. If peace is only ever the absence of war, then violence against women, discrimination against queer people, and the devastation and extinction of non-human species outside of military conflicts can be dismissed as 'peaceful conduct'.[72] Likewise, the narrow understanding of peace in the outer space treaties helps to render non-military forms of violence and oppression against human and non-human subjects, including the environment, in outer space invisible. As discussed below, this has allowed an extractive imaginary, which views nature as an object of human domination and appropriation, to flourish alongside claims of 'peace' in outer space.

Further, by conceiving of peace in outer space through its opposite of war, international space law has helped to uphold and sustain dystopian visions of outer space as a site of warfare. According to Craven, the negative conception of peace in the OST was the result of Cold War fears, in which, at their most extreme, 'it was imagined that a nuclear power might be in a position to launch guided missiles from a space platform to any point on earth . . . or that the moon would become the site of military rocket installations'.[73] Yet, in seeking only to suppress these fears rather than attempting to reimagine human (and non-human) relations, the OST has worked to keep those

68 Dianne Otto, "Rethinking 'Peace' in International Law and Politics from a Queer Feminist Perspective," *Feminist Review* 126, no. 1 (2020): 26–27. This has also been described as a 'negative peace', see Johan Galtung, "What Is Peace Research?" *Journal of Peace Research* 1, no. 1 (1964): 1–4.
69 Otto, "Rethinking 'Peace'," 27.
70 Otto, "Rethinking 'Peace'," 26.
71 Dianne Otto, "Queerly Troubling International Law's Vision of 'Peace'," *AJIL Unbound* 116 (2022): 26.
72 Otto, "Rethinking 'Peace'," 28.
73 Craven, "Other Spaces," 558.

very fears alive.[74] After all, that is how binary thinking works. As queer and feminist thinkers have long shown, by extending rights to the categories of 'women' and 'homosexuals', as defined against 'men' and 'heterosexuals', the law does not simply increase the number of people who have rights. It also works to confirm and stabilise the categories of 'men' and 'heterosexuals', including ideas about their naturalness and dominance.[75] Likewise, by constructing peace through what Judith Butler calls 'frames of war',[76] the OST has preserved the nightmare of outer space becoming a realm of military aggression. Explicit references to military bases, weapons testing, and 'objects carrying nuclear weapons or any other kinds of weapons of mass destruction into orbit' are now encoded into international space law, shaping the way we see outer space.

3.2 The Extractive Imaginary Underpinning International Space Law

The outer space treaty regime also reflects the logics of extraction and commodification. One of the original goals of space lawmaking, at least for some states, was to establish outer space as a 'commons' – that is, as a realm to be enjoyed collectively. However, it should be noted that the notion of an outer space commons has also long been contested, and in recent years, the US has explicitly pushed back against this idea, as discussed further below. Nevertheless, for some of the early proponents of the idea of an outer space commons, Craven observes this was again a reaction to geopolitical fears at the time the treaties were drafted. More specifically, 'drawing upon the history of colonial expansion', the fear was that 'the pathologies of territorial rivalry might well be extended to "the heavens themselves", leading to the planting of flags and claims of sovereignty over the moon and other celestial bodies'.[77] For others, the idea of a space commons was more hopeful, a pathway to a future where expansionism, extractivism, and nationalism would no longer divide humanity from itself.[78]

Yet, the collective vision ultimately enshrined in international space law was highly limited in the way it conceived of humanity's relationship with outer

74 Craven, "Other Spaces," 556.

75 See, e.g., Michele Grigolo, "Sexualities and the ECHR: Introducing the Universal Sexual Legal Subject," *European Journal of International Law* 14, no. 5 (2003): 1025.

76 Judith Butler, *Frames of War: When Is Life Grievable?* (London: Verso, 2010). Otto draws on this framing in her queer feminist critique of the international law and politics of peace on Earth.

77 Craven, "Other Spaces," 551, discussing the views of Oscar Schachter.

78 Sarvepalli Radhakrishanan, "Welcome Speech to Vice President Lyndon B. Johnson" (New Delhi, May 19, 1961) Foreign Affairs Record vol 7(5), 152 ('[I]t is essential for us to rethink our past attitudes, to break with the past traditions of nationalism and militarism').

space. Not only was the collective entity to whom the 'province' of outer space now belonged ('mankind') structured by logics of gender, sexuality, and race, as explored above, but the benefits to be shared centred on the idea of material 'interests'.[79] Article I of the OST, for example, states that the 'exploration and use of outer space, including the Moon and other celestial bodies, shall be carried out for the benefit and in the *interests* of all countries'.[80] The Moon Agreement goes even further. In addition to declaring that 'the exploration and use of the Moon shall . . . be carried out for the benefit and in the *interests* of all countries',[81] Article 4 states that '[d]ue regard shall be paid to . . . the need to promote higher standards of living and conditions of economic and social progress and development', connecting humanity's 'interests' with the idea of economic growth.

Craven argues these provisions construct humanity – or 'mankind' – as a 'commodified form of life identified in and through its relationship to the resources over which it seeks to have control'.[82] What this collective entity has in common is not rights or needs but rather 'a fluid, economy of "interests", the fulfilment of which [is] always more or less and which was open to be bargained, traded, sacrificed and exchanged'.[83] As posthuman feminist scholars have pointed out, the references to 'interests' in the OST and Moon Agreement also place humanity in a position of 'hierarchical supremacy over other subjects – including the environment and nonhumans'.[84] By conceiving of outer space as a realm for pursuing human economic 'interests', the outer space treaties relegate nature to a subordinate status. Emily Jones argues that all feminists should be wary of this kind of anthropocentric thinking in outer space as it is rooted in the same 'humanist' tradition that centres the White, heterosexual, 'rational' man as 'human'.[85]

Beyond structuring the collective vision for outer space around the idea of material interests, the treaty regime leaves the door open to unilateral proprietary claims over space resources. While Article II of the OST prohibits sovereign appropriation 'by means of use or occupation, or by any other means', it does not address 'the question of private ownership and control over minerals and metals'[86] found in outer space. Cait Storr argues that '[t]his permis-

79 Craven, "Other Spaces," 569.
80 Emphasis added.
81 Emphasis added.
82 Craven, "Other Spaces," 569.
83 Craven, "Other Spaces," 569.
84 Emily Jones, *Feminist Theory and International Law: Posthuman Perspectives* (Abingdon: Routledge, 2023), 9, 50–51. See also Rosi Braidotti, *Posthuman Feminism* (Cambridge: Polity Press, 2021), 229–235.
85 Emily Jones, "A Posthuman Feminist Approach to Mars," *International Law Grrls* (blog), October 17, 2018, https://ilg2.org/2018/10/17/a-posthuman-feminist-approach-to-mars/.
86 Cait Storr, "'Space Is the Only Way to Go': The Evolution of the Extractivist Imaginary of International Law," in *Routledge Handbook of International Law and the Humanities*, eds. Shane Chalmers and Sundhya Pahuja (Abingdon: Routledge, 2021), 295.

sive silence' ushered in a new way of thinking about outer space, refiguring it 'as a "new" frontier for resource extraction'.[87] The Moon Agreement of 1979 sought to address the jurisdictional gap regarding claims of property by stating that '[n]either the surface nor the subsurface of the moon, nor any part thereof or natural resources in place, shall become property of any State'.[88] However, the caveat 'in place' in this sentence still leaves open the possibility of such claims over resources once removed.[89] Moreover, although the Moon Agreement committed states to the establishment of 'an international regime, including appropriate procedures, to govern the exploitation of the natural resources of the moon',[90] that agreement ended up as one of the least subscribed UN treaties, with only 18 states ever ratifying it (and one of those states, Saudi Arabia, giving notice of its withdrawal in 2023).[91] As a result, the international regime it proposed to govern the exploitation of natural resources never came into existence.[92]

According to Storr, these gaps and ambiguities in the outer space treaty regime have allowed the 'inherently expansionist logic of capitalism' to turn its sights on the celestial regions.[93] The Space Billionaires mentioned earlier are now heavily investing in space mining technology.[94] Further, the US has recently begun to use these gaps and ambiguities to push for an interpretation of international space law that explicitly allows for the commercial exploitation of outer space. In 2020, for example, US President Donald Trump signed an Executive Order stating that 'Americans should have the right to engage in commercial exploration, recovery, and use of resources in outer space'.[95] This Executive Order also emphasises that, in contrast to some understandings of international space law, 'the United States does not view . . . [outer space] as a global commons'.[96] A few months later, NASA released the Artemis Accords – a non-binding, political agreement between the US and

87 Storr, "Space Is the Only Way to Go," 295.
88 Moon Agreement, Article 11(3).
89 Craven, "Other Spaces," 566.
90 Moon Agreement, Article 11(5).
91 Storr, "Space Is the Only Way to Go," 295. On Saudi Arabia's withdrawal, see Ricky J. Lee, "Saudi Arabia's Withdrawal from the Moon Agreement," *ANZSIL Perspective* (2023), https://anzsilperspective.com/saudi-arabias-withdrawal-from-the-moon-agreement/.
92 In 1994, the UNCOPUOS recommended to the UN General Assembly that it should take no further action in relation to the regime. See Antonella Bini, "The Moon Agreement: Its Effectiveness in the 21st Century," *European Space Policy Institute (ESPI) Perspectives* 14 (2008).
93 Storr, "Space Is the Only Way to Go," 298.
94 See, for example, Sean Captain, "Jeff Bezos Wants to Save Earth by Moving Industry to Space," *Fast Company*, September 5, 2019, www.fastcompany.com/90347364/jeff-bezos-wants-to-save-earth-by-moving-industry-to-space.
95 *Encouraging International Support for the Recovery and Use of Space Resources*, Executive Order 13914 of April 6, 2020 (EO 13914), Section 1.
96 EO 13914, Section 1.

partner states, which aims to 'establish a common vision via a practical set of principles, guidelines, and best practices to enhance the governance of the civil exploration and use of outer space'.[97] While professing to be consistent with 'the Outer Space Treaty and other instruments',[98] the Artemis Accords go further than those treaties by explicitly referring to the 'commercial utilization' of outer space[99] and affirming that 'the extraction of space resources does not inherently constitute national appropriation'.[100]

In putting forward this interpretation of international space law, the Artemis Accords switch out the language of 'mankind' for that of 'humankind'. For example, section 10(1) states that '[t]he Signatories note that the utilization of space resources can benefit *humankind*'.[101] The Preamble also refers to NASA's intention of landing a woman on the Moon as part of its Artemis program.[102] These aspects of the *Artemis Accords* have been depicted by some as a 'women-friendly' approach to international space law. For example, after Colombian Vice President and Foreign Minister Marta Lucía Ramírez signed the Artemis Accords, she stated, 'NASA's Accords are a commitment to our women'.[103] This 'women-friendly' approach follows on from recent attempts by NASA to make the space agency a more inclusive workplace for its LGBTQ staff members.[104]

And yet, NASA's apparent turn towards gender and sexual inclusivity is taking place as part of a wider turn, which is facilitating the transformation of outer space into a site of primitive accumulation. 'Primitive accumulation' refers to the violent process of expropriation through which capitalism establishes itself.[105] Examples of primitive accumulation include the enclosure of the commons, forced migration, and the slave trade, which separated people from the means of subsistence and concentrated wealth in the owners of private property.[106] For some Marxist thinkers, primitive accumulation is an

97 *The Artemis Accords: Principles for Cooperation in the Civil Exploration and Use of the Moon, Comets, and Asteroids for Peaceful Purposes*, 13 October 2020, www.nasa.gov/specials/artemis-accords/img/Artemis-Accords-signed-13Oct2020.pdf, Section 1.

98 *Artemis Accords*, Preamble.

99 *Artemis Accords*, Section 5.

100 *Artemis Accords*, Section 10(2).

101 *Artemis Accords*, Section 10(1) [emphasis added].

102 *Artemis Accords*, Preamble.

103 Marta Lucía Ramírez, "Queremos más colombianas en la NASA y en la industria aeroespacial del país: Vicepresidenta-Canciller tras firma de Artemisa," May 10, 2022, www.cancilleria.gov.co/newsroom/news/queremos-colombianas-nasa-industria-aeroespacial-pais-vicepresidenta-canciller-firma.

104 "LGBTQ Special Emphasis," *NASA Website*, last updated October 6, 2023, www.nasa.gov/offices/odeo/LGBTQ-special-emphasis.

105 Part 8 'The So-Called Primitive Accumulation' in Karl Marx, *Capital: A Critical Analysis of Capitalist Production* (Ware, Hertfordshire: Wordsworth Editions Limited, 2013), 501–542.

106 Marx, *Capital*, 501–542.

ongoing process. For example, Marxist feminists point out that women's labour in producing and maintaining a working class continues to be exploited as a 'free resource' under capitalism.[107] This is achieved through a strategic separation of the 'productive'/'formal' from the 'informal'/social-reproductive sphere (where the conditions of life are (re)produced),[108] as well as logics like 'compulsory heterosexuality'.[109] The domination of nature and the extraction of natural resources is another example of ongoing primitive accumulation: 'naturally produced use-values are plundered for productive consumption as raw materials and treated as commodities in the capitalist circuits of valorization'.[110]

In facilitating the transformation of outer space into a site of primitive accumulation, then, NASA is not only further empowering 'the super wealthy elite white men of techno-mediated capitalism',[111] who are already investing in space mining. It is also paving the way for the infliction of a brutal process of expropriation on the outer space environment that is structurally analogous to the expropriation of social-reproductive labour of women and racialised groups.[112] Viewed in this way, NASA's turn towards gender and sexual inclusivity seems to be little more than a form of 'pinkwashing', designed to conceal its complicity in the violent extension of capitalism out towards the stars.[113]

4. On Straightening and Subversion

4.1 *International Space Law and Politics as an Exercise in 'Straightening'*

When considered together and through a queer and feminist lens, the gendered, militarised, and extractive imaginary embedded in international space law looks like an exercise in 'straightening', aimed at reeling in outer space's queer effects. In her work on queer phenomenology, Sara Ahmed uses

107 Maria Mies, *Patriarchy and Accumulation on a World Scale: Women in the International Division of Labour* (London: Bloomsbury Publishing, 2022).

108 See, for example, Silvia Federici, *Caliban and the Witch: Women, the Body and Primitive Accumulation* (New York: Autonomedia, 2004); Silvia Federici, *Revolution at Point Zero: Housework, Reproduction, and Feminist Struggle*, 2nd ed. (Binghampton: PM Press, 2020).

109 Duc Hien Nguyen, "The Political Economy of Heteronormativity," *Review of Radical Political Economics* 55, no. 1 (2021): 112–131.

110 Johanna Oksala, "Feminism, Capitalism, and Ecology," *Hypatia: A Journal of Feminist Philosophy* 33, no. 2 (2018): 221.

111 Jones, "A Posthuman Feminist Approach to Mars."

112 Oksala, "Feminism, Capitalism, and Ecology," 222.

113 'Pinkwashing' refers to a deliberate strategy of using gay rights to conceal oppressive politics, see, e.g., Sarah Schulman, "Israel and 'Pinkwashing'," *The New York Times*, November 22, 2011. A similar use of women's rights is sometimes referred to as 'purplewashing'.

Merleu-Ponty's description of 'queer' moments, where the world suddenly appears 'off centre' or 'slantwise' and the subject must reorient themselves to once again 'see straight' as a launchpad to explore the relationship between space and sexual orientation.[114] Ahmed argues that we are not born straight but rather become straight and that a 'field of heterosexual objects' helps to bring us 'into line' with heteronormative expectations.[115] In her account, the repetition of objects, such as wedding gifts and family photos in the home, or scenes, such as a resort lined with '[t]able after table'[116] of heterosexual couples, have a 'straightening' effect by putting some desires in reach and others beyond it.

Due to its immensity and infinite diversity, just thinking about outer space can give rise to Merleu-Ponty's 'queer moments', 'where the world no longer appears "the right way up"'.[117] For Ahmed, this kind of disorientation does not inevitably lead to radical politics. Just as '[b]odies that experience disorientation can be defensive', 'the forms of politics that proceed from disorientation can be conservative'.[118] But she does believe 'queer politics might *involve* disorientation': '[t]he point is what we do with such moments of disorientation, as well as what such moments can do – whether they can offer us the hope of new directions'.[119] As we set out in the introduction, the disorienting effects of outer space have the potential to function as an 'imaginal machine',[120] assisting us in conceiving of other ways of doing and being.

In response to these effects, it seems that powerful actors, whether consciously or not, have sought to project the equivalent of wedding gifts and family photos back into outer space. Rather than 'leaving the skies open to the imagination',[121] or acknowledging the many already existing Indigenous laws of the skies,[122] Cold War states proclaimed outer space subject to a singular law on Earth. Further, through that law, outer space was configured

114 Sara Ahmed, *Queer Phenomenology: Orientations, Objects, Others* (Durham, NC: Duke University Press, 2006), 65–67.

115 Ahmed, *Queer Phenomenology*, 87.

116 Ahmed, *Queer Phenomenology*, 82.

117 Ahmed, *Queer Phenomenology*, 65.

118 Ahmed, *Queer Phenomenology*, 158.

119 Ahmed, *Queer Phenomenology*, 158 [emphasis in original].

120 Shukaitis, "Space Is the (Non)Place," 98.

121 We take this phrasing from Eduardo Rothe's observation in 1969 that '[p]ower, which cannot tolerate a vacuum, has never forgiven the celestial regions for being terrains left open to the imagination'. See Eduardo Rothe, "The Conquest of Space in the Time of Power," (1969), translated by Ken Knabb, www.bopsecrets.org/SI/12.space.htm.

122 In Aboriginal and Torres Strait Islander cultures, for example, 'The sky serves as a scientific textbook, a map, a law book, and a canvas on which complex layers of knowledge are interwoven, linked, and recorded for future generations'. See Indigenous Knowledge Institute, "Astronomy," *The University of Melbourne*, accessed December 5, 2023, https://indigenousknowledge.unimelb.edu.au/curriculum/themes/astronomy.

as a site for human use. Refusing to allow humanity to be one small part of a vast universe, outer space became the 'province' of 'mankind'. In turn, the 'mankind' to whom outer space now belonged was shaped by gendered, sexual, racial, and militarised imaginaries. This projection of these imaginaries onto outer space can be seen as an attempt to 'straighten' the celestial regions by putting some futures in reach and others beyond it, helping to re-stabilise earthly power relations.

4.2 The Subversive Potential of the Spectacle of Attempting to 'Straighten' Outer Space

In our view, however, the 'straightening' effects of international space law and politics have not foreclosed the possibility of subverting earthly regimes of normativity or harnessing the radical imaginative potential of the cosmos to do so. This is because the projection of normative imaginaries onto outer space has not simply formed a heterosexual 'background'[123] that orients us in particular directions. Instead, it has tended towards the hyperbolic. The OST's designation of outer space as the 'province of mankind' and astronauts as the 'envoys of mankind', the gender performativity surrounding the early US and Soviet space programs – including the magazine references to 'epochal missions' and 'great men' – and the images of the Space Billionaires today have all been large, overt and spectacular.[124]

Somewhat paradoxically, then, there are aspects of this straightening exercise that resemble Judith Butler's account of drag performances. Butler argues that drag – that is, the 'gender-bending art form in which a person dresses in clothing and makeup meant to exaggerate a specific gender identity'[125] – can play a subversive function by reflecting 'the mundane impersonations by which heterosexually ideal genders are performed and naturalized' and undermining 'their power by virtue of effecting that exposure'.[126] For Butler, the spectacular or hyperbolic nature of drag is central to its ability to expose and subvert: 'As an allegory that works through the hyperbolic, drag brings into relief what is, after all, determined only in relation to the hyperbolic: the understated, taken-for-granted quality of heterosexual performativity'.[127]

123 Ahmed, *Queer Phenomenology*, 101.

124 On the 'theatrics' surrounding Bezos's trip into outer space, see Amy Davidson Sorkin, "The Race to Leave Planet Earth," *The New Yorker*, July 18, 2021, www.newyorker.com/magazine/2021/07/26/the-race-to-leave-planet-earth.

125 "What Is Drag? A Primer on Drag Queens in Popular Culture," *MasterClass*, June 8, 2021, www.masterclass.com/articles/a-primer-on-drag-queens-in-popular-culture.

126 Judith Butler, *Bodies That Matter: On the Discursive Limits of Sex* (London and New York: Routledge, 2011), 243.

127 Butler, *Bodies that Matter*, 237.

Unlike drag, the 'straightening' effects of international space law have not themselves been subversive. Yet, in the attempt to project those power structures beyond the limits of this world, the representations and performances produced have been more spectacular than other 'straightening' exercises. And, like drag, this turn to the larger-than-life can create the possibility of subversion by bringing gendered and sexual (as well as racial and class-based) power relations into focus.

In the late 1960s and 1970s, for example, the starkness of the masculinity surrounding the US space program, as well as the gendered language of 'mankind', became a rallying point for American feminists. After all, at the time, spacefaring was so gendered it seemed 'like some sort of stag club', as an article in *Ms.* Magazine put it in 1973.[128] In response to this overt masculinity, the National Organization for Women (NOW) organised frequent protest activities against NASA. At one of these, in 1970, NOW members picketed outside NASA Headquarters with five enormous placards, which, when lined up, read 'ONE' 'GIANT' 'LEAP' 'FOR HUMAN' 'KIND'.[129] While this statement was responding to US astronaut Neil Armstrong's 'one giant leap for mankind' speech, it demonstrates that even just a few years after the OST opened for signature in 1967, women recognised the term 'mankind' was doing gendered work. These feminist protests attracted media attention, helping the women's liberation movement to both spread its message and expand its numbers, altering politics both on Earth and in outer space – where American women astronauts would eventually go.

A similar story can be found in relation to the civil rights movement in the US, which was not only galvanised by the expense of getting the all-White astronaut corps into outer space but also used the visual contrast between the spectacle of 'Whitey on the Moon'[130] and the poverty experienced by African American communities to draw attention to their cause. In 1969, for example, the day before the Apollo 11 launch, the Poor People's Campaign organised a rally at the launch site, in which they brought along 'scruffy mules' and 'rickety wagons' to expose the wide gulf that existed between rural Black lives and NASA's shiny, white rocket.[131]

The 'straightening' effects of international space law and politics continued to play an illuminating function even after the 'golden age' of space exploration. In 1995, the Association of Autonomous Astronauts (AAA) was formed in response to the 'poverty of thought'[132] its members saw in human

128 Joan McCullough, "13 Who Were Left Behind," *Ms.* 11, no. 3 (September 1973), quoted in Maher, *Apollo in the Age of Aquarius*, 169.

129 Maher, *Apollo in the Age of Aquarius*, 171.

130 'Whitey on the Moon' is the name of a spoken word poem by Gil Scott-Heron in 1970.

131 Maher, *Apollo in the Age of Aquariu*, 11, 14.

132 Luther Blissett, "Sex in Space," *AAA*, 1990s, https://theanarchistlibrary.org/library/association-of-autonomous-astronauts-luther-blissett-sex-in-space.

encounters with outer space to date, in which it seemed earthly norms were simply being reproduced in outer space.[133] As one AAA publication put it, '[w]e are not interested in finding out what's its [sic] like to work in space, to find new ways of killing. We want to find out what dancing or sex feels like in zero gravity'.[134] Another described NASA as 'a patriarchy like all state-agencies' and rejects its 'prioritisation of work over play, of commerce over pleasure'.[135] In response to this overt normativity, the members of AAA set up an international network of 'community space programs' with the goals of building a spaceship and establishing 'a planetary network to end the monopoly of corporations, governments, and the military over travel in space'.[136]

Although the AAA never did build a functioning spaceship, they managed to establish over 30 chapters across Europe, North and South America, and Oceania. They also organised several 'intergalactic conferences', at which members would explore 'sex in zero gravity, space raves, and three-sided football matches'.[137] For many members, it seems, the AAA was not so much about getting to outer space but reclaiming its radical imaginative potential so as to transform social relations on Earth. This can be seen in the group's decision to self-dissolve in 2000, just when the alter-globalisation movement appeared to be gathering momentum.[138] As Neil Disconaut explained: 'So why stop now? . . . We don't want to be the space industry's court jesters when capitalism itself is being openly contested, as seen in Seattle and the City of London in the last year'.[139] Having nourished their imaginations, it appears that members of the AAA now wanted to join in the protests against the World Trade Organisation and other international institutions to use the community they had formed to transform *this* world into something better.

Even more recently, the spectacle of the Space Billionaires and their hyperbolic dreams of 'colonising' the skies have prompted legal scholars to call for a feminist law for Mars. In 2018, Keina Yoshida wrote a post on the international law feminist blog site, 'IntLawGrrls', wondering what would happen if figures like Elon Musk succeeded in their goals of 'colonising' Mars: 'When the first to arrive are the super elite and the wealthy will they do anything

133 Katherine Sammler and Casey Lynch, "Spaceport America: Contested Offworld Access and the Everyman Astronaut," *Geopolitics* 26, no. 3 (2021): 715–716.
134 AAA flyer for J18 Anticapitalist Carnival, 1999, quoted in Shukaitis, "Space Is the (Non) Place: Martians, Marxists, and the Outer Space of the Radical Imagination," 110.
135 Blissett, "Sex in Space."
136 Blissett, "Sex in Space."
137 Sammler and Lynch, "Spaceport America: Contested Offworld Access and the Everyman Astronaut," 716.
138 Shukaitis, "Space Is the (Non)Place," 109.
139 Neil Disconaut, "Mission Accomplished But the Beat Goes On: The Fantastic Voyage of the AAA" (2000), www.uncarved.org/AAA/final/disco.html.

other than impose the capitalist extractivist patriarchy under which we live here and now?'[140] The idea of these power relations being reproduced on Mars was so displeasing to Yoshida that she implored feminist international lawyers to start talking about 'space feminism' and drafting 'the treaties, covenants, and other instruments' that would ultimately 'provide for an alternative and better future'.[141]

Yoshida's blog post was followed by two more on 'IntLawGrrls', by Emily Jones and Kathryn McNeilly, each of which set out to explore what Yoshida's call for 'space feminism' might look like. Jones argued it would need to centre the critical posthuman project by extending legal personality to both the environment, including Mars itself, as well as 'robots or artificially intelligent entities'.[142] McNeilly suggested space feminism should foreground alterity by ensuring 'feminist-inspired attention to social exclusion, marginalisation and the ongoing struggle to challenge such in whatever social and legal system we live within'.[143] Since then, some of these scholars have continued to explore what feminist constitutionalism on a planetary scale might involve,[144] as well as more inclusive legal imaginaries for governing outer space.[145] In this regard, the 'IntLawGrrls' blog series serves as another example of how the 'straightening' project of international space law and politics can facilitate opportunities for subversion by bringing power relations into relief.

5. Conclusion

Since the mid-twentieth century, outer space has been a site of contest for rival imaginaries. On the one hand, through its queerness and infinite diversity, outer space has inspired radical thinking, helping people to conceive of other ways of being and belonging. On the other hand, international space law has facilitated the projection of gendered, militarised, and extractive imaginaries back onto outer space in an apparent attempt to bring the celestial regions into line with earthly power relations. And yet, as we have shown in this chapter, this latter project has not succeeded in stamping out the former.

140 Keina Yoshida, "A Constitution for Mars: A Call for Founding Feminists," *International Law Grrls* (blog), October 4, 2018, https://ilg2.org/2018/10/04/a-constitution-for-mars-a-call-for-founding-feminists/.

141 Yoshida, "A Constitution for Mars."

142 Jones, "A Posthuman Feminist Approach to Mars."

143 Kathryn McNeilly, "What Feminism Can Teach Us About Alterity and Law on Mars," *International Law Grrls* (blog), November 29, 2018, https://ilg2.org/2018/11/29/what-feminism-can-teach-us-about-alterity-and-law-on-mars/.

144 See, e.g., Emily Jones, "Posthuman Feminism and Global Constitutionalism: Environmental Reflections," *Global Constitutionalism* (2022): 1–15.

145 Emily Jones, Cristian van Eijk and Gina Heathcote, "The Common Heritage of Kin-Kind," in *International Law and Posthuman Theory*, eds. Matilda Arvidsson and Emily Jones (Abingdon and New York: Routledge, 2023).

To the contrary, in seeking to project regimes of the normal beyond the limits of this world, the 'straightening' effects of the law and politics of outer space have tended to be overt and hyperbolic. The spectacle created has, in turn, played an illuminating function, helping to bring dominant forms of sociality into relief. Combined with the radical imaginative potential of outer space, this has inspired different groups to contest power structures – whether they be economic, racial, sexual, or gendered. The result has been the development of new and alternative ways of thinking in relation to both life on Earth and in outer space. In this regard, while the future is unknown, the story of 'Cosmic Hope'[146] associated with the celestial regions does not appear to be finished yet.

146 Treviño, "The Cosmos," 19.

Part 2

Queer Encounters with Temporality and Coloniality in International Law

Chapter 5

International Law, Coloniality, and the Temporal Otherwise

Vanja Hamzić[1]

1. Introduction

A decade ago, writing for one of the many anthologies that surfaced as of late with a mission to retell anew the history of international law, Oliver Diggelmann described what seemed to be a common disciplinary trait. 'In the discipline of international law', he proposed, "there is a remarkable inclination towards 'narrations of progress'. I am tempted to speak of a relatively wide consensus that 'the present' – despite its shortcomings – should be understood as a higher stage of evolution than 'the past' and that the history of international law should be told accordingly."[2]

1 I feel close kinship with – and deep, abiding gratitude to – the wonderful folks who have contributed to the *Queering International Law, 2.0* project, which gave rise to this chapter and volume. Our many conversations, particularly those at Deakin in Melbourne in November 2022, have helped me enormously in the process of researching for, and writing, this chapter. Thank you, dear Tamsin Paige and Claerwen O'Hara, not only for spearheading that project, but also for your considerate and intellectually generative stewardship of the present volume, and for your infinite patience with those of us who tarried, to use a biblical term. Finally, thank you, Safet HadžiMuhamedović, for your closeness and unfaltering advice have made this piece possible. All errors and mis-conceptualisations are mine alone.

2 Oliver Diggelmann, "The Periodization of the History of International Law," in *The Oxford Handbook of the History of International Law*, eds. Bardo Fassbender and Anne Peters (Oxford: Oxford University Press, 2012), 997–1011. Linear histories and progressivist narrations of international law are too many to be mentioned here, as are the publications seeking to critically intervene in how the dominant (Euro-American) periodisation and thematic foci were wrought out. For examples of the latter, see, for instance, Matthew Craven, Malgosia Fitzmaurice and Maria Vogiatzi, eds., *Time, History and International Law* (Leiden: Martinus Nijhoff Publishers, 2007); Anne Orford, *International Law and the Politics of History* (Cambridge: Cambridge University Press, 2021); Luis Eslava, Michael Fakhri and Vasuki Nesiah, eds., *Bandung, Global History, and International Law: Critical Pasts and Pending Futures* (Cambridge: Cambridge University Press, 2017).

DOI: 10.4324/9781032645339-7

Indeed, it would be difficult to overlook this narrative dictum in almost any mainstream writings on, or jurisprudence of, international law. Whilst periods and actors may differ, there is a dominant *evolutionary* view of time in international law that privileges the stories of the progress of humankind. Things were ostensibly worse, less developed, in the past, even if certain guiding principles of international legality crystallised along the way.[3] We are to believe that we are in a better place now despite nearly perpetual wars and the ineffectiveness of those principles or the conventions and institutions that coalesced around them. And, even if we do not now, we will prosper eventually if the future brings compliance and further development of the 'international legal norms and standards' aimed at our collective wellbeing.

Such narratives of progress tend not only to overlook the abiding violence of international law – *structural* in its perpetuation of political and economic inequalities and *epistemic* in its primary reliance on Global Northern systems of knowledge production – they also continue to reinforce a distinctly *linear* temporality coterminous with the rise of European imperialism on a global scale and a would-be 'enlightened' international law crafted to enable it.[4] There are surprisingly few critiques of such a long-time investment in an imperial time-reckoning. Upendra Baxi has proposed, for example, that we consider such anthropologies of time that speak of temporalities that are enduring, cyclical, erratic, or accelerated, to name but a few, so as to unsettle the dominant narratives of international legal evolution. He asks, for instance, without attempting to provide any immediate answers, 'How may one write

3 Perhaps the most jarring element of this dominant view are the rules concerning the so-called 'inter-temporality' in international law, which stipulate that the legality of an act or an omission must be judged against the rules of international law that applied *at the time* this happened, so that such judgment is not affected by any subsequent legal changes. This temporal provision could be used, say, against the renewed efforts to seek reparations for former colonial and imperial atrocities. For a brief critical analysis, see Ntina Tzouvala, "The Alibis of History, or How (Not) to Do Things with Inter-temporality," *CIL Dialogues: An International Law Blog*, Centre for International Law, National University of Singapore, February 2023, https://cil.nus.edu.sg/blogs/the-alibis-of-history-or-how-not-to-do-things-with-inter-temporality/.

4 For a critique of international law, not in relationship to diverse forms of violence but of international law *as* violence, see Vanja Hamzić, "International Law as Violence: Competing Absences of the Other," in *Queering International Law: Possibilities, Alliances, Complicities, Risks*, ed. Dianne Otto (Abingdon and New York: Routledge, 2018), 77–99. For the watershed critique of an abiding legacy of European imperialism in international law, see Antony Anghie, *Imperialism, Sovereignty and the Making of International Law* (Cambridge: Cambridge University Press, 2005). For a discussion on the violent legacies of Enlightenment-era European philosophical treatises on international law, see Vanja Hamzić, "After *Homo Narrans*: Botany, International Law and Senegambia in Early Racial Capitalist Worldmaking," in *International Law and Posthuman Theory*, eds. Matilda Arvidsson and Emily Jones (London: Routledge, 2023), 180–199. For a critical history of linear time and its many alternatives, see Carol J. Greenhouse, *A Moment's Notice: Time Politics across Culture* (Ithaca: Cornell University Press, 1996).

the "history" of international law in terms of such temporalities? How may the addition of "messianic" time of the European "civilizing mission" help us in re-exploring the Europe–India interface?'[5] Writing in a similar context, Nathaniel Berman has suggested that 'international legal history has a variety of temporal lines, which the genealogist must disentangle'.[6] For Berman, 'Tony Anghie's story of the reinvention of European sovereignty in relationship to the colonization of the Americas runs on a temporal line that is only obliquely related to other stories', amongst which he lists 'the reconstruction of the Concert of Europe in relationship to the dismantling of the Ottoman Empire' and 'the post-World War II reconstruction of international law's identity in relation to the decolonizing world'.[7] 'Genealogists are interested in how these obliquely related lines diverge and intersect',[8] concludes Berman. Indeed, they are, but Berman does not seem to count himself amongst them, so the reader is left to wonder exactly how such temporal divergences and intersections might be wrought out. Thus, the need to pluralise or qualitatively describe linear time is stated but not necessarily widely followed through. What emerges, instead, is a patchy field of critical engagements, which either consider temporality as it relates to various aspects of *doing* law, in both international and domestic realms, or are concerned specifically with international human rights law (for instance, with its presumptive 'timelessness').[9]

But what if the past and the future of international law, tout court, can be thought of in the temporal *otherwise*; a time that is, as Elizabeth Povinelli would put it, *geontologically* diverse; a time in which the lifeworlds

5 Upendra Baxi, "India-Europe," in *The Oxford Handbook of the History of International Law*, eds. Bardo Fassbender and Anne Peters (Oxford: Oxford University Press, 2012), 751–752. For the influential work Baxi had in mind concerning the anthropology of time, see Alfred Gell, *The Anthropology of Time: Cultural Constructions of Temporal Maps and Images* (Abingdon: Routledge, 2001).

6 Nathaniel Berman, *Passion and Ambivalence: Colonialism, Nationalism, and International Law* (Leiden: Martinus Nijhoff Publishers, 2012), 69.

7 Berman, *Passion and Ambivalence*, 69. See also, Anghie, *Imperialism, Sovereignty and the Making of International Law.*

8 Berman, *Passion and Ambivalence*, 69.

9 Engagements with temporal aspects of how law is done include critical studies of adjudicative temporality, for instance, in the times of war and peace, in litigation around affirmative action and reparations, or in criminal responsibility ascription; Zinaida Miller, "Time, Law, and Judgment," *Temple International and Comparative Law Journal* 32, no. 1 (2018): 53–67; Zinaida Miller, "The Injustices of Time: Rights, Race, Redistribution, and Responsibility," *Columbia Human Rights Law Review* 52, no. 2 (2021): 647–737; Tanzil Chowdhury, *Time, Temporality and Legal Judgment* (Abingdon: Routledge, 2020). For a discussion on would-be 'timelessness' and of other temporal aspects of international human rights law, see Fleur Johns, "The Temporal Rivalries of Human Rights," *Indiana Journal of Global Legal Studies* 23, no. 1 (2016): 39–60. For another thorough engagement with temporality as it relates to human rights law, see Kathryn McNeilly and Ben Warwick, eds., *The Times and Temporalities of International Human Rights Law* (Oxford: Hart, 2022).

of resistance to the violence of colonial and postcolonial international law can be (re-)encountered and re-centred to inform a novel, *queerer* theorising of the international, the legal, and the subjecthood they prop up and legitimise?[10] In particular, what could such temporal refuges yield vis-à-vis an extractive, forcefully universalised linear time in which the canons and 'foundational principles' of international law anchored their logics and claims to authority?

This chapter engages a distinct temporal and material locale – that of 'proto-colonial' eighteenth-century Senegambia – not only to ponder a circum-Atlantic early capitalist economy of enslavement and human fungibility in the making, in which international legal theory and practice of the time were fully complicit, but also to retell the story of radically different, insurrectionary West African conceptualisations of time and personhood.[11] Dwelling on the example of gender-nonconforming Mande griots (*jeliw*) and their increasingly precarious lifeworlds, and learning from the Black radical tradition and decolonial queer and trans/feminist critique, I query what is construed as 'recent', and what as 'distant', in temporal inflections of international law.[12] Or, rather, the chapter asks whose stories and experiences matter and whose do not and cannot, along an inherently hegemonic, cisheteropatriarchal timeline.[13]

10 Elizabeth A. Povinelli, "Routes/Worlds," *e-flux* 27 (September 2011); Elizabeth A. Povinelli, "Geontologies of the Otherwise," *Cultural Anthropology* (January 2014).

11 This exploration is based on my long-term archival and ethnographic research of gender nonconformity and the forceful making of the (proto-)colonial gender binary in eighteenth-century Senegambia. See, for example, Hamzić, "After *Homo Narrans*."

12 For a recent queer critique of the temporality of law in a different register, see Anthony J. Langlois, "Queer Temporalities and Human Rights," in *The Times and Temporalities of International Human Rights Law*, eds. Kathryn McNeilly and Ben Warwick (Oxford: Hart, 2022), 159–177. Langlois deals specifically with international human rights law and argues that, in order to recuperate a politics of liberation after the loss, or at least serious disruption, of the 'last utopia' of human rights, queer and trans scholarship, and activism need to recall the long history of abjection and marginalisation of queer and trans legal subjects and consider how this history continues to structure queer and trans lives in the present.

13 Queer theorists have recently proposed temporary, special, and people's tribunals as particularly generative in disrupting and rethinking the linear time of international law. Relying on queer and international relations scholarship on other-than-linear time, Caitlin Biddolph re-reads the memories of the genocidal violence in Srebrenica and elsewhere in Bosnia and Herzegovina in the 1990s contained within the paradigm of the International Criminal Tribunal for the former Yugoslavia as a traumatic experience of time 'that is complicated, layered, and out of joint'. At the time of finalising the present chapter, such critical re-reading of the temporalities of genocidal violence seems particularly urgent, given the *ongoing* genocide against Palestinians in Gaza. In another example, Claerwen O'Hara critically revisits two people's tribunals held in 1976 in Brussels and Sydney, respectively, to re-establish 'links between queer theory and the ideas underpinning the gay and women's liberation movements, despite the gap in time between the two and the emergence of the gay rights movement in between', which, in turn, enables O'Hara's

In Section 2, I revisit the distinct role played by European natural law theories in undergirding the colonial project of an extractivist linear time and show how this led to the systemic dispossession of enslaved Senegambians of their senses of selfhood, freedom, *and* time, exemplified in *jeliw*'s complex cosmology and sociality, and their lingual, bodily, and gender nonconformity. In Section 3, I turn to *jeliw*'s regional diplomatic and legal function to recall an otherwise to the linear telling of the international legal past and propose a queerer approach to temporality that privileges diverse nonconforming communities' own cosmologies and articulations of personhood and more-than-personhood in time. Finally, in the Coda, I reflect on the need for a sustained focus on the local and the particular that can interrupt the making of the dominant past. To that end, I reiterate my hope that a queerer work on the temporal otherwise – in its manyfold emanations and guises – can trouble international law's suspect claim to the universal.

Against the abiding imperial intimacies and technologies of subjectivation that saturate the dominant projects of international legal time-reckoning and meaning-making, what can the stories and ways of being-in-the-world that emerge from the temporal otherwise tell us, in Lisa Lowe's words, about 'the connections that could have been but were lost and are thus not yet'?[14] In other words, if one can abandon, even for a short while, the dominant timeline and mainstream histories of legal international meaning-making, can the emergent remnants of the lifeworlds past – such as those of eighteenth-century Senegambia – speak to the explorations in a queer and trans otherwise that saturates today's critical approaches to gender, sexuality, and subjectivity, in law and beyond? And, if so, what (early, speculative, still-in-the-making) interconnections and intimacies between these temporally distant worldings, beyond and against empire and its onto-epistemic violence, can such work yield?

interpretative disruption of 'the linear progress narrative that helps to naturalise the current LGBTI rights framework'. Caitlin Biddolph, "Queering Temporalities of International Criminal Justice: Srebrenica Remembrance and the International Criminal Tribunal for the Former Yugoslavia (ICTY)," *Griffith Law Review* 29, no. 3 (2020): 410; Claerwen O'Hara, "In Search of a Queerer Law: Two People's Tribunals in 1976," *Australian Feminist Law Journal* 49, no. 1 (2023): 24.

14 Lisa Lowe, "History Hesitant," *Social Text* 33, no. 4 (2018): 107. For Lowe, 'imperial intimacies' relate to 'the many of the liberal concepts that were used to justify slavery [but] were also employed differently at other times to justify settler occupation, theft of land, imperial war, and overseas empire', at 90. However, for Hazel Carby, imperial intimacies denote also 'a story of the everyday ties, relations and intricate interdependencies of empire and colonialism'; Hazel V. Carby, *Imperial Intimacies: A Tale of Two Islands* (London: Verso, 2019), i. See also, Lisa Lowe, *The Intimacies of Four Continents* (Durham: Duke University Press, 2015).

2. European Natural Law, Senegambia and Proto-colonial Distemporalisation

To arrive at these junctures, one must first pay a brief visit to the philosophical contours of eighteenth-century international law. Following the generations of TWAIL[15] scholarship and other critical, decolonial, and postcolonial studies, it may no longer be surprising or controversial to assert that the European Enlightenment project in general, and its reflections in European natural law theories in particular, have enabled, rather than impeded, the rise of Euro-American colonialism and imperialism. As Sylvia Wynter has contended, these concerted, systemic efforts resulted in the figurations of the human as onto-epistemically divisible and governable along the imposed racialised, gendered, sexed, classed, abled, and other fault lines – and they were either explicitly legal or lawlike.[16] The hierarchical subjectivities in the making were given – all at once – a particular legal, natural, and scientific veneer. As I have argued elsewhere, this ordering gave rise to such abiding constructs as the (colonial) gender binary.[17] But it also ushered in and touted a singular conceptualisation of linear time as 'universal'.

In their efforts to construe sovereign states as possessing moral personhood, proponents of European natural legal theories took a 'pragmatic' view of legal, social, and political history. For example, the German jurist Samuel Freiherr von Pufendorf advocated an approach to statecraft that Martti Koskenniemi describes as a what-history-taught-as-wise policy.[18] Empire, in this scheme, was not an inevitable, timeless type of polity but 'simply what history had produced'.[19] One needed to learn about would-be 'universal histories' of humankind in order to discern lessons for the future.

Another German jurist and philosopher, Christian Wolff, proposed that a nation's 'civility' and 'worth' were directly dependent on its ability to preserve the memories of its past. 'So the Chinese gave their best efforts to

15 Third World Approaches to International Law (TWAIL) is an influential, multigenerational critical current in international legal scholarship, comprising, in particular, histories 'from below' of Euro-American colonialism and imperialism and centre on Global Southern experiences of the international legal order. See, for instance, James Thuo Gathii, "TWAIL: A Brief History of Its Origins, Its Decentralized Network and a Tentative Bibliography," *Trade, Law and Development* 3, no. 1 (2011): 26–48.

16 Sylvia Wynter, "The Ceremony Found: Towards the Autopoetic Turn/Overturn, Its Autonomy of Human Agency and Extraterritoriality of (Self-)Cognition," in *Black Knowledges/Black Struggles: Essays in Critical Epistemology*, eds. Jason R. Ambroise and Sabine Broeck (Liverpool: Liverpool University Press, 2015), 184–252.

17 Hamzić, "After *Homo Narrans*."

18 Samuel Freiherr von Pufendorf, *De jure naturae et gentium, libri octo* (Amsterdam: Johann Paul, 1698 [1672]).

19 Martti Koskenniemi, "A History of International Law Histories," in *The Oxford Handbook of the History of International Law*, eds. Bardo Fassbender and Anne Peters (Oxford: Oxford University Press, 2012), 949.

training in manners and to statecraft', he averred, 'and so from the most ancient times they have been prominent among the more civilized nations and are so to-day'.[20] However, such praises for non-European nations were rare and could, as in Wolff's case, lead to reprisals and disciplinary actions. Instead, as with Wolff's epistolary correspondent, the philosopher Gottfried Wilhelm von Leibniz, it was much more common to see such polities and people as bereft of the necessary civilisational markers precisely because they did not master the art of linear time. Leibniz, for his part, revelled in the trope of 'Muḥammadan fatalism' (*fatum mahometanum*), which portrayed Islam and the Ottoman Empire in particular as 'isolated from a past it does not inquire into and a future it does not care about, [so that] it lies adrift in a sea of Oriental passivity'.[21] Such dispassion for and outsideness of the 'civilising' linear time could render a nation, in Emer de Vattel's words, deserving of being 'extirpated as savage and pernicious beasts'.[22] Or, in other instances, enslaved or colonised.

Combined with early colonial aspirations and conquests, natural law theories wielded distinct power to project 'a single and coherent reality', deployed within universal linear time, that made multiple forms of dispossession both moral and lawful.[23] In eighteenth-century Senegambia, extractive (un)gendering, racialisation and dehumanisation of the enslaved bound for the trans-Atlantic commerce – undertaken systematically in the local French and British entrepôts – became commonplace markers of the new order.[24] Still unable to fully colonise these vast West African territories, the French and the English built their forts at Saint-Louis and James Island, respectively, the small but strategically important islands in the estuaries of Senegal and the Gambia. Their additional fortified trading posts, such as Saint-Joseph de Galam in Gajaaga on the upper Senegal River, ensured that the flow of enslaved people and goods from the interior of the continent towards the river's mouth could be as secure as possible. And finally, a small but strategically important French entrepôt was located on Île de Gorée, which oper-

20 Christian Wolff, *The Law of Nations Treated According to the Scientific Method*, trans. Joseph H. Drake (Carmel: Liberty Fund, 2017 [1749]), 51.

21 Ian Almond, "Leibniz, Historicism, and the 'Plague of Islam'," *Eighteenth-Century Studies* 39, no. 4 (2006): 470.

22 Emer de Vattel, *The Law of Nations or Principles of the Law of Nature Applied to the Conduct of Nations and Sovereigns*, trans. Charles G. Fenwick (Washington, DC: Carnegie Institution of Washington, 1916 [1758]), I, 37.

23 Martti Koskenniemi, "'Not Excepting the Iroquois Themselves . . .': Machiavelli, Pufendorf and the Prehistory of International Law," *Max Weber Lecture Series* (Florence: European University Institute, 2007), 30.

24 Hamzić, "After *Homo Narrans*," 189–190. Writing about the same geo-temporal locale, Jessica Marie Johnson also describes 'the violent ungendering of the slave trade'; Jessica Marie Johnson, *Wicked Flesh: Black Women, Intimacy, and Freedom in the Atlantic World* (Philadelphia: University of Pennsylvania Press, 2020), 81.

ated its own network of trading villages along the Senegalese Petite Côte. In these militarised proto-colonial outposts, the enslaved would be ordinarily stripped of the bodily markers of their gender difference (these included specific adornments, accessories, attire, and hairstyles) and re-assigned within the crude gender binary, directly linked to the (racialised human) unit of value known as *pièce d'Indie*, which governed the quotas and tariffs of the trans-Atlantic trade in enslaved humans and undergirded the early formations of racial capitalism.[25]

Enslaved West Africans were also denied their idiosyncratic, qualitatively different notions of time – they were *distemporalised*.[26] Each of these concomitant forms of dispossession gravely affected an endogamous artisanal status group found across diverse Senegambian populations. As *ɲamakalaw* – their collective name in Mande languages – suggests, members of this status group were believed to possess extraordinary access to the foundational life force, *ɲama*, and be beings with their own special temporality, contact with history, and bodily and gender-variant properties. Such properties were cosmologically specific; for instance, a gender-variant water spirit, Faro, was central to diverse Mande expressions of selfhood and spirituality.[27] And *ɲamakalaw*'s bodily, gender, and temporal difference in Mande society also meant that they

25 Hamzić, "After *Homo Narrans*," 189–190. For a more detailed study, see Vanja Hamzić, "Labors in Time and Subjectivity: Gender Nonconformity and Racial Capitalism in the Making of Eighteenth-Century New Orleans," in *Beyond Inequality: New Paradigms for Addressing the Future of Work*, eds. Karen Engle and Neville Hoad (New York: Columbia University Press, forthcoming 2024).

26 Safet HadžiMuhamedović and I have described *distemporalisation* as a project of denial of time – a denial of historicity, futurity, or change, which is a significant element of various constructions of 'otherness'. We have also taken distemporality to signify a refusal of, and intervention into, qualitatively specific temporal lifeworlds, such as those of the Senegambian polities and subjectivities in what is known, elsewhere, as 'the eighteenth century'. See Safet HadžiMuhamedović and Vanja Hamzić, "Distemporalities: Collisions, Insurrections and Reorientations in the Worlding of Time," panel organised for the Biennial Conference of the Finnish Anthropological Society, Helsinki, Finland, August 29–30, 2019. For a study of colonial and postcolonial distemporalisation of the gender-nonconforming *khwajasara* community in South Asia, see Vanja Hamzić, "Temporal Nonconformity: Being There Together as *Khwajasara* in a Time of One's Own," in *Pakistan Desires: Queer Futures Elsewhere*, ed. Omar Kasmani (Durham: Duke University Press, 2023), 125–145.

27 See, for example, Germaine Dieterlen, *Essai sur la religion Bambara* (Paris: Presses universitaires de France, 1951), 40–56. For a wider discussion of gender diversity amongst the Mande and other Senegambian communities, see Hamzić, "After *Homo Narrans*," 190. For an exploration of the remnants, reverberations, and rearticulations of such diversity in colonial and postcolonial Senegal, see Babacar M'Baye, "Afropolitan Sexual and Gender Identities in Colonial Senegal," *Humanities* 8, no. 4 (2019): 1–16; Babacar M'Baye, "The Origins of Senegalese Homophobia: Discourses on Homosexuals and Transgender People in Colonial and Postcolonial Senegal," *African Studies Review* 56, no. 2 (2013): 109–128; Aminata Cécile Mbaye, "Queer Political Subjectivities in Senegal: Gaining a Voice within New Religious Landscapes of Belonging," *Critical African Studies* 10, no. 3 (2018): 301–314.

'could behave "outrageously" and dress "showily", with no particular regard to what may have been socially construed as "male" or "female" attire, manners and hairstyles'.[28] This was true not only for the members of the artisanal status group amongst the Mande but also for the members of equivalent artisanal 'castes' across diverse Senegambian populations, including the Wolof, Fulɓe, Arabo-Berbers, and many others.

Within *ɲamakalaw*, many occupational sub-groups existed, of which *jeliw* (sing. *jeli*), or griots, were most well-known. Temporality was, in fact, griots' chief domain since past events were often believed to be in a causal relationship with present and future happenings. Owing to griots' *ɲama*-laden storytelling, oral histories were socially constructed and understood as both the history of today and the history of tomorrow – with the body of the oral historian mediating any potential temporal and mystical borders between them. An accomplished griot storyteller (*ŋara*) excelled in a wide variety of ritualised speech (*kilisi*), which could either benefit or harm those to whom it was directed. The power of *kilisi* could sometimes also be enhanced by means of various potent substances known to possess *ɲama*, including those that were believed to cause physical harm (*korote*).[29] Thus, a griot's power extended across the material and spiritual domains, just as their stories traversed and connected multiple temporalities and forms of life.

Jeliw's unique wordsmithery also meant that their *ɲama*-laden bodies were considered volatile. They could be a blessing, or they could wreak havoc.[30] Perhaps because of this unique property, they were exceptionally feared by European enslavers. From very early on, European travelogues warned their readers of *jeliw*'s 'otherness', in life as much as in death. Travelling up the Gambia River in 1620, the English explorer Richard Jobson seemingly sympathised with Gambian griots because, 'when any of them die, they doe not vouchsafe them buriall, as other people have; but set his dead corps upright in a hollow tree, where hee is left to consumme'.[31] John (Jean) Barbot, an employee of the Compagnie du Sénégal, attributed to griots' 'infamy' that the Wolof and Serer people "will scarce allow [griots] a grave when they die; believing the earth would never produce any fruit or plants, should it be defiled with their dead carcasses, nor will they throw their corps into ponds or rivers, for fear of

28 Hamzić, "After *Homo Narrans*," 191.

29 Hamzić, "After *Homo Narrans*," 190–192. For an anthropological perspective on Senegambian griots' speech and its many mystical properties, including those relative to multiple temporalities of the communal past, see Barbara G. Hoffman, *Griots at War: Conflict, Conciliation, and Caste in Mande* (Bloomington: Indiana University Press, 2000).

30 See, generally, David Courtney Conrad, "The Role of Oral Artists in the History of Mali" (PhD Thesis, SOAS University of London, 1981).

31 Richard Jobson, *The Golden Trade, or a Discovery of the River Gambra and the Golden Trade of the Æthiopians* (London: Nicholas Okes, 1623), 137.

killing the fish, and therefore they only thrust them into the hollow trunks or stumps of trees."[32]

Similar accounts continued to be published well into the eighteenth century, and beyond. For example, René-Claude Geoffroy de Villeneuve, who spent a total of four years in the region in the 1780s in service to a French governor and penned a popular four-tome description of Senegal, concluded that griots 'cannot obtain the honours of the sepulchre', because the Senegalese 'believe them to be related to the malicious spirit, [and] regard them as sorcerers'.[33] Denounced as 'sorcerers', *jeliw* and other *ɲamakalaw* were particularly harshly punished for any act of rebellion – but this did not deter them from leading several known revolts, including onboard enslavers' ships sailing towards the 'New World'.[34] Their bodily, gender, temporal, and cosmological difference aided such insurrectionary efforts considerably, rupturing – even if for a short while – an Atlantic racial capitalist world in its making. In life as well as in death, *jeliw*'s presence disturbed the formations of colonial racialisation, gendering, and linear time.

3. *Jeliw*'s Legal Function, Chrononormativity, and the Trouble with 'Queer Time'

What can this brief episode in by now ubiquitously linear history of international law tell us of the temporal and subjective *otherwise*? Curiously, perhaps, *jeliw* had an idiosyncratic international legal role to play in amongst diverse Senegambian polities prior to full-scale European colonisation. Much like emissaries in some other lifeworlds, griots were 'living otherwise' within a complex regional political and legal constellation of the Greater Senegambia.[35] Their volatile life force made their bodies inviolable and, therefore, apt to serve as negotiators and messengers between warring polities – effectively, an international diplomatic and legal function.[36] For instance, in the Gambia, '[t]he mutilation of a griot was a particularly outrageous act. The body of

32 John Barbot, *A Description of the Coasts of North and South-Guinea and of Ethiopia Inferior, Vulgarly Angola* (London: Messrs Churchill, 1732), 55.

33 René-Claude Geoffroy de Villeneuve, *L'Afrique, ou histoire, mœurs, usages et coutumes des Africains* (Paris: Nepveu, 1814), IV, 195.

34 For example, onboard *Le Courrier de Bourbon*, sailing in 1723 from Senegambia to Louisiana, a 45-year-old enslaved Senegambian was identified as 'the sorcerer' (*sorcier*) – and, therefore, likely a griot – who sought to instigate a rebellion amongst the ship's enslaved, which led to this person's gruesome death. See Hamzić, "After *Homo Narrans*," 192.

35 That is, of Senegambia in its broadest sense, incorporating as faraway regions as Ɓundu, Futa Jallon, and Futa Toro – the traditional Fulɓe heartlands – as well as the Mande 'cultural zone', extending as far east as Bamako and Timbuktu and as far south as the Southern Rivers region, framed to the north by the Arabo-Berber Trarza and Brakna communities in present-day Mauritania.

36 Conrad, "Role of Oral Artists," 20.

a griot was normally inviolable, and griots could pass freely through enemy lines to parley with the enemy without fear of molestation'.[37] For this reason, the 'injury or murder of a griot would arouse feelings of horror and outrage', an equivalent to a diplomatic scandal that would arise in some other parts of the world if an emissary were wounded or killed on their mission.[38] And yet, no history of international law 'remembers' this episode from a geontologically different place and time. And, even if it did, would it be possible to 'recover' what has been so systemically distemporalised? Or, to paraphrase C. Riley Snorton, a historian of transness and Blackness, would it suffice to recall that at least such lives and temporalities were 'liveable'?[39]

Much of more recent scholarship in the distinct but interrelated Black radical, decolonial queer, and trans/feminist traditions deals with the problem of time. Against the (usually) colonial, postcolonial, or neoliberal *chrononormativity*, which Elizabeth Freeman has memorably described as 'the use of time to organize individual human bodies toward maximum productivity' – a central preoccupation of European enslavers working towards ungendering and distemporalising the Senegambians bound for the trans-oceanic commerce in the eighteenth century – Kara Keeling has proposed *queer temporality* as 'a dimension of time that produces risk'.[40] 'Queer temporality', explains Keeling, describes 'that dimension of the unpredictable and the unknowable in time that governs errant, eccentric, promiscuous, and unexpected organizations of social life'.[41] It chimes well with the generous description of queerness by Muñoz as that irreverent 'mode of desiring that allows us to see beyond the quagmire' of the postcolonial present or perhaps beyond and outside the chrononormative time altogether.[42]

Critical voices have, however, warned against prefiguring such all-too-hopeful dimensions of time. To that end, Rahul Rao, for example, has called for renewed attention to the ways sexually and gender-nonconforming

37 Gordon Innes, *Sunjata: Three Mandinka Versions* (London: School of Oriental and African Studies, 1974), 317.

38 Innes, *Sunjata*, 317.

39 C. Riley Snorton, *Black on Both Sides: A Racial History of Trans Identity* (Minneapolis: University of Minnesota Press, 2017), 7. Snorton aptly observes that, for multiple historical racialised gender-nonconforming subjectivities, what little can be 'recovered' are but scattered remnants of the past that were either purposely disappeared in the (proto-)colonial archive or subjected to a form of European categorical and hierarchical historical empiricism, in which the existence of such subjectivities would be seen as outright unbelievable. See Hamzić, "After *Homo Narrans*," 192.

40 Elizabeth Freeman, *Time Binds: Queer Temporalities, Queer Histories* (Durham: Duke University Press, 2010), 3; Kara Keeling, *Queer Times, Black Futures* (New York: New York University Press, 2019), 37.

41 Keeling, *Queer Times, Black Futures*, 37.

42 José Esteban Muñoz, *Cruising Utopia: The Then and There of Queer Futurity* (New York: New York University Press, 2009), 1.

subjects inhabit categories of their own making, including such constructs as 'queer time', which, as I proposed elsewhere, are not inherently unidirectional or proleptic and can have both decolonising and recolonising effects.[43] The less totalising visions of queerness and transness *in time* allow for disparate, multifarious dealings with the human in its environment(s).[44] This, in turn, can help uncover exactly how, in their temporal-material specificity, the nonconforming communities respond to the dominant cisheteropatriarchal time-reckoning, reliant on colonial linear time, and in so doing, relate to the other (bodily, agential, economic, legal, social . . .) prescriptive and dispossessive tendencies embedded in hegemonic worldmaking – such as that, say, of eighteenth-century proto-colonial racial capitalism in Senegambia, founded on predatory Enlightenment natural law. Marquis Bey has described this as an approach cognisant of a 'spectral historicality' of the nonconforming subjectivities and communities, a view of their plural, localised, idiosyncratic pasts that refuses the hold of mainstream histories (and other hegemonic dealings with the temporal) over the forms of personhood and existence that, as Keeling points out, 'were never meant to survive *as such*'.[45] Or, as I would argue, what is necessary is a critical approach to the historical (and to temporality, as such) that privileges those nonconforming communities' own cosmologies and articulations of personhood and more-than-personhood in time.

Subjectivities, such as the Senegambian *jeliw*, contingent on both *ɲama* and interrupted access to the temporal otherwise, exceeded and therefore rendered superfluous any purely bodily aspects of selfhood. This, uncannily perhaps, resonates with recent works in decolonial queer and Black/trans/feminist critique. Bey has argued, for example, for 'an engagement that is not determined wholly by or confined to the surface of corporeality', so that 'if aspects of the body have come to be that which are formed by violent forces, it is necessary to find liberation in the aspects that are not confined to the body'; that is to say, 'it is necessary to find liberation in the aspects of

43 Rahul Rao, *Out of Time: The Queer Politics of Postcoloniality* (Oxford: Oxford University Press, 2020), 17–18; Hamzić, "Temporal Nonconformity," 140–141. M. Jacqui Alexander has theorised *recolonisation* as a process related to sexual and gender diversity in her critical writings about Caribbean state nationalism; see, for example, M. Jacqui Alexander, "Erotic Autonomy as Politics of Decolonization: An Anatomy of the Feminist and State Practice in the Bahamas Tourist Economy," in *Feminist Genealogies, Colonial Legacies, Democratic Futures*, eds. M. Jacqui Alexander and Chandra Talpade Mohanty (New York: Routledge, 1997), 63–100.

44 For the exploration of transness as an invitation to recover and chart anew the interconnections and transits between human bodies and nonhuman natures, see Stacy Alaimo, *Bodily Natures: Science, Environment, and the Material Self* (Bloomington: Indiana University Press, 2010).

45 Marquis Bey, *Black Trans Feminism* (Durham: Duke University Press, 2022), 93; Keeling, *Queer Times, Black Futures*, i.

subjectivity that exceed and ooze out of the body'.[46] The resistance of the Senegambian *jeliw* and other gender-nonconforming subjectivities to the (proto-) colonial gender binary, distemporalisation, and other extractivist interventions relied, in no small part, on such 'excessive', trans-temporal, both human and more-than-human subjectivity. European enslavers, explorers, merchants, and imperial officers branded and feared it as all-too-powerful 'sorcery', capable of causing insurrection and ruptures in their circum-Atlantic early capitalist economy of enslavement and human fungibility in the making, propped up by Enlightenment technologies of subjectivation, including that of international law.

4. Coda: Localities of the Subjective and the Temporal

Just as they did *then*, in the chrononormative construct known as 'the long eighteenth century', the dominant projects of international *legal* time-reckoning and meaning-making continue to rely on law's would-be salvatory powers – the powers rendered both natural and scientific in that same, 'eighteenth-century' timeframe. This was made possible, in part, by the rise of 'global histories', including those of international law, whose totalising view centred some people and their stories at the expense of many others. Is there a way to challenge such harmful, normative time-reckoning and meaning-making?

Two modest critical interventions come to mind. First, a sustained, queerer focus on the local and the particular could challenge and substantively alter what constitutes a dominant past, a lasting canon, or a foundational principle in any given international legal context. This might unearth, in turn, different legalities, such as that of eighteenth-century Senegambian *jeliw* in their role as negotiators and messengers between warring West African polities, a legal function rooted in their cosmological and gender-bodily difference. Second, a sustained, queerer research of the temporal otherwise – wherever, however it occurs – could trouble what or who is rendered 'recent', and what or who 'distant', in international law and its suspect claim to the universal. Stories from geontologically different lifeworlds and temporal orders could thus rekindle different perspectives on the international legal order and its relationship with the human and its environment(s) in time.

Either of these pursuits strikes me as potentially more generative than seeking to 'queer' the dominant figures, and their legal interventions, however potentially *temporarily* beneficial to queer and trans communities, appearing along the hegemonic temporal linear trajectory of international law. This is because, to echo Elizabeth Freeman, linear time

46 Bey, *Black Trans Feminism*, 3–4.

binds in that it renders certain forms of life and legal conduct infinitely more present – and, therefore, both liveable and believable – than the entire lifeworlds and subjectivities it purposely has left and continues to leave, *behind*, in the temporal, cosmological, social, political, and legal otherwise.[47] Given the manifold ravages of linear law and temporality, such lifeworlds and subjectivities may not be fully 'recoverable', but their resistive remnants abide and speak volumes to the nonconforming and insurrectionary across time.

47 Freeman, *Time Binds.*

Chapter 6

Rewriting Queer Markers of Identity

International Cultural Heritage Law, Criminalisation, and the Other

Lucas Lixinski

1. Introduction

Much of our thinking about queering international law is focused on two things: queer subjects and narratives, on the one hand;[1] and genealogies and critiques of power, on the other.[2] These two projects are often closely intertwined on much of the (still relatively incipient) literature on the subject, which seems to aim, like most critical projects, at shedding light on the power structures that we take for granted and underscore their contingency, as a first step towards ultimately undoing and reimagining those power relationships.

In this chapter, I draw on this literature but seek to take it one step further (or at least one step differently). First, I do not focus on queer subjects and narratives, at least not ostensibly; instead, I attempt to imagine the impact of queering international law in a subfield of international law that has not, to date, been imagined as queer: international cultural heritage law (ICHL). In doing so, I highlight queer as a verb rather than a noun.[3] I queer ICHL. I do so in these pages by bringing a queer sensitivity to reimagine the import of kinship into how we engage with the law that enables and channels identity in ways that are wary of and resist the law's inherent violence as an authorising force. For the most part, I focus on the interests of states and their deployment of cultural heritage (or cultural property, as some – particularly in the United States of America – still refer to it, despite significant changes in the field)[4] and not on the interests of human beings (queer or otherwise).

1 Aeyal Gross, "Homoglobalism: The Emergence of Global Gay Governance," in *Queering International Law: Possibilities, Alliances, Complicities, Risks*, ed. Dianne Otto (New York: Routledge, 2018), 148–170, 150.

2 See, for example, Dianne Otto, "Introduction: Embracing Queer Curiosity," in *Queering International Law: Possibilities, Alliances, Complicities, Risks*, ed. Dianne Otto (New York: Routledge, 2018), 1–11, 2.

3 Robert Leckey and Kim Brooks, "Introduction," in *Queer Theory: Law, Culture, Empire*, eds. Robert Leckey and Kim Brooks (Abingdon: Routledge, 2010), 1–18, 2.

4 Janet Blake, "On Defining the Cultural Heritage," *International and Comparative Law Quarterly* 49 (2000): 61.

DOI: 10.4324/9781032645339-8

For that reason, ICHL has so far escaped a queer (re-)reading. I attempt to correct that scenario.

A queer reading of ICHL is useful not just because it is novel but because it also aids goals in both ICHL and international law more broadly. From an ICHL perspective, it being queered helps because we can imagine additional ways to map and undo the power structures that underpin our relationship to heritage and identity. For international law more broadly, a queered ICHL is useful because ICHL is at present a battleground for reimagining international law away from a state-centric institutional framework to one that can and should serve identities and human interests (the so-called 'human dimension' of ICHL).[5] Therefore, ICHL can work as a bridge between the prevailing mode of analysis in queering international law scholarship (one centred on queer subjects and narratives) and a broader analytical project that engages with the queerness of international law more pervasively.

I will undertake this effort to queer ICHL through its institutional intersection with international criminal law (ICL), an encounter of different bodies of law that in itself can be a bit queer if it can avoid imperial co-option of one regime by the other.[6] To be sure, there is a fair amount of thinking about queer ICL, but to the best of my knowledge and with few exceptions, most of that thinking centres on sexual crimes and queer (or at least feminine or feminised) subjects.[7] While that literature will be useful, I am less interested in what ICL does in relation to the body and its sexual constitution and more in its impacts on institutions and power more broadly and how queer theory can help shed light on how identities are constituted, negotiated, and the power around them co-opted and brokered by different actors.

Further, ICL and its intersection with ICHL gives me the opportunity to do this queering exercise through the language of a judgment and, specifically, what reimagining a certain judgment might mean for adding a queer perspective to (international) law's operation. While there is a vast literature on rewriting judgments from feminist and other critical perspectives (such as Indigenous, child-centric, and nature-centric perspectives), only now are scholars invested in queer theory grappling with the narrative power of judgments.

5 Francesco Francioni, "The Human Dimension of International Cultural Heritage Law: An Introduction," *European Journal of International Law* 22, no. 1 (2011): 9, https://doi.org/10.1093/ejil/chr018Francioni.

6 Nicholas Bamforth, "An 'Imperial' Strategy? The Use of Comparative and International Law in Arguments about LGBT Rights," in *Queer Theory: Law, Culture, Empire*, eds. Robert Leckey and Kim Brooks (Abingdon: Routledge, 2010), 157–172, 157.

7 Caitlin Biddolph, "Queering Temporalities of International Criminal Justice: Srebrenica Remembrance and the International Criminal Tribunal for the Former Yugoslavia (ICTY)," *Griffith Law Review* 29, no. 3 (2020): 401. See also Caitlin Biddolph, "Queering (Un)Certainty in International Law: Reflections on the International Criminal Tribunal for the Former Yugoslavia," this volume.

I am one of the participants in the pilot (or first) phase of the Queer Judgments Project. While judgments (and critical judgment rewriting) can be limited, as I note further on, it is also useful, particularly in our thinking about queering international law more broadly, in that it allows (in fact, requires) us to channel the critique into certain normative commitments.

My contribution to the queer judgments project has been to rewrite *Prosecutor v Al Mahdi*,[8] a case in which the International Criminal Court (ICC) had its first opportunity to engage with the destruction of cultural heritage as an international crime. The destruction in question happened during an internal armed conflict in Mali and consisted of attacks on mausoleums in Timbuktu, a World Heritage Site, by insurgents affiliated with Muslim extremist ideologies. In taking this opportunity, the ICC both reinforced and problematised a series of binaries about cultural heritage (tangible or intangible?), its role in shaping identity (religious or secular?), who owns or controls heritage (state or the international community?), and the role of the law in preventing and punishing the destruction of cultural heritage (reparations or non-repetition?). The reliance on these binaries both creates hierarchies of heritage (and consequently those cultural practices and subjectivities it channels), and the reliance on binaries excludes and disallows practices that do not fit within either of the categories.

A queer reading and rewriting of this judgment and ICHL more broadly allows us to articulate the role of queer theory in debunking the binaries upon which legal argument often relies. These binaries, while ostensibly only heuristic, have deep constitutive effects. They catalyse much of the power and violence of international legal projects and deserve closer scrutiny through a queer prism.

A queer reading of *Al Mahdi* also allows us to challenge the way the law grapples with and constructs identities and the artefacts that anchor these identities. I argue that a queer perspective on ICHL liberates the law to capture better the fluidity of the power immanent to cultural heritage. This chapter also contributes to our thinking about queer legal theory in mapping pathways through which binaries can be analytically debunked or tactically deployed.

In what follows, I will first engage with the idea of queer judgments and their potential contributions to queer thinking in international legal scholarship. Second I will queer the basic ideas and premises of ICHL and ICL (the latter inasmuch as it intersects with ICHL). Next, I will move to

8 Judgment and Sentence, *Prosecutor v Al Mahdi*, International Criminal Court Trial Chamber VIII, ICC-01/12–01/15 (September 27, 2016); Reparations Order, *Prosecutor v Al Mahdi*, International Criminal Court Trial Chamber VIII, ICC-01/12–01/15 (August 17, 2017); and Judgment on the appeal of the victims against the 'Reparations Order', *Prosecutor v Al Mahdi* (International Criminal Court Appeals Chamber, ICC-01/12–01/15 A (March 8, 2018).

a queer analysis of *Al Mahdi*, which reveals the cracks created by bringing together different fields (ICL and ICHL), as well as different modes of analysis (critical legal scholarship and judgment rewriting). Through these cracks, one can seep imagination, subversion, and a more radical normativity.

2. Why Queer Judgments?

The Queer Judgments Project's first output, an edited volume, was going to press as this chapter was going to press.[9] I am fortunate to be in the pilot of this project as one of the few international law scholars involved – several of the contributors to this volume are also part of the queer judgments project (Alexandra Grolimund, Odette Mazel, Claerwen O'Hara, and Joanne Stagg), even if not contributing rewritten international law judgments. Given the novelty of this project, it is worth contextualising it. The project follows the impulse of multiple other critical judgment projects, spanning human rights integrationist, bioethical, feminist, Indigenous, children's, and environmental perspectives.[10] Their shared impetus is to rewrite well-known judgments within a jurisdiction from a perspective that centres on different ethical and legal commitments. These rewritings do away with a purported view of the neutrality of legal decision-makers and foreground certain political commitments as the premises for describing and interpreting the law and legal system.

Many of these critical judgments projects, at least those with distinctively anthropocentric goals (therefore, excluding the environmental projects), focus on identities as catalysts for critical re-examination of the law. They start from the basic premise of the law being created (and, particularly, adjudicated) predominantly by and for white, cisgender, able-bodied, heterosexual, property-owning men (what I will call the 'neutral avatar'). These men operate as the 'neutral' baseline of the legal process. By displacing that perspective and proactively resisting its embedded appeal, judges adopt different identities to query the way the law operates, free it of its contingencies, and imagine different legal possibilities that cater to a broader humanity. As a result, many of these rewritten judgments tend to focus on cases that directly affect these 'others.'

Among these critical judgments projects, perhaps the most prominent is the Feminist Judgments Project (or projects). The latter has spanned many

9 Nuno Ferreira, Maria F. Moscati and Senthorun Raj, eds., *Queer Judgments* (Coventry: Counterpress, forthcoming 2024).

10 For a website collecting many of these projects, as well as associated scholarship, see "Home," *Critical Judgments*, last modified April 6, 2022, accessed March 25, 2024, https://criticaljudgments.com/.

iterations[11] and even international law-specific versions.[12] Given the alignments (and misalignments) between queer and feminist theories,[13] it is worth scrutinising the feminist judgments project further, and for present purposes, at least in relation to its intersections with international law.

As Hilary Charlesworth has put it, feminist-judgment writing is a form of 'prefiguring,' or a mode of activism that evokes and prompts change.[14] It is a practice that does not require mobilising multiple actors and institutions since the judge gets to implement their own view of what the law ought to be and how it should be applied.

This formula offers 'a powerful vehicle for demonstrating what is plausible within the bounds of legal formalism.'[15] It is a challenge to orthodox ways of thinking without entirely upending the basic structures of the legal system. In other words, it requires us to observe the same rules and constraints of the original judges, meaning being bound by the same facts and substantive and procedural rules. These facts and rules can be re-read and reinterpreted (and such is the point) but not rejected outright.[16] It is thus a reformist, and decidedly less radical, rendering of the contribution of feminist (or, here, queer) theory to how we imagine the law, which is often cast in the image of the impossibility of using the master's tools to dismantle their house.[17] But, precisely because it forces operating within certain boundaries, it can force greater creativity within queer legal projects and a way of queering institutions from within. There are trade-offs, of course, but these can,

11 These include projects in Australia, Canada, England, Ireland, New Zealand, Scotland, and the United States. See "Feminist Judgments Projects," *Critical Judgments*, last modified April 6, 2022, accessed March 25, 2024, https://criticaljudgments.com/feminist-judgment-projects.

12 These include not only international law in general but also a specific International Criminal Law project. See "Feminist Judgments Projects."

13 Mapped extensively in Martha Albertson Fineman, Jack E. Jackson and Adam P. Romero, eds., *Feminist and Queer Legal Theory: Intimate Encounters, Uncomfortable Conversations* (Farnham: Ashgate, 2009). I also note that many contributors to feminist judgment projects have brought queer sensibilities to bear on their feminist rewritings, further reinforcing alignment and misalignments. See, for instance, Damian Gonzalez-Salzberg, Loveday Hodson, and Paul Johnson, "Christine Goodwin v the United Kingdom," in *Feminist Judgments in International Law*, eds. Loveday Hodson and Troy Lavers (Oxford: Hart Publishing, 2019).

14 Hilary Charlesworth, "Prefiguring Feminist Judgment in International Law," in *Feminist Judgments in International Law*, eds. Loveday Hodson and Troy Lavers (Oxford: Hart Publishing, 2019), 479, 492.

15 Rosemary Grey, Kcasey McLoughlin and Louise Chappell, "Gender and Judging at the International Criminal Court: Lessons from 'Feminist Judgment Projects'," *Leiden Journal of International Law* 34, no. 1 (2021): 247, 255.

16 Kathryn Gooding, "How Can the Methodology of Feminist Judgment Writing Improve Gender-Sensitivity in International Criminal Law?" *LSE Law Review* 5 (2020): 115, 120.

17 Zoi Aliozi, Bérénice K. Schramm and Ekaterina Yahyaoui Krivenko, "Germany v Italy," in *Feminist Judgments in International Law*, eds. Loveday Hodson and Troy Lavers (Oxford: Hart Publishing, 2019), 117, 145–146.

in my view, be worth accepting if it means it is harder, from the perspective of the mainstream neutral adjudicator avatar I conjured previously, to avoid these perspectives (and therefore easier to change the neutral avatar's sensibilities and sensitivities). After all, changing sensitivities is an open objective of feminist judgments.[18]

As to the methodology of these judgments, it seems generally applicable to queer thinking as well. The methodology developed for feminist judgments generally requires us to: (1) centre the identity meant to displace the neutral avatar and ask questions that force that displacement (also known as 'asking the woman question' [or, in our case, 'asking the queer person question']); (2) ensure that women (queer persons) are included in the decision-making process; (3) challenging discriminatory biases in judicial reasoning; (4) paying attention to women's (queer) lived experience; (5) actively seek to overcome injustices created by these discriminatory lines; and (6) being informed by feminist (queer) scholarship.[19]

One of the key contributions of feminist judgments in thinking about cases involving gendered subjects but with broader implications is the conclusion that a party to a case can be simultaneously vulnerable and have autonomy (in other words, that victimhood does not strip away agency).[20] While this lesson is somewhat antithetical to much international law practice (particularly in the field of international human rights law),[21] it aligns with feminist thinking and allows us to reconceptualise victims of violations of (international) law as not being fully in the hands of international institutions from the moment they are found to be victims. Rather, they continue to be actors in the process of applying and shaping international law (a point to which we will return later).

Feminist judgment rewriting does not always cover women or gendered subjects, however. There are multiple examples of feminist rewriting of judgments in international that do not involve women directly. The contribution of feminist thinking can be simply to remind us to seek alternative and richer narratives.[22] Doing so can make us 'answerable to the dead'[23] and avoid the sanitisation of tragedy that international law often requires. Feminist rewriting thus raises the

18 Gooding, "How Can the Methodology of Feminist Judgment Writing Improve," 120.

19 Rosemary Hunter, "An Account of Feminist Judging," in *Feminist Judgments: From Theory to Practice*, eds. R. Hunter, C. McGlynn and E. Rackley (Oxford: Hart Publishing, 2010), 30, 35.

20 Gooding, "How Can the Methodology of Feminist Judgment Writing Improve," 122.

21 Lucas Lixinski and Noam Peleg, "Paternalism in International Human Rights Law," *Duke Journal of Comparative & International Law* 33, no. 1 (2022): 1.

22 Kathryn Greenman and Troy Lavers, "The Lockerbie Case (Libyan Arab Jamahiriya v United States of America)," in *Feminist Judgments in International Law*, eds. Loveday Hodson and Troy Lavers (Oxford: Hart Publishing, 2019), 83, 84.

23 Greenman and Lavers, "The Lockerbie Case," 87.

human stakes and forces a discussion about how power is created and distributed by international institutions without abandoning the institutions altogether since they are important sites to confer identity.[24] It can also force analysing international law and its effects through the public/private divide, rendering this divide both visible and permeable.[25] The same kind of thinking extends naturally to binaries in general,[26] which is a valuable tool for queer rewriting as well.

Indigenous critical judgments, too, can contribute to queer judgment rewriting. Specifically, Insights from Indigenous judgment rewriting help centre questions and cast doubt on assumptions about jurisdictional commitments, applicable bodies of law, resistance to colonial forms, and the centring of subjects rendered subaltern on account of their culture.[27]

Importantly for our purposes, therefore, a judgment-rewriting version of queering international law does two things: it forces normative commitments, and, despite being suspicious of rights language, it still humanises institutional frameworks in international law without rejecting them altogether. After all, queer theory 'encounters its limits if it fails to pay attention to the role of institutions.'[28] On the former, as indicated previously, there is a reformist impulse which works with, but also separate from, queer theoretical critique. Queer theorists are often reluctant to make normative commitments[29] and have even blatantly described queer theory as 'a critical anti-normative project';[30] the judgment-rewriting process forces these commitments, which can be useful in terms of advancing thinking about the consequences of critical agendas, regardless of whether these commitments are subsumed within the reformist parameters of judgment rewriting. On the latter, this humanisation comes in part from resisting the urge in international law to exercise violence against an 'other,' by centring the 'other' and their narratives.[31]

Having established the perspectives that queer judgment rewriting can bring us to how we queer international law more broadly, we can now move to queering international law's substantive and institutional frameworks. Specifically, the next section attempts to queer ICHL and ICL, particularly the former, as the bodies of substantive law that operate in the *Al Mahdi* case.

24 Bruno Perreau, *Queer Theory: The French Response* (Stanford: Stanford University Press, 2016), 9.
25 Aliozi et al., "Germany v Italy," 118.
26 Aliozi et al., "Germany v Italy," 123–124.
27 See generally Nicole Watson and Heather Douglas, eds., *Indigenous Legal Judgments: Bringing Indigenous Voice into Judicial Decision Making* (Abingdon: Routledge, 2021).
28 Perreau, *Queer Theory*, 80.
29 Lorenzo Bernini, *Queer Theories: An Introduction from Mario Mieli to the Antisocial Turn* (Abingdon: Routledge, 2021), 47.
30 Ratna Kapur, "The (Im)possibility of Queering International Human Rights Law," in *Queering International Law: Possibilities, Alliances, Complicities, Risks*, ed. Dianne Otto (Abingdon: Routledge, 2018), 131–147, 132.
31 Greenman and Lavers, "The Lockerbie Case," 88.

3. Queering International Cultural Heritage Law (and International Criminal Law)

Queering substantive bodies of international law is an important mechanism through which to upend the basic premises and contingencies underlying certain normative commitments. We can thus map and problematise dichotomies, add narratives and perspectives, and, in the specific case of ICHL, ponder how international law forms identities through a queer identity perspective. It also allows us to question how the legacies of empire and its violence operate[32] and queer their ongoing influence on international law-making, starting from the premise that bigotry and the rejection of the 'other,' in one way or another, have always underpinned international law-making.[33]

In a judgment rewriting context, this step also allows us to tease out these commitments better before we get to the specific constraints of the case and the step of displacing and replacing the purportedly neutral avatar. Separating institutions and substantive law can be a problematic heuristic, to be sure, because it turns us blind to how institutional goggles shape what is possible in substantive law.[34] But, for our purposes, this separation allows us to articulate the dual registers of critique and normative commitments more distinctively and in a way that is arguably better conducive to both of those enterprises.

Even though there is a relatively robust body of literature that engages with queering ICL and its institutions, there is less so on ICHL, so I will devote the bulk of this section to the latter. On the former, it is worth stating from a queer critical perspective that ICL institutions, to the extent they rely on an international security paradigm for their existence, are themselves a form of juridical violence.[35] A queer critical view would suggest looking for 'alegal' spaces and imagining a life beyond the law through 'productive voids' that signal the 'absence' of international law and the violence it engenders.[36] But other work operates within the constraints of these institutions, instead recasting the jurisprudence of bodies like the International Criminal Tribunal for former Yugoslavia (which was created by the United Nations Security Council, being therefore a prime example of the enforcement of violence) through queer lenses.[37] The focus on securitisation (particularly in war crimes like heritage destruction)

32 Vanja Hamzić, "International Law as Violence: Competing Absences of the Other," in *Queering International Law: Possibilities, Alliances, Complicities, Risks*, ed. Dianne Otto (Abingdon: Routledge, 2018), 77–90, 78.
33 Nan Seuffert, "Queering International Law's Stories of Origin: Hospitality and Homophobia," in *Queering International Law: Possibilities, Alliances, Complicities, Risks*, ed. Dianne Otto (Abingdon: Routledge, 2018), 213–235.
34 From a general critical legal studies perspective, particularly embracing feminist critiques, see Karen Knop, *Diversity and Self-Determination in International Law* (Cambridge: Cambridge University Press, 2002).
35 Hamzić, "International Law as Violence," 79–80.
36 Hamzić, "International Law as Violence," 80–81.
37 Biddolph, "Queering Temporalities."

itself engenders very problematic consequences, which queer theory helps expose.[38] At the same time, however, testimony within ICL institutions can help resist and challenge narratives,[39] which can illuminate reified discursive threads within ICHL. Highlighting these gaps can also operate within ICL to allow narratives around culture, often neglected within the regime, to emerge and be centred.[40]

The move towards criminalisation and criminal law as a form of redress for international legal wrongs can be criticised from a feminist and queer perspective. In fact, both queer and feminist scholars have shown dissatisfaction with the use of criminal mechanisms to advance the rights of women and queer persons,[41] particularly in the queer context, where criminal law has often been used to punish and oppress queer persons and identities.[42] This dissatisfaction stands in tension with the idea within ICHL that international criminal institutions offer a rare and much-needed avenue for the enforcement of ICHL commitments, which, in one view, seek to protect identity.

Identities, however, are, for the most part, seen as a secondary (or at least non-normative) objective of ICHL. I understand, for present purposes, ICHL to be the body of law structured around five international treaties (and their protocols) administered by the United Nations Educational, Scientific and Cultural Organisation (UNESCO), each covering a specific form of heritage (or, in UNESCO parlance, a domain): heritage in wartime;[43] cultural objects;[44]

38 Tamsin Phillipa Paige, "The Maintenance of International Peace and Security Heteronormativity," in *Queering International Law: Possibilities, Alliances, Complicities, Risks*, ed. Dianne Otto (Abingdon: Routledge, 2018), 91–109.

39 Maria Elander, "In Spite: Testifying to Sexual and Gender-Based Violence During the Khmer Rouge Period," in *Queering International Law: Possibilities, Alliances, Complicities, Risks*, ed. Dianne Otto (Abingdon: Routledge, 2018), 110–127, 111.

40 On this gap, see generally Evelyne Schmid, *Taking Economic, Social and Cultural Rights Seriously in International Criminal Law* (Cambridge: Cambridge University Press, 2015), 3. Note, however, that this argument was made before the *Al Mahdi* case and may not be as strong on the surface any longer.

41 Grey et al., "Gender and Judging at the International Criminal Court," 250.

42 See Karen Engle in this volume's sibling collection, *Queer Encounters with International Law: Lives. Communities, Subjectivities*, eds. Tamsin Phillipa Paige and Claerwen O'Hara (Abingdon: Routledge, 2025).

43 Convention for the Protection of Cultural Property in the Event of Armed Conflict with Regulations for the Execution of the Convention 1954, 249 UNTS 240 (adopted May 14, 1954, entered into force 7 August 7, 1956); Protocol to the Convention for the Protection of Cultural Property in the Event of Armed Conflict, 249 UNTS 358 (adopted May 14, 1954, entered into force August 7, 1956); and Second Protocol to the Hague Convention of 1954 for the Protection of Cultural Property in the Event of Armed Conflict, 2253 UNTS 172 (adopted March 26, 1999, entered into force March 9, 2004).

44 Convention on the Means of Prohibiting and Preventing the Illicit Import, Export and Transfer of Ownership of Cultural Property 1970, 823 UNTS 231 (adopted November 14, 1970, entered into force April 24, 1972).

world heritage;[45] underwater cultural heritage;[46] and intangible cultural heritage.[47] The most relevant domains for our present purposes are heritage in wartime, world heritage, and intangible cultural heritage since they come up more clearly in the *Al Mahdi* context.

ICHL protects identities inasmuch as they are cast as national identities because it is eminently a state-centric endeavour, despite proclamations of heritage being of value to all of humanity.[48] This problematic dichotomy turns us blind to even seeing that there are other actors (particularly communities) for whom heritage matters most to create and galvanise identity, even mobilising that identity for political purposes.[49] Queer theory destabilises the concepts of global and local and, with it, the centring of state narratives.[50] And, within the state, subaltern identities are only protected via heritage in sanitised forms that strip away any radical content or emancipatory claim, so they can be packaged to serve an authorised form of national identity.[51] Queer theory, as (a relatively small and underexplored) part of the package of critical projects that form critical heritage studies,[52] allows us to not only note this displacement of subaltern identity but also to imagine what recentring it might look like, whether it is in relation to the state or the experts that often speak instead of communities in heritage contexts.[53] This call for inclusion also exists in the (relatively small) subfield of queer archaeology,[54] whether it applies to specific queer sites or beyond.[55]

Part of the effect of the five domains of ICHL is that they reinforce a fiction of different categories. Legal formalism propels states and international institutions to treat each of these domains as separate entities, seldom acknowledging intersections despite relationship clauses in most of the major

45 Convention concerning the Protection of the World Cultural and Natural Heritage 1972, 1037 UNTS 151 (adopted November 23, 1972, entered into force December 15, 1975).
46 Convention on the Protection of the Underwater Cultural Heritage 2001, 2562 UNTS 3 (adopted November 2, 2001, entered into force January 2, 2009).
47 Convention for Safeguarding of the Intangible Cultural Heritage 2003, 2368 UNTS 3 (adopted October 17, 2003, entered into force April 20, 2006) ('ICHC').
48 Lucas Lixinski, *International Heritage Law for Communities: Exclusion and Re-Imagination* (Oxford: Oxford University Press, 2019).
49 On a critique of this binary more broadly, see Lucas Lixinski, "A Third Way of Thinking About Cultural Property," *Brooklyn Journal of International Law* 44, no. 2 (2019): 563.
50 Perreau, *Queer Theory*, 183.
51 Laurajane Smith, *Uses of Heritage* (Abingdon: Routledge, 2006).
52 Colin Sterling, "Critical Heritage and the Posthumanities: Problems and Prospects," *International Journal of Heritage Studies* 26, no. 11 (2020): 1029, 1030.
53 Lixinski, *International Heritage Law for Communities*.
54 Dawn M. Rutecki and Chelsea Blackmore, "Towards an Inclusive Queer Archaeology: An Overview and Introduction," *The SAA Archaeological Record* 16, no. 1 (2016): 9.
55 For a collection of essays on queer sites in history, see David Higgs, ed., *Queer Sites: Gay Urban Histories since 1600* (Abingdon: Routledge, 1999).

treaties.[56] The most prominent division is the binary that separates heritage between tangible (that is, physically existing) and intangible (what one might call folklore, a term rejected by UNESCO). This binary effectively works to separate heritage from the people who practice and live in, with, or around it.[57] It engenders a false notion that heritage exists on its own, has intrinsic value, and should be defined and safeguarded by experts at the behest of states, ultimately serving state narratives and uses for this heritage. A critical perspective forces us to be suspicious of this binary and its clear division and allows us to understand that heritage is not a thing but a relationship, and, in this way, all heritage is, in fact, intangible.[58] What queer theory adds to this conversation is the idea of heritage as being created by affective relationships, which forces us to query not only the divide between heritage, but also the consequences of doing away with it: that heritage matters to communities first and foremost, and that it is intangible practices that both are heritage and keep it alive and relevant.

Heritage stems not only from culture as a secular-humanistic endeavour, but also often from religious roots. Much heritage that is legally protected nationally or internationally is associated with religious buildings, sites, and practices.[59] International humanitarian law, in protecting cultural monuments, often also associates them with religious buildings. Queer theory is also suspicious of religion and culture, in no small part because of the history of oppression and violence wielded against queer persons in the name of both of those things. But queer theory also helps us untangle the secular and the sacred in religion, which is useful in the *Al Mahdi* context because it refers to the destruction of Muslim mausoleums. Queer theory reminds us that relational and kinship practices are multifaceted and can exist beyond the constraint of authorising forces and institutions like heritage and religion. Even while kinship is normally constructed in international law as having a biological reproduction component, queer theory can help us liberate it and focus on social and cultural ties instead,[60] which are not dependent on institutions like the state or organised religion.

56 For a mapping of these clauses, see generally Lucas Lixinski, "Article 3(a): Relationship to Other International Heritage Instruments," in *The 2003 UNESCO Intangible Heritage Convention: A Commentary*, eds. Janet Blake and Lucas Lixinski (Oxford: Oxford University Press, 2020), 100–116.

57 Lixinski, *International Heritage Law for Communities.*

58 Smith, *Uses of Heritage.*

59 For instance, about 20% of 1,000-plus monuments and sites on the World Heritage List have important religious aspects connected to them and contribute to a monument or site's 'outstanding universal value.' See UNESCO World Heritage Center, "Initiative on Heritage of Religions Interest," accessed March 26, 2024, http://whc.unesco.org/en/religious-sacred-heritage.

60 Dianne Otto, "Resisting the Heteronormative Imaginary of the Nation-State: Rethinking Kinship and Border Protection," in *Queering International Law: Possibilities, Alliances,*

The question of the role of regimes in the enforcement of international legal rules is also central to ICHL, particularly its intersection with ICL. As indicated previously, ICHL has no internal enforcement mechanisms beyond political pressure on states. Instead, it is a regime that focuses on implementation.[61] The external enforcement mechanisms that are receptive to international heritage treaties often rely on the language of rights. As indicated previously, feminist judgments are marked by a scepticism of rights discourse and rejection of how these discourses naturalise dichotomies of agency and victimhood.[62] The same happens with queer perspectives,[63] which are also suspicious of the language of rights, but this time for the ability of rights regimes to water down the radical political potential that exists otherwise in exchange for 'the lure of normativity and glitter of respectability.'[64] Taken to an ICHL context, the language of rights subjects the identity and political organisation power of cultural heritage to a soft cultural paradigm that does little to emancipate and instead strips away the power of communities, particularly minorities.[65] Others have articulated these issues, however, using other forms of critical legal theory.

Where the unique contribution of queer theory may lie, instead, is in problematising how the law remedies the destruction of cultural heritage. ICHL decries the destruction of heritage as an affront to humanity, and enforcement mechanisms like those in ICL borrow from that language to elevate the destruction of heritage to a crime of sufficient gravity to fall under the purview of bodies like the ICC. But then what this mechanism of enforcement suggests is a focus on reparations for harm that are generally individual (or individualised) and only indirectly collective. Collective forms of reparation get us closer to imagining reparations in the form of guarantees of non-repetition, whereas ICL institutions themselves admit that non-repetition (in the form of reintegration of the offender in society, which is already much narrower than examining the state's role in enabling that violence in the first place) is only a secondary objective (if at all) of their activities.[66] What queer theory can do

Complicities, Risks, ed. Dianne Otto (Abingdon: Routledge, 2018), 236–257, 251. And, specifically on the potential of kinship in reimagining reparations in international courts' judgments, see Damian A. Gonzalez-Salzberg, "Queering Reparations Under International Law: Damages, Suffering, and (Heteronormative) Kinship," *AJIL Unbound* 116 (2022): 5.

61 Evan Hamman and Herdis Hølleland, *Implementing the World Heritage Convention: Dimensions of Compliance* (Cheltenham: Edward Elgar, 2023).

62 Gooding, "How Can the Methodology of Feminist Judgment Writing Improve," 124.

63 Paige, "The Maintenance of International Peace and Security Heteronormativity."

64 Ratna Kapur, "The (Im)Possibility of Queering International Human Rights Law," 131–147, 132.

65 As powerfully articulated in a broader critical context by Karen Engle, *The Elusive Promise of Indigenous Development: Rights, Culture, Strategy* (Chapel Hill: Duke University Press, 2010).

66 Judgment, *Al Mahdi*, para. 67.

in this context is help us think of the broader violence the law generates[67] and how a narrow focus on reparations can be part of that violence.

Critical legal studies and critical heritage studies are key to unpacking the work that ICHL does. They also do much of the heavy lifting in the existing literature. What queer theory does that these larger critical traditions fail to do, at least as fully as queer theory, is to recentre debates around the idea of violence (rather than simply power), which forces us to query assumptions about whether the power contained in and wielded through heritage, identity, and the legal regimes around it is desirable in the first place. Further, queer theory helps identify and problematise binaries in ways that other approaches only do indirectly or less overtly. Also, queer theory calls stronger attention to subaltern narratives of heritage in its value in a way that is warier of the language of rights. The language of rights is often seen in critical heritage contexts as a pathway to spelling out the fact that heritage embodies and channels power and shifts that power in favour of communities and away from states. A wariness of rights borrowed from queer theory, however, also calls attention to the trade-offs in that embrace of rights and the agency-stripping consequences of that language.

Many of these binaries I problematised in my description of ICHL (and ICL) are triggered in the *Al Mahdi* case. The next two sections highlight how these issues appear in the case and what queer theory can do to recast the ICC's judgments.

4. The *Al Mahdi* Case

Rewriting the *Al Mahdi* case involves engaging with a queered ICHL.[68] It also involves revisiting the methodology from feminist judgment rewriting I spelled out previously to see if the added value of queer theories to ICHL (and ICL) compels any changes. I suggest they do.

The methodology of feminist judgments, as I articulated previously, drawing from Hunter requires six things, in no particular order and rephrased in a queer context: (1) centring the queer person question; (2) ensuring participation in decision-making; (3) challenging discriminatory biases; (4) paying attention to lived experience which is a problem in a judicial context that tends to overlook sexuality in the composition of courts;[69] (5) actively seeking to overcome injustices based on discriminatory lines while, I would add from a queer perspective, being wary of how equality can engender problematic

67 Hamzić, "International Law as Violence."

68 I note that this case is also the object of a forthcoming (at the time of writing) volume on feminist international criminal law judgments, to be published in 2024 by Cambridge University Press. My thanks to one of the anonymous reviewers for the comment.

69 Leslie Moran, "The Judicial Virtue of Sexuality," in *Queer Theory: Law, Culture, Empire*, eds. Robert Leckey and Kim Brooks (Abingdon: Routledge, 2010), 86–101.

'tolerance' by flattening difference through a colonial prism;[70] and (6) being informed by queer scholarship. Based on the lessons from queering ICHL, I would add the following steps: (7) identifying and problematising binaries underlying the status quo of the law's operation; (8) recasting the work of the law in terms of violence to introduce a certain wariness about the cavalier or saviour role of the law and lawyers.

The most central tenet of the methodology, too, merits some revision. In asking the queer question, it is important, given the lessons we learned previously, that we should widen the queer question not just to think of queerness as an identity anchored in sexual orientation and/or gender identity but more broadly to reimagine and centre otherness. It is fairly obvious that asking the queer question and centring queer people, bodies, and lives means asking 'whose experiences are excluded when the crime is applied in the real world,' and it can easily apply to crimes such as the destruction of heritage.[71] So, imagining the queer question in terms of queerness as otherness compels us to unpack the othering effects of international law and institutions across the board, which is relevant in thinking about the *Al Mahdi* case.

The *Al Mahdi* case involves charges of destruction of heritage in the context of a non-international armed conflict, in potential breach of Article 8(2)(e)(iv) of the Rome Statute.[72] It is also the first guilty plea in the ICC's history. As a guilty plea, there is relatively little discussion about the elements of the crime and their application to the facts, at least in relation to weighing evidence. Nonetheless, the ICC undertook some interpretation of the crime and its elements because it was the first time it appeared on the docket.[73] The ICC discussed the context of the conflict and Al Mahdi's participation in a morality brigade[74] as an expert on religion.[75] Even though he initially advised against the destruction of the mausoleums (with an eye to keeping good relations between the insurgents and the local population),[76] he ultimately directed the attack.[77]

The ICC established the site as 'an integral part of the religious life of its inhabitants' that is 'frequently visited by the residents.'[78] They were also

70 Ratna Kapur, "De-Radicalising the Rights Claims of Sexual Subalterns Through 'Tolerance'," in *Queer Theory: Law, Culture, Empire*, eds. Robert Leckey and Kim Brooks (Abingdon: Routledge, 2010), 37–52, 46–47.
71 Grey et al., "Gender and Judging at the International Criminal Court," 259.
72 The provision addresses the crime of 'Intentionally directing attacks against buildings dedicated to religion, education, art, science or charitable purposes, historic monuments, hospitals and places where the sick and wounded are collected, provided they are not military objectives.'
73 Judgment, *Al Mahdi*, para. 13.
74 Judgment, *Al Mahdi*, para. 31.
75 Judgment, *Al Mahdi*, para. 32.
76 Judgment, *Al Mahdi*, para. 36.
77 Judgment, *Al Mahdi*, para. 37.
78 Judgment, *Al Mahdi*, para. 34.

mostly part of a UNESCO World Heritage Site[79] and, as such, had 'special importance to international cultural heritage.'[80] Nonetheless, Al Mahdi saw his role as more broadly contributing to eliminating superstition and 'backwards' practices, particularly those based on invented myths.[81] He also referred to the international prominence of the site as being created by '[t]hose UNESCO jackasses,'[82] in a rejection of international legal regimes and their imposition of rules onto local contexts.

The ICC generally focuses primarily on retribution and deterrence by its own admission.[83] As such, it examines aggravating and mitigating circumstances of the crime,[84] but it does not consider rehabilitation of the accused to be an objective worth pursuing.[85] This focus on only certain objectives of criminal law, as I indicated previously, speaks directly to reasons why queer theorists are increasingly wary of criminalisation as a legal response since it limits the possibilities of social transformation by relying too heavily simply on the punishment of undesirable others.

In *Al Mahdi*, the ICC stated that crimes against heritage are of less gravity than crimes against persons.[86] It also relied heavily on experts to speak on behalf of the local community in Timbuktu.[87] In doing so, it undervalued culture as an element of kinship despite professing the importance of heritage for the local community, and even when it seemed willing to consider these communities' voices, it only did so through the filtered voices of expertise.

The ICC also used the language of 'rights' to articulate the value of heritage for the local and international community,[88] concluding that the crime of destruction of heritage was, after all, of 'significant gravity.'[89] The court found that there were mitigating circumstances (particularly Al Mahdi's professed remorse about the destruction of the mausoleums)[90] and sentenced Al Mahdi to 9 years of imprisonment.[91]

Less than one year later, in *Al Mahdi* reparations, the ICC was presented with a better opportunity to speak to the value of heritage and the actual impact its destruction had on the lives of communities. Confronted with 139

79 Judgment, *Al Mahdi*, para. 39.
80 Judgment, *Al Mahdi*, para. 46.
81 Judgment, *Al Mahdi*, para. 38(viii).
82 Judgment, *Al Mahdi*, para. 46.
83 Judgment, *Al Mahdi*, para. 66.
84 Judgment, *Al Mahdi*, para. 70.
85 Judgment, *Al Mahdi*, para. 67.
86 Judgment, *Al Mahdi*, para. 77.
87 Judgment, *Al Mahdi*, para. 78.
88 Judgment, *Al Mahdi*, para. 79–80.
89 Judgment, *Al Mahdi*, para. 82.
90 Judgment, *Al Mahdi*, para. 105.
91 Judgment, *Al Mahdi*, para. 109.

reparations applicants,[92] it had to engage with their voices, as well as with their calls for individual and collective reparations measures.[93] The defence attempted to undermine these efforts by requiring a demonstration of 'direct kinship between the people claiming the harm and the deceased whose mausoleums were attacked,'[94] a call which the ICC rejected based on a broader (and queerer)[95] understanding of kinship. The defence also called for predominantly collective reparations and the use of modern and traditional justice mechanisms, among other forms of relief.[96] After considering the importance of cultural heritage[97] and laying out principles on reparations,[98] the ICC determined the relevant victims of the case[99] and outlined the harm suffered and the modalities of reparations.[100] It determined that reparations amounted to 2.7 million euros[101] and gave instructions for implementation of the order.[102]

The representatives of the victims appealed against the reparations order, challenging the way in which the ICC limited access to individual reparations only to certain types of victims, as well as the powers of the Trust Fund for Victims to hold identifying information about victims applying for individual reparations.[103] The ICC Appeals Chamber amended the reparations order to the effect that applicants to individual reparations should be able to challenge the decisions of the Trust Fund for Victims on their eligibility and that these applicants should be entitled to be still considered for individual reparations even if they ask that their identities be kept confidential.[104] Understandably, on the grounds of litigation mechanics, this appeal focuses on the individualised or individualisable victims of the case, but, in doing so, it takes attention away from the collective reparations ordered in the case. In centring some victims (who, as individuals, have voices) over others (who, as part of collective reparations, are diffuse and thus more likely to be silent or silenced), the ICC opens the door for seeking alternative narratives even within its own legal-formal boundaries.

92 Reparations, *Al Mahdi*, para. 9.
93 Reparations, *Al Mahdi*, para. 9.
94 Reparations, *Al Mahdi*, para. 11.
95 Otto, "Resisting the Heteronormative Imaginary of the Nation-State."
96 Reparations, *Al Mahdi*, para. 12.
97 Reparations, *Al Mahdi*, 13–22.
98 Reparations, *Al Mahdi*, 23–38.
99 Reparations, *Al Mahdi*, 39–41; 51–56.
100 Reparations, *Al Mahdi*, 42–50; 57–133.
101 Reparations, *Al Mahdi*, 134.
102 Reparations, *Al Mahdi*, 135–148.
103 Reparations appeal, *Al Mahdi*, para. 23.
104 Reparations appeal, *Al Mahdi*, paras. 1–2.

5. Queerly Rewriting *Al Mahdi*

Among the many issues raised across these three ICC decisions, I focus on two sites where queer-informed recasting is useful: the discussion on the value of heritage and the decision on the available modes of reparation. Both these issues appear in the reparations order. They are important for present purposes because they connect us to reconsidering the very core of ICHL (value of heritage), as well as who it serves and how it operates in international law more generally (modes of reparation). In queering those findings, I also occasionally rely on elements from the other decisions.

In relation to the value of heritage, the ICC anchored the value of heritage on the right to cultural life.[105] It brought together tangible and intangible heritage to assess value and tie it to the ways that communities define themselves and bond together.[106] At the same time, despite speaking to the human dimension of heritage, the Chamber said that it is 'exceptional quality which warrants . . . labelling as cultural heritage,'[107] and that World Heritage is a 'most important category.'[108] The Chamber also characterised the destruction of heritage as an 'irreplaceable loss that negates humanity.'[109]

These views speak closely to the traditional paradigm underpinning ICHL. Even if the ICC Chamber attempted to pierce the veil separating tangible and intangible heritage, it still relied on tangible heritage tropes of exceptionality that render heritage intelligible to a Western reader. This rendering essentialises identity and flattens difference in ways that queer theorists have long criticised.[110] Further, foregrounding these views undercuts the primacy of the importance of heritage to the local community, which is particularly relevant considering that the ICC draws most of these views from the expert reports submitted to it rather than communities or victims themselves. In doing so, the ICC decentres victims' voices in favour of the usual suspects of governmentality, which further reinforces the importance of Western tropes. It then neutralises the politics of how heritage is used in favour of a stance that, for being ostensibly neutral, is also passive and casts these communities further into a victim position from whence they have relatively little agency.

Queering this issue would instead suggest a view that focuses more, if not entirely, on the role of heritage for the local community. One effect of doing so is to downplay, if not altogether eliminate, the relevance of Timbuktu as a World Heritage Site in assessing whether the 'international community'

105 Reparations, *Al Mahdi*, para. 14.
106 Reparations, *Al Mahdi*, paras. 14–15.
107 Reparations, *Al Mahdi*, para. 16.
108 Reparations, *Al Mahdi*, para. 17.
109 Reparations, *Al Mahdi*, para. 22.
110 Nikki Sullivan, *A Critical Introduction to Queer Theory* (Edinburgh: Edinburgh University Press, 2003) 23.

is a victim (a finding which the ICC did make, despite UNESCO's protests and calls to focus on the local community,[111] granting the international community a symbolic one euro in reparations).[112] The issue of international status remains relevant from the perspective of the gravity of the crime, and it would speak to the direct economic loss of victims who relied on tourists (who, aside from religious pilgrimage, came to Timbuktu at least partly because of World Heritage status). But it would not be a determinant of the value of heritage per se. In other words, queering the value of heritage would have the effect of recentring the local community (however inherently impossible community is, from a queer theory perspective)[113] and their interests, rather than tropes about international relevance that at best muddy the issue and, at worst, displace local voices.

On the matter of modes of reparation, the ICC Chamber determined that, when possible, 'reparations should reflect local cultural and customary practices unless they are discriminatory or exclusionary or they deny victims equal access to their rights.'[114] Doing so addresses an important step in a queer judgment methodology, which is to consider the discriminatory impacts of a judgment. In doing so, the ICC is also aware of the tensions between traditional cultural practices and discrimination of subaltern subjects.

Reparations for the ICC include restitution, compensation, and rehabilitation. Compensation is primarily money awarded to victims 'in recognition of the harm they suffered.'[115] Rehabilitation aims at 'restoring the victims and their communities to their former condition'[116] which is difficult in the present case, given the ICC's insistence on the irreplaceability of heritage, as I indicated previously. And reparations can be individual or collective[117] and also symbolic, the latter being 'particularly appropriate to repair the harm caused to a community.'[118]

The ICC stipulates that collective reparations are due as guarantees of non-repetition but does not specify what they should be since the buildings have already been reconstructed by UNESCO.[119] In doing so, the ICC avoids delving further into the role of culture and cultural heritage in social resilience, assuming it rather than shoring it up. In this way, it behaves exactly like ICHL, which also takes the role of heritage for resilience largely for granted. A queerer version might pay greater attention to the lived experiences of

111 Reparations, *Al Mahdi*, para. 52.
112 Reparations, *Al Mahdi*, 107.
113 Sullivan, *A Critical Introduction*, 148–149.
114 Reparations, *Al Mahdi*, para. 34.
115 Reparations, *Al Mahdi*, para. 47.
116 Reparations, *Al Mahdi*, para. 48.
117 Reparations, *Al Mahdi*, para. 45.
118 Reparations, *Al Mahdi*, para. 49.
119 Reparations, *Al Mahdi*, para. 67.

those in the community in terms of articulating guarantees of non-repetition, even while being consciously wary of the limits of the law in this context (the latter being the effect of the ICC's silence on the matter, but it is unclear to what extent that silence is intentional to avoid imperialism and violence in relation to heritage safeguarding).

The ICC also made economic reparations primarily collective in *Al Mahdi* reparations, including 'community based educational and awareness raising programmes,' 'return/resettlement programmes,' 'a "microcredit system" that would assist the population,' and 'other cash assistance programmes to restore some of Timbuktu's lost economic activity.'[120] These measures extended to the population at large while restricting individual reparations to 'those whose livelihoods exclusively depended upon the Protected Buildings.'[121] This decision foregrounds the broader systemic harm caused by the destruction of heritage and helps with ensuring participation in decision-making. However, advocates for the victims disagreed via their appeal to the reparations order discussed previously. Representatives of the victims sought to problematise the view of kinship in the community to broaden the category of victims eligible for individual reparations.[122] They also sought to de-territorialise reparations to account for the rights of those who had fled Timbuktu and did not seek to return, which would render them ineligible for individual reparations and unable to benefit from collective reparations.[123] Doing so is an important queer move in that it challenges 'the monochromatic lens through which the 'Other' . . . is viewed along such rigid boundaries,'[124] but in this case, it comes at the expense of collective reparations. Victim representatives sought to further individualise reparations in a way that promoted more direct input, based largely on the language of the rights of individual victims, as opposed to the diffuse interests of the communities. Here, the goal of queer judging of highlighting participation in decision-making comes in tension with a wariness of the language of rights, and I suggest that the latter should prevail and force a reconciliation of these two interests that reframes reparations primarily as collective in nature.

Despite the ICC largely rendering the value of the heritage in *Al Mahdi* reparations through the eyes of experts, when it came to the determination of moral harm it relied on victims' voices, using multiple quotes taken from victims' application forms.[125] These quotes are taken at face value to underscore the 'kinds of distress' experienced by the community.[126] The ICC

120 Reparations, *Al Mahdi*, para. 83.
121 Reparations, *Al Mahdi*, para. 83.
122 Reparations appeal, *Al Mahdi*, paras. 18–19.
123 Reparations appeal, *Al Mahdi*, para. 31.
124 Kapur, "De-Radicalising the Rights Claims of Sexual Subalterns Through 'Tolerance'," 37.
125 Reparations, *Al Mahdi*, para. 85.
126 Reparations, *Al Mahdi*, para. 87.

Chamber distinguishes between those who experienced religious harm and those who suffered harm on the basis of disruption of culture.[127] But in doing so, it holds on to the instability of the relationship between heritage and religion. The ICC ignores that some of the religious suffering articulated by some of the victims is based on a misunderstanding of the harm caused by the attacks. Specifically, the attacks destroyed the mausoleums above the surface but kept the actual interred remains intact. Therefore, the harm to the bodies of those Saints was relatively minimal, and only the built additions were compromised. In other words, the core of the religious belief was left intact, and religious harm should, in my view, not have been separated from cultural harm. To do so elevates the role of institutionalised religion in a way that can be harmful because it foregrounds the interests of professed believers over those who have exclusively cultural ties to the site, fracturing kinship on factually inaccurate grounds. To be sure, the ICC did, by taking community voices at face value, centre their narratives, but it may have done so at the cost of engendering and reinforcing discrimination.

In conclusion, the ICC ordered a number of reparations, individual and collective, across direct damage to the heritage, economic loss, and moral harm.[128] It also stressed the importance that 'these reparations must be implemented in a gender and culturally sensitive manner which does not exacerbate – and in fact addresses – any pre-existing situation of discrimination preventing equal opportunities to victims.'[129] This latter objective, in particular, aligns with a queer judgment methodology. But, at the same time, the ICC, in multiple instances, decentred local voices in favour of Western tropes at critical moments in the judgment, and relied on categories that can, in fact, lead to discriminatory effects. Despite the ICC's best efforts, therefore, a queer rewriting of this reparations order can help make sense of some of the problematic impacts and internal contradictions of this judgment.

6. Concluding Remarks

Imagining heritage, and ICHL, beyond the constraints of authorised narratives that anchor heritage's value, can foreground community interests and agency, as well as their voices. To be sure, many of these voices, particularly in a judicial context like the ICC's, pull towards the language of rights, which itself can have distorting effects. But a queerer ICHL forces us to think beyond binaries of tangible and intangible, western or non-western, international or domestic. It also helps us better understand the relationships between heritage and other forms of kinship, like institutionalised religion, which can be

127 Reparations, *Al Mahdi*, para. 90.
128 Reparations, *Al Mahdi*, para. 104.
129 Reparations, *Al Mahdi*, para. 105.

deeply problematic and lead to discriminatory effects. All along, a queerer ICHL can show us pathways to unpack and wield power differently.

The adjudication of heritage via ICL also shows us the possibilities of bringing together not only these two fields but also the possibilities of critique in the specific genre of judgment rewriting. To reimagine and recast ICHL and the power it engenders can open us to more imaginative and radical possibilities while simultaneously confronting the possibilities and limits of turning queer critique into normative commitments. To liberate identity and its political potential is at the core of queer critique and ICHL. To wield those potentials towards change is the next natural step.

Chapter 7

The Filipina in the Shadows of International Law

A Case Study of Philippine Court Decisions

Ruby Rosselle L. Tugade

1. Introduction

On 13 September 2020, Philippine President Rodrigo Roa Duterte granted an absolute pardon to Lance Cpl. Joseph Scott Pemberton, a United States Marine who was found guilty by a Philippine court of killing transgender woman Jennifer Laude.[1]

At the time of the killing, Pemberton was 19 years of age. The manner of killing, as established in court and reported in the media, was gruesome. Pemberton met Laude on the night of 11 October 2014 in Olongapo City – a Philippine city infamous for its red-light district and sex tourism catering to American servicemen.[2] According to Elias Gallamos, the front desk attendant of Celzon Lodge, he saw Jennifer and another transgender woman whom he identified as 'Barbie' enter the motel with a 'foreigner with white complexion'. Laude, Barbie, and the foreigner, later identified as Pemberton, entered Room 1 of the lodge. Barbie left the room shortly thereafter. Gallamos later saw the white male individual leave the door of Room No. 1 ajar and then proceeded to check on his companion. He then saw the head of Laude slumped inside the toilet bowl. When police arrived at the scene, the accompanying Red Cross team checked on Laude but found her already dead.[3]

The criminal information filed against Pemberton during the indictment stage stated that the serviceman knowingly attacked, assaulted, boxed, beat up, strangled, and choked Laude from behind until she stopped moving.[4] Laude sustained multiple injuries from the assault. Pemberton repeatedly

1 Azer Parrocha, "Duterte Grants Absolute Pardon to Pemberton: Palace," *Philippine News Agency*, September 7, 2020, www.pna.gov.ph/articles/1114675.

2 Allan Macatuno, "Party Is Over in 'Gapo'," *Inquirer.net*, October 22, 2014, https://globalnation.inquirer.net/113122/party-is-over-in-gapo.

3 *People v Pemberton*, CA-G.R. No. 38620 (April 3, 2017), 6.

4 *People v Pemberton*, 3.

DOI: 10.4324/9781032645339-9

dunked her head over the rim of the toilet, ultimately drowning Laude, whose cause of death was ruled as 'asphyxia due to drowning and strangulation'.[5]

The Regional Trial Court (RTC) of Olongapo City, on 18 November 2015, found Pemberton guilty of the crime of homicide and appreciated 'passion and obfuscation' as mitigating circumstances to the killing. According to the RTC, 'Pemberton had a motive to kill Laude as he found his experience of having been kissed and orally stimulated by a man so revolting and disgusting'.[6] In the appeal brought by Pemberton before the Court of Appeals, one of the determined errors of the RTC was not appreciating his invocation of self-defence.[7] Pemberton interposed the defence 'that he was molested by Laude who pretended to be a woman and which prompted Pemberton to defend his dignity and self-respect'.[8] The Court of Appeals gave no credence to Pemberton's allegations, denied the appeal, and affirmed the conviction.

Laude's killing is hardly the first sensational crime committed by an American serviceman that made it to Philippine national news. In 2006, Lance Corporal Daniel Smith was accused of raping a Filipina named Suzette Nicolas inside the Subic Bay Freeport Zone, Olongapo City. Smith was later convicted of the crime in the lower court[9] but acquitted on appeal.[10]

The Laude and Nicolas cases brought to the fore the continuing struggle of the Filipina beneath the shadows of the United States military empire and, in particular, how – part of what fuels modern-day conquest is the subjugation of bodies in the post-colony. It goes without saying that the history between the two states runs deep. In fact, the Philippines has had the longest security arrangements and foreign relations with the United States in the Asia Pacific Region.[11]

These high-profile crimes led to a groundswell among progressive movements informed by various political positions – nationalist, racial, and gendered. Two main demands emerged from their contraction into a political moment: *first,* to uphold Filipina women and queer people's rights, and *second,* to reject the Visiting Forces Agreement (VFA) between the Philippines and the United States of America.[12]

5 *People v Pemberton*, 3.
6 *People v Pemberton*, 16.
7 *People v Pemberton*, 20.
8 *People v Pemberton*, 23.
9 *Nicolas v Romulo*, G.R. No. 175888 (February 11, 2009).
10 *People v Smith*, CA-G.R. C.R. H.C. No. 02587 (April 23, 2009).
11 Ronald Simbulan, "People's Movement Responses to Evolving U.S. Military Activities in the Philippines," in *The Bases of Empire: The Global Struggle against U.S. Military Posts* (New York: New York University Press, 2009), 152.
12 David Myles and Kelly Lewis, "Constructing Injustice Symbols in Contemporary Trans Rights Activisms," *Kvinder, Køn & Forskning*, no. 3–4 (September 30, 2019): 24–42, 29.

In ruling on cases involving international law issues, Philippine courts have avoided feigning a liberatory task from foreign yoke. For even when profound international legal norms are on the line, the Supreme Court is ready to assert its limits and the finite nature of its powers: 'What is within [the court's] purview is not the effectivity of laws among states, but the effect of international law on the Constitution and our municipal laws'.[13] Judicial decisions emanating from this interpretive stance on international law thus only serve to reinforce the logics of 'inequitable conventional orderings'[14] and overtly racial and sexual hierarchies.

This chapter attempts at queering *some* aspects of the Philippine practice of international law. If queering international law means to offer 'a fundamental challenge to the usual way of framing international legal problems and crafting solutions',[15] then the legal outcomes in the Laude and Nicolas cases present a starting point for a disruption in the normative interpretations of international law underpinning empire. By way of an aside, the chapter is keenly aware of the extractive dangers of writing about Filipina bodies – especially about a trans body silenced by death.[16] Thus, the present attempt – more than anything else – is towards fielding questions on how courts help maintain an asymmetrical international legal order implicating Filipina bodies. The cost to the Filipina of maintaining international law's province is and has always been incalculable.

2. Keeping the Colony Ensnared: A Legal History of US-Philippine Military Relations

Four centuries' worth of colonial rule and foreign occupation have shaped the Philippines' engagement with international law. The 'law of nations' has attended the birth of the Philippine state and its epochs of political change, producing a local method of interpreting international law sources.[17] International law has, in overt and covert ways, accommodated power dynamics rooted in the country's colonial past.

The Philippine-United States military arrangements embodied in international legal instruments are the pinnacle of this complex and delicate dance.

13 *Pangilinan v Cayetano*, G.R. No. 238875 (March 16, 2021).

14 Dianne Otto, "Introduction: Embracing Queer Curiosity," in *Queering International Law: Possibilities, Alliances, Complicities, Risks*, ed. Dianne Otto (London: Routledge, 2018), 1–11, 5.

15 Otto, "Introduction," 1.

16 Curran Nault, "Documenting the Dead," *TSQ: Transgender Studies Quarterly* 8, no. 1 (February 1, 2021): 32.

17 Raul C. Pangalangan, ed., "Introduction," in *Philippine Materials in International Law* (Boston: Brill Nijhoff, 2021), 1.

Thus, this inter-state relationship, resilient in contemporary times, warrants an examination of its legal history.

The victory of the United States over Spain in the Battle of Manila Bay marked the consolidation of its power in the Philippines. The Philippine-American War ensued in the aftermath of Spain's relinquishment of sovereignty over the Philippines to the United States, with warfare subsiding after 1906.[18] The Spanish empire had ruled over the Philippines for over three centuries. The Americans took over the military bases previously occupied by the Spanish, including what is now portions of Subic Bay, Zambales, and the Clark Air Base in Pampanga.[19]

Policy towards the Philippines was couched in terms such as 'benevolent assimilation', where Filipinos were treated as the 'little brown brothers' of their American counterparts.[20] The advent of American colonial rule has, in many ways, consisted of a rationalisation of the colonial state built by the Spanish. The American colonial enterprise was held up by various interconnected pillars – 'a professional civil service, public education to unify the country and build capacity, and the formation and training of a Philippine Constabulary to keep the peace'.[21]

Benevolent assimilation, as the Filipino scholar Reynaldo Ileto argues, was in itself a mode of warfare far from being pacifist: it was characterised by a 'reordering of society' marked by surveillance and suppression accompanied by the presence of United States troops on Philippine soil.[22] The United States military presence was a decisive factor in keeping the colony of the Philippine islands at bay. Thus began the long-standing affair that sustained the United States' imperial fantasies and the Philippines' entanglement in the desires of its empire.

In 1934, the United States Congress created the *Tydings-McDuffie Act*, also known as the *Philippine Independence Act*. Under that law:

> [T]he President of the United States . . . withdr[e]w and surrender[ed] all right of possession, supervision, jurisdiction, control, or sovereignty then existing and exercised by the United States in and over the territory and people of the Philippine Islands, including all military and other reservations of the Government of the United States in the Philippines.[23]

18 Patricio N. Abinales and Donna J. Amoroso, *State and Society in the Philippines*, 2nd edn, State and Society in East Asia (Lanham, Boulder, New York and London: Rowman & Littlefield, 2017), 119.

19 *Saguisag v Ochoa* G.R. No. 212426 (January 12, 2016).

20 Reynaldo Ileto, "Knowing America's Colony," in *Philippine Studies Occasional Paper No. 13* (Hawai'i: Center for Philippine Studies, 1999), 22.

21 Abinales and Amoroso, *State and Society in the Philippines*, 119.

22 Ileto, "Knowing America's Colony," 40.

23 *The Philippine Independence Act 1934, also known as Tydings-McDuffie Act, 1934* (The Philippines, 1934), para. 10, https://govtrackus.s3.amazonaws.com/legislink/pdf/stat/48/STATUTE-48-Pg456.pdf.

The Act, however, made exceptions as to certain naval reservations and fuelling stations.

The aftermath of World War II produced the security arrangements that would govern the military relations between the United States and the Philippines going forward. In 1947, the two countries signed the Military Bases Agreement (MBA) 'which formalized, among others, the use of installations in the Philippine territory by United States military personnel'.[24] A Mutual Defense Treaty (MDT) was subsequently entered into, where both states 'agreed to respond to any external armed attack on their territory, armed forces, public vessels, and aircraft'.[25] The MBA expired in 1991, forcing the Philippine government to confront the question of the presence of United States military forces.

A proposed Treaty of Friendship, Cooperation, and Security was drafted and negotiated in 1991 but ultimately rejected by the Philippine Senate.[26] Senator Agapito Aquino, speaking on the Senate floor, painted the chamber's vote as the 'end [to] a political adolescence tied to the purse strings of America',[27] invoking the symbolic and material value of the withdrawal.

By the time the MBA expired, the Philippines had ushered in a new Constitution. The 1987 Philippine Constitution contained the following provision in Article XVIII, Section 25:

> After the expiration in 1991 of the Agreement between the Republic of the Philippines and the United States of America concerning military bases, foreign military bases, troops, or facilities shall not be allowed in the Philippines except under a treaty duly concurred in by the Senate and, when the Congress so requires, ratified by a majority of the votes cast by the people in a national referendum held for that purpose, and *recognized as a treaty by the other contracting State*.[28]

The legal import of the last part of Article XVIII, Section 25, was articulated during the drafting of the Constitution in 1986, with particular attention to United States bases and troops. Succinctly put by Fr. Joaquin Bernas, one of the framers of the 1987 Constitution, the United States must 'complete the process by accepting [the agreement] as a treaty through ratification by [its] Senate as the United States Constitution requires'.[29] The Supreme

24 *Bayan v Zamora*, G.R. No. 138570 (October 10, 2000).
25 *Bayan v Zamora*.
26 *Saguisag v Ochoa*.
27 Philip Shenon, "Philippine Senate Votes to Reject U.S. Base Renewal," *The New York Times*, September 16, 1991, www.nytimes.com/1991/09/16/world/philippine-senate-votes-to-reject-us-base-renewal.html.
28 *The Constitution of the Republic of the Philippines* (1987) art. XVIII, sec. 25 [emphasis added].
29 "IV Record," *Constitutional Commission* (September 16, 1986).

Court has stated that this constitutional provision is designed to ensure equal bindingness between the Philippines and the foreign state.[30]

In 1997, a United States panel met with a Philippine panel to exchange notes on 'the complementing strategic interests of the United States and the Philippines in the Asia-Pacific region'.[31] The negotiations resulted in the Visiting Forces Agreement (VFA) that allowed elements of the United States armed forces to enter the Philippines from time to time.[32] Pursuant to the 1987 Constitution's formal requirements for treaty validity and effectivity,[33] the Philippine Senate expressed its concurrence to the VFA on May 27, 1999.[34]

The first constitutional challenge to the VFA was in *Bayan v Zamora*, which was decided on October 10, 2000. Petitioners, claiming standing as citizens, taxpayers, and legislators, came before the Supreme Court to argue that the VFA was an abdication of Philippine sovereignty and a violation of the 1987 Constitution. In particular, the pivotal legal issue was whether or not the VFA complied with the constitutional requirement that any agreement on foreign bases or troops be 'recognized as a treaty by the other contracting State' as it was, on the part of the United States, concluded as an *executive agreement*.[35]

The Philippine Supreme Court, in the end, dismissed the petition:

> With the ratification of the VFA, which is equivalent to final acceptance, and with the exchange of notes between the Philippines and the United

30 *Nicolas v Romulo*.

31 *Bayan v Zamora*.

32 Agreement Between the Government of the Republic of the Philippines and the Government of the United States of America Regarding the Treatment of United States Armed Forces Visiting the Philippines (February 10, 1998).

33 See, *The Constitution of the Republic of the Philippines*, art. VII, sec. 21: 'No treaty or international agreement shall be valid and effective unless concurred in by at least two-thirds of all the Members of the Senate'.

34 Michael Bueza, "EXPLAINER: Visiting Forces Agreement," *Rappler*, January 31, 2020, www.rappler.com/newsbreak/iq/250406-explainer-visiting-forces-agreement/.

35 See, Merlin Magallona, "The Supreme Court and International Law: Problems and Approaches in Philippine Practice," *Philippine Law Journal* 85, no. 1 (2010): 8. Professor Magallona breaks down the legal requirements under the 1987 Constitution regarding foreign bases and troops:

(1) It is required that the foreign military bases, troops, or facilities be "under a treaty," as provided in this constitutional provision.
(2) The term treaty is to be understood as subject to concurrence by the Senate under Section 25, Article XVIII of the fundamental law.
(3) The term treaty is to be interpreted as requiring concurrence by the Senate by a vote of at least two-thirds of all the members of the Senate under Section 21, Article VII of the Constitution.
(4) The agreement is mandated to be recognized as a treaty by the other contracting State.

> States of America, it now becomes obligatory and incumbent on our part, under the principles of international law, to be bound by the terms of the agreement. Thus, no less than Section 2, Article II of the Constitution, declares that the Philippines adopts the generally accepted principles of international law as part of the law of the land and adheres to the policy of peace, equality, justice, freedom, cooperation and amity with all nations.
>
> As a member of the family of nations, the Philippines agrees to be bound by generally accepted rules for the conduct of its international relations. While the international obligation devolves upon the state and not upon any particular branch, institution, or individual member of its government, the Philippines is nonetheless responsible for violations committed by any branch or subdivision of its government or any official thereof. As an integral part of the community of nations, we are responsible to assure that our government, Constitution and laws will carry out our international obligation.[36]

The body of the decision relied on the reasoning that for as long as the United States 'accepts or acknowledges the VFA as a treaty and binds itself further to comply with its obligations under the treaty, there is indeed marked compliance with the mandate of the Constitution'.[37] The court then anchored the case to the principle of *pacta sunt servanda*, stressing that there must be faithful observation of the VFA as a treaty between both states.

The VFA would once more be challenged in the *Nicolas v Romulo*, tackling, for the most part, the criminal jurisdiction aspect based on the facts of the Subic Bay rape case described earlier. Lance Cpl. Smith was found guilty by the Regional Trial Court of Makati City of rape in a decision rendered on December 4, 2006. The disposition of the RTC of Makati included the following portion:

> Pursuant to Article V, paragraph No. 10, of the Visiting Forces Agreement entered into by the Philippines and the United States, accused L/CPL. DANIEL J. SMITH shall serve his sentence in the facilities that shall, thereafter, be agreed upon by appropriate Philippine and United States authorities. Pending agreement on such facilities, accused L/CPL. DANIEL J. SMITH is hereby temporarily committed to the Makati City Jail.[38]

However, on December 29, 2006, Smith was 'taken out of the Makati jail by a contingent of Philippine law enforcement agents, purportedly acting under orders of the Department of the Interior and Local Government, and

36 Magallona, "The Supreme Court and International Law."
37 Magallona, "The Supreme Court and International Law."
38 *Nicolas v Romulo*, 598 Phil. 262, 277 (2009).

brought to a facility for detention under the control of the United States government'.[39] The new arrangement was supposedly 'provided for under new agreements between the Philippines and the United States, referred to as the Romulo-Kenney Agreement of December 19, 2006'.[40]

Thus, the crux of the renewed constitutional challenge to the VFA in the *Nicolas* petition was that the Philippines should have custody of Smith. Questions of ratification previously resolved in *Bayan v Zamora* aside, petitioners in *Nicolas v Romulo* argued that the VFA violated Article VIII, Sec. 5 (5) of the 1987 Philippine Constitution and the equal protection clause under the Bill of Rights.[41]

The petitioners asserted that only the Supreme Court had the power to adopt rules of procedure for all courts in the Philippines. Petitioners argued that allowing Smith's transfer to the custody of a foreign power 'is to provide a different rule of procedure for the accused'.[42] This, in turn, violated the guarantee of equal protection under the 1987 Constitution. In the end, the Supreme Court found no violation of the 1987 Constitution:

> The equal protection clause is not violated, because there is a substantial basis for a different treatment of a member of a foreign military armed forces allowed to enter our territory and all other accused.
>
> The rule in international law is that a foreign armed forces allowed to enter one's territory is immune from local jurisdiction, except to the extent agreed upon. *The Status of Forces Agreements involving foreign military units around the world vary in terms and conditions, according to the situation of the parties involved, and reflect their bargaining power.* But the principle remains, i.e., the receiving State can exercise jurisdiction over the forces of the sending State only to the extent agreed upon by the parties.
>
> As a result, the situation involved is not one in which the power of this Court to adopt rules of procedure is curtailed or violated, but rather one in which, as is normally encountered around the world, the laws (including rules of procedure) of one State do not extend or apply – except to the extent agreed upon – to subjects of another State *due to the recognition of extraterritorial immunity given to such bodies as visiting foreign armed forces.*[43]

Nicolas appears to rely on two things to justify the response to the petitioners' arguments: the difference in treatment of members of foreign armed forces

39 *Nicolas v Romulo*, 598 Phil. 262, 278 (2009).

40 *Nicolas v Romulo.*

41 *The Constitution of the Republic of the Philippines*, art. III, sec. 1.

42 *Nicolas v Romulo.*

43 *Nicolas v Romulo.*

and recognising immunity from some aspects of jurisdiction. Parenthetically, the latter prong of the decision fails to recall an earlier case decided by the Supreme Court, where it clearly held that American officers who commit a crime or tortious act are not covered by immunity.[44] In the end, the Supreme Court deferred to the text of the VFA:

> It is clear that the parties to the VFA recognized the difference between custody during the trial and detention after conviction, because they provided for a specific arrangement to cover detention. And this specific arrangement clearly states not only that the detention shall be carried out in facilities agreed on by authorities of both parties, but also that the detention shall be 'by Philippine authorities.'[45]

Despite finding the Romulo-Kenney Agreement not in accordance with the VFA, the Supreme Court only made the disposition that the 'Secretary of Foreign Affairs is hereby ordered to forthwith negotiate with the United States representatives for the appropriate agreement on detention facilities under Philippine authorities as provided in Art. V, Sec. 10 of the VFA'.[46] The court did not directly ask the United States embassy to return Smith to Philippine authorities, once again highlighting the devil in the details – that the relations between the two states would concede to the strength of each's bargaining power in the historically steeped power dynamic.

The 'written ambiguities' in the VFA 'allowed for differing interpretations and implementations and whose prevailed depended on who had the power to enforce or ignore the other's requests'.[47] In reaffirming that the Philippines and the United States both treat the VFA as a treaty and, therefore, compliant with the 1987 Constitution and international law, the Supreme Court held that:

> It was simply required that the treaty be recognized as a treaty by the other contracting State. With that, it becomes for both parties a binding international obligation and the enforcement of that obligation is left to the normal recourse and processes under international law.[48]

In making such an assertion, the Supreme Court cedes the fate of the VFA to what it considers as the body of objective international law. The interpretation in *Nicolas* is thus insidious as it relies on a 'distortion' of treaty

44 *Wylie v Rarang*, G.R. No. 74135 (May 28, 1992).
45 *Nicolas v Romulo*.
46 *Nicolas v Romulo*.
47 Victoria Reyes, ed., "Money and Authority," in *Global Borderlands: Fantasy, Violence, and Empire in Subic Bay, Philippines* (Stanford: Stanford University Press, 2020), 35.
48 *Nicolas v Romulo*.

principles and a 'mythical formula' to qualify the VFA under Article XVIII, Sec. 25.[49] Asymmetrical power relations are at the heart of these cases – while the Philippines enforces the VFA as a treaty, the United States does not, given its federal law.[50] Chief Justice Reynato Puno's dissenting opinion in *Nicolas* minces no words: 'such dichotomy would render our sovereignty in tatters'.[51]

In 2014, Philippine President Benigno Aquino III ratified the Enhanced Defense Cooperation Agreement (EDCA), yet another instrument between the Philippines and the United States dealing with military presence on Philippine soil. The EDCA 'authorizes the U.S. military forces to have access to and conduct activities within certain "Agreed Locations" in the country'.[52] The petitioners in *Saguisag v Ochoa*, in challenging the EDCA, maintained that the agreement was unconstitutional as it was not concurred with by the Senate. The petitions in *Saguisag* were ultimately dismissed on the basis that the President may enter into an executive agreement – without the need of Senate concurrence – 'if (a) it is not the instrument that allows the presence of foreign military bases, troops, or facilities; or (b) it merely aims to implement an existing law or treaty'.[53] The earlier MDT and VFA were merely implemented by the EDCA, and the latter already allowing the presence of foreign military troops.

By way of epilogue, the decision in *Saguisag v Ochoa* acknowledged that the petitioners' arguments were borne out of a 'genuine desire for self-determination, nationalism, and, above all, a commitment to ensure the independence of the Philippine Republic from any foreign domination'.[54] 'Mere fears', the Supreme Court notes, 'cannot curtail the exercise by the President of the Philippines of his Constitutional prerogatives in respect of

49 Magallona, "The Supreme Court and International Law," 22.

50 See *Medellín v Texas*, 552 U.S. 491 (March 24, 2008), where the United States Supreme Court ruled that treaty sources do not create binding federal law 'in the absence of implementing legislation, and no such legislation has been enacted'. See also Justice Carpio's dissenting opinion in *Nicolas:* 'Under *Medellin*, the VFA is indisputably not enforceable as domestic federal law in the United States. On the other hand, since the Philippine Senate ratified the VFA, the VFA constitutes domestic law in the Philippines . . . In short, the Philippine Constitution bars the efficacy of such a treaty that is enforceable as domestic law only in the Philippines but unenforceable as domestic law in the other contracting State. The Philippines is a sovereign and independent State. It is no longer a colony of the United States. This Court should not countenance an unequal treaty that is not only contrary to the express mandate of the Philippine Constitution, but also an affront to the sovereignty, dignity and independence of the Philippine State'.

51 Dissenting Opinion of Justice Reynato Puno, *Nicolas v Romulo*, G.R. No. 175888 (February 11, 2009), 598 Phil. 262, 307.

52 *Saguisag v Ochoa*, 777 Phil. 280, 343 (2016).

53 *Saguisag v Ochoa*.

54 *Saguisag v Ochoa*.

foreign affairs. They cannot cripple him when he deems that additional security measures are made necessary by the times'.[55]

Saguisag then cited the geopolitical sensitivities surrounding the decision, as if self-aware of the criticisms it will attract: the war against terror from local bandits and insurgents, peace negotiations with a secessionist group, the looming threats posed by China in the West Philippine Sea, and the assistance extended by United States military troops in times of natural disasters. The last point, the court emphasised, 'brought to the fore the value of having friends in the international community'.[56] Once again, through an affirmative decision, Philippines-United Nations relations are given a premium, legitimised, and accepted as a necessity.

From the presence of United States bases and military personnel on Philippine soil emerged a complex, twisted relationship. For the United States, the presence of their bases meant palpable power over its former colony.[57] It also meant maintaining strategic power in the war against communism and, much later, the war against terror. For succeeding Philippine administrations, however, the relationship meant different things. Notably, it was the regime of former Philippine President Ferdinand Marcos, Sr. – whose iron-fisted rule during the Martial Law era marked repression and abuse – that benefitted greatly from the complicated state-to-state relationship. Washington extended military and economic assistance to the Philippines under Marcos' rule, thus helping to legitimise the latter and maintain the crony dictatorship.[58] This is but a snapshot of the stories and complicated relationship between former coloniser and colonised.

While increasing claims to sovereignty in military agreements were somewhat present in succeeding administrations, this did not translate to equality between the Philippines and the United States.[59] Indeed, the consequences of the military arrangements between the Philippines and the United States – arguably semi-permanent in character – are wide and far-reaching. As Neferti Xina Tadiar puts it,

> the Philippines has served the US fantasy to the extent that its labour, its natural resources, its territory and symbolic presence, together with those of other US colonies and territories, have served to guarantee precisely those social and economic conditions promised by 'America'.[60]

55 *Saguisag v Ochoa.*
56 *Saguisag v Ochoa.*
57 Reyes, *Global Borderlands*, 32.
58 Alexander Cooley, "Base Politics," *Foreign Affairs* 84, no. 6 (2005): 82.
59 Reyes, *Global Borderlands*, 47.
60 Neferti Xina M. Tadiar, *Fantasy Production: Sexual Economies and Other Philippine Consequences for the New World Order* (Hong Kong: Hong Kong University Press, 2004), 27.

The Philippines, among other former US colonies, continued to generate symbolic and material power for the United States.

The reasoning employed in Supreme Court decisions affirming the constitutionality of instruments setting forth military arrangements largely defer to general principles of international law, even as its power refers to determinations within the confines of the Constitution.[61] While the decisions emphasise conformity with international law, they ultimately mask a complex dynamic.

United States military bases in the Philippines – and foreign military presence in general – have created sexual economies[62] and generations of abandoned racially mixed children raised solely by Filipina mothers.[63] In the sanitised and legitimising language of international law, Filipina bodies are invisibilised. The true cost of these international agreements, borne by Filipina women, remains obscured.

3. The Filipina Body as Victim

By now, the stance of the branches of the Philippine government regarding the military agreements with the United States is firm and resolute – there is no infringement on sovereignty on the basis of compliance with the Constitution and international law. What is blurred and made opaque by these decisions, however, is the way in which victimhood is discussed and represented.

The *Subic Bay Rape Case* involving Suzette Nicolas was surrounded by large media coverage. She would be given the pseudonym 'Nicole' in media reports. Nicolas' case did not begin in the Subic Bay Freeport Zone, where the events of the sexual assault took place. As the narrative goes, Nicolas was a resident of Zamboanga, a province in the south of the Philippines, where she managed the canteen owned by her parents, which was frequented by United States servicemen.[64] At the time, the United States presence in Zamboanga was attributed to various humanitarian missions in the conflict-ridden province of Mindanao. The media reports go on to narrate that Nicolas herself stated that at the time of the incident, she had a relationship with a United States Marine named Brian Goodrich.[65] Nicolas ended up going to Subic Bay,

61 *The Constitution of the Republic of the Philippines*, art. VIII, sec. 4(2).

62 Jonalyn Paz, "Pipe Dream for the Ladies: Constructs of Rights of Prostituted Women among Social Actors in the Sex Industry of Olongapo City, Zambales," *Philippine Journal of Public Policy: Interdisciplinary Development Perspectives* 2020 (2020): 36.

63 P. C. Kutschera, Jose Maria Pelayo III and Mary Grace Talamera-Sandico, "The Continuing Conundrum of Southeast Asia's 50,000 Filipino Military 'Amerasians'," *International Proceedings of Economics Development and Research* 48 (2012): 62–67.

64 Tadiar, *Fantasy Production*, 378.

65 GMA News Online, "'Nicole': I Had a Boyfriend When Rape Happened," *GMA News Online*, July 6, 2006, www.gmanetwork.com/news/topstories/nation/10165/nicole-i-had-a-boyfriend-when-rape-happened/story/.

thousands of miles away from Zamboanga, at the invitation of two navy officers who were regular customers of her family's business.

It is worth noting how the Court of Appeals characterised Nicolas in the decision that ultimately acquitted Smith. In the portion summarising the evidence for the prosecution, the Court of Appeals deemed it necessary to portray her initially as a rural lass hungry for a change of scenery away from 'the drudgery of their everyday life in Zamboanga'.[66] The navy officers who invited Nicolas and her sisters, Carlos Ocasio and Chris Mills, promised to pay for their accommodation in Subic. The following passage from the Court of Appeals decision is of particular interest:

> Not to waste time for what they came for, on their first night in Subic on the 30th of October, 2005 after dinner at the Grand Leisure Hotel, Nicole, AA, and Ocasio immediately went bar-hopping. First, at the Scuba Shack, Ocasio ordered rhum and coke and she took a sip and so did AA, but they never left the place when Nicole was miffed after she noticed a Filipina sitting on the lap of an American and saw another couple kissing. At Pier 1, where they went to next, Ocasio ordered Vodka Sprite which she and AA consumed, one glass each. When Mills arrived, he ordered two shots of alcoholic drinks but both girls did not like the taste. Still, not to hurt Mills' feelings, Nicole took them as if on a spree and drank two shots, after which she embraced AA, complaining she felt dizzy.
>
> From Pier 1, they hopped to Neptune Club and Nicole enjoyed it because she liked to dance. She wanted to dance with Ocasio but he did not feel like dancing and instead introduced her to a friend who danced with her . . .
>
> Obviously, they were having a good time of their young lives.[67]

It is not unusual for the surrounding media circus in the case to characterise the events in a sensational manner, especially in a high-profile case where the Philippines' and United States' military relations were at stake and in discussion. However, what sticks out from the foregoing characterisation by no less than the Court of Appeals is that it played into language that helped bury Nicolas' victimhood, portraying her first as a naïve lady and then later reversing the narrative and turning her into a not-so-innocent woman who had what happened to her clearly coming.

In ultimately absolving Smith of the crime of rape, the Court of Appeals relied on the reasoning that Nicolas herself was not a credible witness. The Court of Appeals held:

> In a prosecution for Rape, the credibility of the private complainant becomes the single, most important issue considering her testimony alone 'if

66 *People v Smith.*
67 *People v Smith*, 5–6.

> credible, natural, convincing, and consistent with human nature and the natural course of things' (citations omitted) is sufficient for conviction . . .
>
> But then, this is not without exception. When there appears on record that the trial has overlooked, ignored, or disregarded some fact or circumstance of weight or significance that, if considered, would alter the results, this Court may disregard the findings of the trial court and make its own conclusions.[68]

The clincher of the Court of Appeals' decision is found in the succeeding paragraphs of the body's text:

> The Court finds it deceptively posturing Nicole's portrayal of herself as a demure provinciana lass . . . On hindsight, we see this protestation of decency as a protective shield against her own indecorous behavior when she did exactly as testified by Smith himself in a straight-forward manner and affirmed by Carpentier and Silkwood. Her going to Subic far away from Zamboanga with her step-sister allowing two American friends whom they met only about three months earlier, and accepting their offer of free hotel accommodations and other things as well, in her words – 'to enjoy' – do not coincide with the demure provinciana lass we are talking about . . .
>
> As she dramatized her ordeal, in-between sobs, the court repeatedly asking if she wanted to exclude the public but she refused and preferred to testify at a full-packed gallery and yet, when asked by the court how Smith kissed her breasts, she coyly answered, 'I am ashamed.' These vacillating behaviors infuse ambivalent messages that surely inflict damage to the trustworthiness of her testimony.[69]

Clearly, the Court of Appeals' logic, according to its observations, drill into the character of Nicolas as a victim, obscuring the bigger push-and-pull behind the scenes of geopolitical dynamics and a long history of racialisation and exoticisation of Filipina women. Filipina women and their bodies are frequently subject to harmful stereotypes that portray them as inherently suited only for sex work and care work.[70]

Further, what the Court of Appeals decision has effectively done was more than absolve Smith of the crime of rape. As Winter observed, 'What one might have discounted as a 'typical' sexist interpretation by some unknown man writing on a relatively obscure blog is, in this case, given an official

68 *People v Smith*, 60–61.

69 *People v Smith*, 61.

70 Aren Z. Aizura, "Trans Feminine Value, Racialized Others and the Limits of Necropolitics," in *Queer Necropolitics*, eds. Jin Haritaworn, Adi Kuntsman and Silvia Posocco (New York: Routledge, 2014), 135.

imprimatur by the Court of Appeals decision'.[71] The tenor of the decision affirms a victim-shaming dynamic, perhaps cognisant of the fact that the case itself placed in a precarious position on the Philippine-United States dynamic from the lens of popular social movements taking place outside the court system.

Indeed, the *Subic Bay Rape Case* placed front and centre the policy considerations surrounding the VFA within the larger arena of public consciousness, with the courts providing institutional legitimacy and structure to the continued dependence on the United States' military strength through its decisions. In the aftermath of the case, Nicolas recanted her testimony. Her lawyer accepted a settlement and later on, departed for the United States.[72]

Textually, the decision of the Court of Appeals in the rape case plays into gendered mores deeply ingrained in the Philippine legal system. Across judicial decisions on rape decided by Philippine courts, Gatmaytan distils two prevailing stylistic and legal patterns: 1) that the 'typical Filipina' is a romanticised archetype that exists in the real world, whose identity is fixed, and 2) that only a 'sincere quest for justice' justifies the filing of rape cases where the Filipina-victim stands to lose materially and reputationally.[73]

The judicial doctrine on rape in the Philippines is partially anchored on character and reputation, and victims can only be either 'good' or 'bad' girls.[74] Meanwhile, the perpetrator's identity and motivations are not fanned out in the narrative. The construction of Filipina identity as a recurring theme in Philippine case law on rape clearly produces essentialisms that are politically valuable for the Philippine State. Expectations of meekness and submission from the Filipina have their provenance in the logics of power underpinning colonial rule – the *Maria Clara* doctrine, as it is also known, borrows from revolutionary-era literature repudiating Spanish rule.[75] In the continuity with neo-colonialism by way of complex geopolitical arrangements, the connections are not entirely unambiguous.

Jennifer Laude's killing, which took place a few years after the *Subic Bay Rape Case* and a few months after the signing of the EDCA, once again surfaced the intricacies arising from Philippine-US relations and what it means

71 Bronwyn Winter, "Guns, Money and Justice," *International Feminist Journal of Politics* 13, no. 3 (2011): 384.

72 Allan Macatuno, "Olongapo Folk Remember 'Nicole'," *Inquirer*, October 16, 2014, https://globalnation.inquirer.net/112711/olongapo-folk-remember-nicole.

73 Dante B. Gatmaytan, ed., "Character, Credibility, and Contradiction: Rape Law and the Judicial Construction of the Filipina," in *Underclass: Public Interest Law Practice and Perspectives* (Quezon City: UP Law Complex, 2018), 243–287, 261.

74 Gatmaytan, "Character, Credibility, and Contradiction," 281.

75 Kristine Joy Patag, "SC Has Not Abandoned Ruling on Maria Clara Doctrine," *Philstar*, February 21, 2018, www.philstar.com/headlines/2018/02/21/1789994/sc-has-not-abandoned-ruling-maria-clara-doctrine.

for Filipina women. Perhaps what further complicates the case is the fact that Laude was a transgender woman. However, nowhere in the court decisions, whether of the Court of Appeals or Supreme Court, is the crime characterised as a hate crime. This discursive silence on the gender identity of Laude rings loudly.

In the Court of Appeals decision convicting Pemberton of the crime of homicide, it is worth noting that Laude was consistently referred to using he/him pronouns and putting the word *woman* in quotation marks. Pemberton's defence in the criminal trial for homicide mainly hinged on his feeling of being violated, deceived, and even 'molested' by Laude, 'who pretended to be a woman and which prompted Pemberton to defend his dignity and self-respect'.[76] While the Court of Appeals ultimately did not give credence to the legal argument of Pemberton from the lens of general criminal law, it did little to make a pronouncement to address the 'trans panic' defence raised by the accused. The Court of Appeals could have used the Pemberton case as an opportunity to protect LGBTQIA+ rights 'with respect to the invocation of a defence premised on homophobia and transphobia'.[77] This it did not do, instead further rendering invisible the plight of Filipina transgender women. More so, it has done little to place Laude's victimisation in context – as a crime that occurred in the auspices of a geopolitical power dynamic.

As Reyes argues, the 'more appropriate observation is whether U.S. servicemen *stay* convicted and are required to adhere to the original punishments handed down by Philippine courts'.[78] Thus, the presidential pardon granted to Pemberton and the acquittal of Smith from rape charges leave much to be desired in terms of how the justice system moves for victims of United States servicemen. All in all, these circumstances amplify further the inequities in power underlying the two cases. The cases are not merely isolated acts of violence; rather, they drip with symbolic meaning, considering how Nicolas and Laude were seen as representations of the Philippine state and its subservience to a dominant military global power.

4. The Filipina Body as Site of Resistance

The decisions of the Philippine courts relating to the Subic Bay rape case and the Laude killing merit their own analysis from a critical perspective. The text of the decisions, relying heavily on the judges' interpretation of Philippine and international law, stealthily reproduced asymmetrical relations of power. Not

76 *People v Pemberton*, 23.

77 Christine Faith Tango and Juan Paolo Artiaga, "The Transplantation of the Trans 'Panic' Defense in the Philippines as a Consequence of People v. Pemberton," *Ateneo Law Journal* 65, no. 2 (2020): 827.

78 Reyes, *Global Borderlands*, 71.

only do they repeat clichéd narratives of victimhood, but they also affirm the context in which the crimes took place – that the military presence of another sovereign power on Philippine soil is free from problematic consequences.

In both *Pemberton v Laude* and *Nicolas v Romulo*, for instance, the thorny issue of custody of the accused was central. On the one hand, it is possibly a question for treaty interpretation. However, it is also a question of sovereign power dealt with by bargaining, closed-door arrangements, and symbolic might. These are all sites of power that constitute one another. One crucial point to note, however, is that an analysis of power as such must go beyond viewing it as merely compulsory in nature. Power may also be diffuse and productive, oozing into the construction of identities.[79]

The protests launched by progressive groups parallel to the court proceedings are a reflection of what bringing United States servicemen to justice meant for the country and for Filipinos. *Bagong Alyansang Makabayan* (BAYAN) – an organisation with members in Congress – had this to say about Pemberton's confinement in the United States Embassy:

> The US refusal to surrender Pemberton to Philippine authorities shows how it regards our country. The US doesn't look at us on an equal footing. The entire Visiting Forces Agreement is premised on unequal relations. There is no mutuality in our relations.[80]

Meanwhile, the Subic Bay rape case also helped launch a broad feminist-led coalition for the repeal of the VFA.[81]

The Filipina body means so much more than the victimhood ascribed to them in the court cases discussed thus far. It is important to note that economic and political relations, while establishing the material reality of the relationship between the Philippines and the United States, also inform the '*desiring* or libidinal character of these relations'.[82] Thus, these relations are constitutive of notions of race, gender, sexuality, and other symbolic meanings that inform the Philippines' 'contemporary world realities'.[83] Military base politics, in other words, go deep into the fantasies of empire, with the United States having the upper hand in these relations, deploying and asserting power. The deep affirmation by Philippine courts of international law norms reveals how law endorses these global hierarchies and orders, often

79 Michael Barnett and Raymond Duvall, eds., *Power in Global Governance* (Cambridge: Cambridge University Press, 2004), 12.

80 Dennis Carcamo, "Groups to Storm US Embassy for Pemberton's Turnover," *Philstar*, October 16, 2014, www.philstar.com/headlines/2014/10/16/1380851/groups-storm-us-embassy-pembertons-turnover.

81 Winter, "Guns, Money and Justice," 372.

82 Tadiar, *Fantasy Production*, 30.

83 Tadiar, *Fantasy Production*, 30.

racialised and sexualised.[84] The United States military presence in the Philippines produces many consequences for many lives, soaked in disparity.

It is within this context that greater attention must be given to the feminist-led and queer interventions made to resist the presence of the United States military on Philippine soil. At the height of the anti-bases movement in the 1980s, women's groups 'contributed actively in the formulation of the official comprehensive bases-conversion program on the alternative uses of the U.S. military bases commissioned by the Philippine government'.[85] Groups like Women's Education, Development, Productivity, and Research Organisation (WEDPRO) proposed programs that would help, support, and empower victims of forced sex work and sex trafficking living and located in the former United States bases.[86]

In the aftermath of Laude's death, what was seen was a coalescing of pro-nationalist activism and trans activism, taking into account the intersection of 'cissexism, racism, and colonialism' surrounding the case.[87] Digital activism also saw this moment, with online users participating in calls for justice for Laude along with the renewed activism for the junking of the VFA.

Feminist voices remain crucial to 'expose the numerous instances of gendered and racialised violence committed against Filipina women as a result of continued U.S. military presence in the Philippines'.[88] While pro-nationalist activists have also been steadfast in their advocacy for asserting sovereignty, voices from those most caught up in the desires of empire need amplification more than ever. And while the court cases and legal battles that ensued in the Subic Bay rape incident and Laude killing have been concluded in one way or another, it is important to highlight as well that the construction of international law and international relations do not remain in the exclusive province of the courts. In the daily lives of those who resist, interpretations of the law bear heavily.

5. Conclusion

The sexualised form in which Philippine-United States relations have shaped up to be warrants consideration. In a relationship attended by highly

84 Doris Buss and Blair Rutherford, "'Dangerous Desires': Illegality, Sexuality and the Global Governance of Artisanal Mining," in *Queering International Law: Possibilities, Alliances, Complicities, Risks*, ed. Dianne Otto (London: Routledge, 2017), 36.

85 Simbulan, "People's Movement Responses to Evolving U.S. Military Activities in the Philippines," 165.

86 Simbulan, "People's Movement," 165.

87 Myles and Lewis, "Constructing Injustice Symbols in Contemporary Trans Rights Activisms," 30.

88 Zachary Frial, "Transgender, Transnational, Transpinay: Jennifer Laude and Trans Necropolitics in the Philippines" (PhD Diss., Honors thesis, Georgetown University, 2018), 47.

sexualised, racialised, and colonial hierarchies, it cannot be denied that the judicial interpretations that came out of the Subic Bay rape and Laude cases are constituted by practical and highly symbolic relations of power. The Supreme Court and the Court of Appeals decisions examined in this chapter cannot be divorced from the context of power and desire in which they took place.

State-centric discourses of 'security' and 'national interest' within which military arrangements are rationalised deeply rely on international law for their legitimacy. When domestic courts, in turn, give their imprimatur to prevailing normative interpretations to uphold these agreements, they conceal the profound human cost. How Philippine courts engaged in intricate legal reasoning, heavily reliant on interpretations of international law, to justify the preservation of 'friendly relations' and 'international obligations' is emblematic as much as it is symptomatic. Just as it was plain to see the United States' dissimilar legal treatment of the VFA, it was equally clear how Philippine courts took pains to reconcile their own confusion.

Far from being neutral interpreters in the outcomes of cases, courts and their decisions are implicated in the constitution of power, especially when projected on a global scale. Espousing queer engagements with international law then means testing the limits of structures that brace it. In the lives of Filipina women whose fates have come under the contours of law's prescription, relief lies in imagining an inversion of unilateral civilising, securitising missions.

Part 3

Queering International Law's Imaginaries

Reflections on Legal Myths and Methods

Chapter 8

Queering (Un)Certainty in International Criminal Law

Reflections on the International Criminal Tribunal for the Former Yugoslavia

Caitlin Biddolph

1. Introduction

International criminal law (ICL) deals in the currency of (un)certainty; its purpose is ostensibly to establish legal truths, decisions, and certainties in response to the uncertain excesses of violence. In other words, ICL is and has been developed and applied in response to, and because of, global violence. Its tribunals and courts provide a way to refract messy, complicated violence(s) into the coherent certainties of law. Elizabeth Dauphinée writes that 'the war crimes tribunal has a certain seduction associated with it . . . there is something reassuringly simple about what takes place there . . . victims and perpetrators are identified, evidence is presented, and judgment is returned'.[1] There is an appeal, a seduction to this story of certainty in ICL, to the demarcation of violence into factual evidence, legal categories, and judgments of innocence or guilt.[2] But there is something uncertain, destabilising, and *queer* about ICL, even as it attempts to excise the messy and uncontained from its governing practices. In this chapter, I grapple with the (un)certainties of ICL, engaging queer approaches to disrupt the fiction of law as fixed and certain. Drawing on my reading of the International Criminal Tribunal of the former Yugoslavia (ICTY or 'the Tribunal'), I queer (un)certainty in

1 Elizabeth Dauphinée, "War Crimes and the Ruin of Law," *Millennium: Journal of International Studies* 37, no. 1 (2008): 50.

2 In this chapter, my discussion of (un)certainty in international law diverges from the concept of 'legal certainty' and 'legality' used in international law scholarship and practice. For an example of scholarship on legal certainty, see Alexia Solomou, "Comparing the Impact of the Interpretation of Peace Agreements by International Courts and Tribunals on Legal Accountability and Legal Certainty in Post-Conflict Societies," *Leiden Journal of International Law* 27, no. 2 (2014): 495–517. I approach 'certainty' as it relates to its meaning and etymology, c. 1300, *certeynte*, 'surety, pledge', from Anglo-French *certeinté*, meaning 'that which is certain, a clear fact or truth'. See also 'certain', from Vulgar Latin *certanus*, extended form of Latin *certus* meaning 'determined, resolved, fixed, settled'; "Certainty," *Online Etymology Dictionary*, accessed March 22, 2024, www.etymonline.com/search?q=certainty.

DOI: 10.4324/9781032645339-11

ICL, in dialogue with feminist, postcolonial, and queer approaches that have problematised the 'comforting language' of juridical certainty.[3]

This chapter is sparked by a 'queer curiosity',[4] suspicion of, and discomfort with, law's appeal to truth,[5] order,[6] and stability,[7] of what I see in ICL as the always already uncertain, plural, and political governance of violence. It is also a provocation to notice the violence of ICL and its gendered, sexualised, and racialised invocations of law and 'legitimate' violence as 'normal', and 'illegitimate' violence as 'perverse'. A queer approach necessitates a critique of these violences and the carceral logics they both hinge on and enable, but it is also a commitment to seeing these as uncertain so that we might envision alternative modes of justice beyond ICL. I argue that the ICTY and ICL more broadly cleave to a fallacy of certainty in attempts to position law as distinct from violence, in its construction of (gendered, sexualised, racialised) legal subjects, in its rendering of culpability, and in the deliverance of those guilty to prison. However, a queer reading reveals that uncertainties permeate every aspect of ICL, even through these same appeals to certainty. Thus, the ICTY and ICL are *both* certain *and* uncertain. I use queer to expose the (gendered, sexualised, racialised, carceral) violences of their appeals to certainty and to consider what possibilities for queerer, more liberatory visions of justice arise when we understand international law as a practice in uncertainty.

3 Christine E. J. Schwöbel, "The Comfort of International Criminal Law," *Law and Critique* 24, no. 2 (2013): 170. While not the subject of this chapter, I note the important and relevant discussions within critical international legal scholarship on international law's indeterminacy, that its 'rules . . . cannot be identified with certainty', Cameron A. Miles, "Indeterminacy," in *Concepts for International Law*, eds. Jean d'Aspremont and Sahib Singh (Cheltenham, UK: Edward Elgar Online, 2019), 447.

4 Dianne Otto, "Introduction: Embracing Queer Curiosity," in *Queering International Law: Possibilities, Alliances, Complicities, Risks*, ed. by Dianne Otto (Abingdon and New York: Routledge, 2018), 6.

5 Stina Bergman Blix and Alessandra Minissale, "(Dis)passionate Law Stories: The Emotional Processes of Encoding Narratives in Court," *Journal of Law and Society* 49, no. 2 (2022): 246; Martti Koskenniemi, *From Apology to Utopia: The Structure of International Legal Argument* (Cambridge: Cambridge University Press, 2005), 520; Dianne Otto, "Beyond Legal Justice: Some Personal Reflections on People's Tribunals, Listening and Responsibility," *London Review of International Law* 5, no. 2 (2017): 225; Schwöbel, "The Comfort," 178.

6 Anna Carline and Zoe Pearson, "Complexity and Queer Theory Approaches to International Law and Feminist Politics: Perspectives on Trafficking," *Canadian Journal of Women & Law* 19 (2007): 73–118; Luis Eslava, "Istanbul Vignettes: Observing the Everyday Operation of International Law," *London Review of International Law* 2, no. 1 (2014): 11, 27.

7 Elizabeth Philipose, "Prosecuting Violence, Performing Sovereignty: The Trial of Dusko Tadic," *International Journal for the Semiotics of Law* 15, no. 2 (2002): 162; Juliana Santos de Carvalho, "The Powers of Silence: Making Sense of the Non-Definition of Gender in International Criminal Law," *Leiden Journal of International Law* (2022): 13; Schwöbel, "The Comfort," 181.

This chapter proceeds in three parts. First, I introduce the queer approach that orients this chapter. Second, I queer the (un)certainties of ICL through the case of the ICTY, identifying three areas of plurality and ambivalence that constitute international law: the law/violence dichotomy, the plural discourses of gender and sexuality that constitute legal subjects, and the queer logics that make violence legible in ICL. Each of these examples from the ICTY provides insights into the messy and uncertain logics of ICL, including the various gendered, sexualised, and 'perverse' bodies that embody this site. Finally, I offer concluding remarks, arguing that queer insights and orientations help to revel in these (un)certainties and to find in these 'in-between spaces'[8] a 'more fluid, non-binarised and multitudinous idea within the discourse of international law'.[9] By exposing the fiction of certainty, critiquing law's violence, and embracing messy legal subjects, I hope to disrupt legal hierarchies and seek out more inclusive, uncertain practices within and beyond international law.

Critical approaches to international law, including feminist perspectives, have crafted strategies for calling out law's violence, sitting within the uncertain, and imagining more inclusive ways of doing international law.[10] Through these and other contributions, uncertainty is not a *bad thing*; it is a way 'to imagine and practice relationships and power in new and creative ways'.[11] Uncertainty can be uncomfortable, discomforting,[12] and 'disquieting'.[13] But revealing and revelling in the uncertain, even if, and precisely because it is uncomfortable, affords opportunities to affirm 'the vibrant multiplicity of life, whereas absolute truth or certainty cannot endure the existence of alternatives'.[14] As I demonstrate in my reflections on the ICTY, embracing

8 Dianne Otto, "Handmaidens, Hierarchies, and Crossing the Public-Private Divide in the Teaching of International Law," *Melbourne Journal of International Law* 1, no. 1 (2000): 54, quoted in Carline and Pearson, "Complexity," 93.

9 Kathyrn McNeilly, "Sex/Gender Is Fluid, What Now for Feminism and International Human Rights Law? A Call to Queer the Foundations," in *Research Handbook on Feminist Engagement with International Law*, eds. Susan Harris Rimmer and Kate Ogg (Cheltenham and Northhampton: Edward Elgar, 2019), 437.

10 Luis Eslava, "Istanbul Vignettes," 3–47; Luis Eslava and Sundhya Pahuja, "Beyond the (Post)Colonial: TWAIL and the Everyday Life of International Law," *Verfassung in Recht und Übersee* 45, no. 2 (2012): 221; Gina Heathcote, *The Law on the Use of Force: A Feminist Analysis* (Abingdon: Routledge, 2011), 15; Anne Orford, "Feminism, Imperialism and the Mission of International Law," *Nordic Journal of International Law* 71, no. 2 (2002): 275–291; Ntina Tzouvala, *Capitalism as Civilisation: A History of International Law* (Cambridge: Cambridge University Press, 2020), 37–38.

11 Eva Mackey, "Unsettling Expectations: (Un)certainty, Settler States of Feeling, Law, and Decolonization," *Canadian Journal of Law and Society* 29, no. 2 (2014): 237.

12 Schwöbel, "The Comfort," 183.

13 Enrike Van Wingerden, "Unmastering Research: Positionality and Intercorporeal Vulnerability in International Studies," *International Political Sociology* 16, no. 2 (2022): n2.

14 Van Wingerden, "Unmastering Research," n2.

uncertainty opens possibilities for plural legal encounters, non-binary perspectives, and messy, uncertain, and queer futures of international law.[15]

2. Queer Orientations, (Un)Certainty, and International Law

Building on and in dialogue with these pluralist, feminist, and postcolonial perspectives, my own strategy of queering (un)certainty in ICL depends on three queer orientations. First, queer is uncertain. As Eve Kosofsky Sedgwick argues, 'queer is a continuing moment, movement, motive – recurrent, eddying, troublant',[16] the 'open mesh of possibilities, gaps, overlaps, dissonances and resonances, lapses and excesses of meaning when the constituent elements of anyone's sexuality aren't made (or *can't be* made) to signify monolithically'.[17] Queer is anti-normative, disruptive, and resists articulation. It is, in other words, 'open to uncertainty'.[18] In its etymological meaning, queer not only refers to the strange but, as a verb, means to twist or to cross,[19] and so there holds within queer an open refusal to conform and stabilise our plural life-worlds. This first queer orientation, then, is a direct counter to claims of certainty in international law, including, for example, that ICL, as an internationalised model of incarceration and imprisonment, is 'an inevitable and permanent feature of our social lives'.[20] In addition to queer abolitionist perspectives (see more further on in relation to my second queer orientation), I also draw on queer and pluralist approaches that 'emphasize the fundamental importance of dialogue, openness, uncertainty, and inclusivity . . . in international law'.[21] Queer as uncertain is not only about disturbing the violent hierarchies of international law, as well as the fiction of certainty they depend on,

15 See also Philipp Kastner and Elisabeth Roy Trudel, "Unsettling International Law and Peace-Making: An Encounter with Queer Theory," *Leiden Journal of International Law* 33, no. 4 (2020): 911.

16 Eve Kosofsky Sedgwick, *Tendencies* (Durham: Duke University Press, 1993), xii.

17 Eve Kosofsky Sedgwick, *Epistemology of the Closet* (London: Penguin, 1994), 7.

18 Kastner and Trudel, "Unsettling International Law," 913.

19 "Queer," *Online Etymology Dictionary*, accessed March 22, 2024, www.etymonline.com/search?q=queer.

20 Angela Y. Davis, *Are Prisons Obsolete?* (New York: Seven Stories Press, 2003), 9. See also Kate Grady, "Towards a Carceral Geography of International Law," in *Routledge Handbook of International Law and the Humanities*, eds. Shane Chalmers and Sundhya Pahuja (Abingdon: Routledge, 2021), 360; Alexandre Martins and Caia Maria Coelho, "Notes on the (Im)possibilities of an Anti-Colonial Queer Abolition of the (Carceral) World," *GLQ: A Journal of Lesbian and Gay Studies* 28, no. 2 (2022): 216; Ruth Wilson Gilmore, *Golden Gulag: Prisons, Surplus, Crisis, and Opposition in Globalizing California* (Berkeley: University of California Press, 2007).

21 Carline and Pearson, "Complexity," 74.

but it also invites 'efforts toward disruption, creativity, and hope'[22] in queer engagements with international law. This queer approach frames the broader deconstructive and uncertain orientation in this chapter, reminding me that in sites of ICL, plurality and openness animate practices of law and justice, and so there is always already the possibility to seek out more inclusive and nourishing ways of doing international law, both within and beyond it.

The second queer orientation I speak from challenges cis-heteronormative, racist, and carceral hierarchies and violences in ICL.[23] It is concerned with questions of embodiment, expressed through various entangled assemblages of gender, sexuality, race, ethnicity, class, able-bodiedness, geography, and Indigeneity, to name but a few relational modes of being. This queer orientation allows me to destabilise certainty by exploring the plural discourses of gender and sexuality that constitute legal subjects at/of the ICTY. This approach to queer is also about recognising how all these performatively constructed markers of identity and embodiment constitute the authority and practice of international law.[24] Taking these embodied and relational vectors of empowerment and oppression seriously means understanding that 'power and violence are authorized and legitimized'[25] through international law in ways that construct ideas about what (and who) is 'normal' and what (and who) is 'perverse'.[26] Doris Buss and Blair Rutherford, in their analysis of small-scale artisanal mining in Africa, see these logics of normal and perverse manifest along vectors of race, coloniality, gender, and sexuality, vectors which manifest through and reproduce 'contemporary discourses of self and other, order and criminality'.[27] As I explore later in this chapter, a queer orientation to gendered, sexualised, and civilisational logics of 'normal' and 'perverse' at/of the ICTY has violent ramifications, including the construction of 'uncivilised' bodies as criminal and therefore subject to (carceral) punishment. I thus also adopt a queer orientation that is necessarily anti-carceral

22 Odette Mazel, "Queer Jurisprudence: Reparative Practice in International Law," *AJIL Unbound* 116 (2022): 10.

23 On the gendered, sexual, Eurocentric, colonial, and racial foundations of international law, see, for instance, Doris Buss and Blair Rutherford, "'Dangerous Desires': Illegality, Sexuality and the Global Governance of Artisanal Mining," in *Queering International Law: Possibilities, Alliances, Complicities, Risks*, ed. Dianne Otto (Abingdon and New York: Routledge, 2018), 43; Carline and Pearson, "Complexity," 92; Eslava and Pahuja, "Beyond the (Post) Colonial," 197; Heathcote, *The Law*, 34; Kastner and Trudel, "Unsettling International Law," 919; Otto, "Introduction," 6; Santos de Carvalho, "The Powers of Silence," 13.

24 See, for example, Lys Kulamadayil, "Ableism in the College of International Lawyers: On Disabling Differences in the Professional Field," *Leiden Journal of International Law* 36, no. 3 (2023): 549–563.

25 Kastner and Trudel, "Unsettling International Law," 919.

26 Heathcote, *The Law*, 9.

27 Buss and Blair Rutherford, "Dangerous Desires," 43.

and abolitionist, one that 'aim[s] at abolishing not only punishment but also the racist, gendered, and sexual reproduction of this colonial world'.[28]

The final queer orientation I espouse is one that embraces and recognises plural, non-binary logics and realities, including the relational and paradoxical ways in which these logics and realities emerge. I follow Cynthia Weber's concept of queer logics, which embraces the *and/or*, that is, '*both* one thing *and* another (plural/perverse) while *simultaneously* one thing *or* another (singular, normal)'.[29] Queer logics resist the 'stabilising "slash" in . . . binaries', and instead emphasise the 'multiplying and complicating connections, figures, and orders rather than reducing and simplifying them'.[30] Engaging with queer logics, I seek out examples where fleshy, human bodies in/of ICL are plurally embodied, messy, and refuse or fail to conform to the cis-heteronormative, abiding legal subject as the common sense. This is a queer orientation that sees bodies as 'non-binary, fluid and always existing in excess of attempts to contain [them]',[31] and crucially, it is one that seeks 'to resist the ways of thinking that have so distorted our relationships with each other and the non-human world, and to celebrate instead the many different ways of being human'.[32] I engage this queer orientation to explore how ICL is contradictory and paradoxical through the example of bodies that *do both*, that is, who both reinforce and subvert violence. More broadly, I also engage and/or argue that ICL is both certain *and* uncertain.

Taken together, the queer orientations I have mapped out allow me to problematise claims of certainty in ICL, claims that have been incisively challenged by pluralist, feminist, and postcolonial perspectives. Drawing on these approaches and queer analyses of international law, I queer (un)certainty through attention to the messy, plural, and contingent practices of law. In the analysis that follows, I reflect on the queer insights that stem from queering (un)certainty at/of the ICTY, a site that embodies the violent, cis-heteronormative, civilisational, and paradoxical logics of ICL.

3. Reflections on the International Criminal Tribunal for the Former Yugoslavia

ICL is an illustrative example of how practices of international law are attempts at achieving certainty. It proclaims objectivity, neutrality, and a sense

28 Martins and Coelho, "Notes," 219.

29 Cynthia Weber, *Queer International Relations: Sovereignty, Sexuality, and the Will to Knowledge* (Oxford: Oxford University Press, 2016), 40 [emphasis in the original].

30 Weber, *Queer International Relations*, 40.

31 McNeilly, "Sex/Gender," 430.

32 Dianne Otto, "Queerly Troubling International Law's Vision of 'Peace'," *AJIL Unbound* 116 (2022): 13.

of predictability,[33] evident in the application of laws to measure criminal culpability.[34] ICL also maintains an appearance of certainty through the normalisation of criminal accountability as the assumed approach to addressing mass atrocity.[35] As with other examples of ICL, the ICTY is a fitting case for queer (un)certainty. As a criminal body, there is an appeal to certainty in its delineation of guilt, as I discuss shortly. The ICTY is also an appropriate case to explore, given its claim as the first ICL body in the contemporary era of international criminal justice mechanisms.[36] The ICTY's interpretation and application of the law lay the foundations for subsequent international courts and tribunals, mechanisms that would refer to the established (read: certain) jurisprudence of the ICTY.[37] The Tribunal was created in 1993 through United Nations Security Council (UNSC) Resolution 827 in response to the conflicts that occurred in the former Yugoslavia during the 1990s, and it formally closed in 2017, with the remaining cases transferred to the International Residual Mechanism for Criminal Tribunals.[38] The ICTY was created for the purpose of holding individuals criminally responsible for war crimes, grave breaches of the Geneva Conventions of 1949, crimes of genocide, and crimes against humanity committed in the former Yugoslav territories.[39] The invocation of preestablished international humanitarian laws, the task of assigning criminal responsibility, and the call to make sense of violence all position the ICTY as an example of ICL's appeal to certainty. As I have argued elsewhere, 'international criminal justice attempts to capture suffering in ways that make pain legible as international crimes that meet established

33 Grietje Baars, "Making ICL History: On the Need to Move Beyond Pre-Fab Critiques of ICL," in *Critical Approaches to International Criminal Law: An Introduction*, ed. Christine Schwöbel (Abingdon: Routledge, 2014), 198; Kamari Maxine Clarke, "Affective Justice: The Racialized Imaginaries of International Justice," *PoLAR: Political and Legal Anthropology Review* 42, no. 2 (2019): 245.

34 Kamari Maxine Clarke, "Refiguring the Perpetrator: Culpability, History and International Criminal Law's Impunity Gap," *The International Journal of Human Rights* 19, no. 5 (2015): 595.

35 Karen Engle, "Anti-Impunity and the Turn to Criminal Law in Human Rights," *Cornell Law Review* 100, no. 5 (2015): 1070; Engle, *The Grip*, 3.

36 Karen Engle, *The Grip of Sexual Violence in Conflict: Feminist Interventions in International Law* (Stanford: Stanford University Press, 2020), 81.

37 Engle, *The Grip*, 82.

38 This decision was prefaced by calls as early as 1991 from Yugoslav and international journalists, human rights organisations, and State Representatives to establish a tribunal in response to the violence in the former Yugoslavia, Galina Nelaeva, "Establishment of the International Criminal Tribunal in the former Yugoslavia (ICTY): Dealing with the 'War Raging at the Heart of Europe'," *Romanian Journal of European Affairs* 11, no. 1 (2011): 100–108.

39 Resolution 827, S/RES/827. United Nations Security Council. May 25, 1993, www.icty.org/x/file/Legal%20Library/Statute/statute_827_1993_en.pdf, para. 2.

legal criteria',[40] the effects of which include the concealment of those bodies and practices that do not, cannot, or refuse to fit within the classificatory schema of international law.[41] This translation of suffering into the language of ICL is not just an effect but an intentional practice, done so that the Tribunal can criminalise particular people and groups and exonerate others.[42] In other words, ICL is deliberately structured to produce victims, perpetrators, and crimes out of the messy and complicated realities of violence it is mandated to prosecute.[43] In this section, I explore three ways my queer approach can expose and revel in the (un)certainties of ICL at/of the ICTY: through disrupting the law/violence binary, by tracing the plural discourses of gender and sexuality that constitute legal subjects, and by embracing the queer logics of ICL.[44]

3.1 Law/Violence

Queer orientations can render uncertain and destabilise the law/violence dichotomy that constitutes ICL, revealing that 'law [is] intimately co-opted in violence – dividing that which is authorised from that which is regulated and outlawed'.[45] In this way, there is no certainty about law as distinct from violence; ICL is always already violent, established, and practiced in response to ('illegitimate') violence through violent juridical practices. It is these acts of juridical violence that I explore in my reflections on (un)certainty at/of the ICTY. In this section, I first analyse racialised denunciation as an example of

40 Caitlin Biddolph, "Queering Crimes of Torture: A (Re)imagining of Torture in International Criminal Tribunal for the Former Yugoslavia Jurisprudence," *Australian Journal of Human Rights* 27, no. 2 (2021): 386.

41 Elsewhere, I have written about the erasure of queer bodies and LGBTQIA+ persons from the ICTY texts, an exclusion in large part owing to the binary, cis-heteronormative common sense that constitutes international law, Caitlin Biddolph, "Queering Governance at/of the International Criminal Tribunal for the former Yugoslavia (ICTY): Discourses of Gender, Sexuality, and Violence" (PhD Diss., University of New South Wales, 2022); Caitlin Biddolph, "Haunting Justice: Queer Bodies, Ghosts, and the International Criminal Tribunal for the former Yugoslavia," *International Feminist Journal of Politics* 26, no. 2 (2024): 216–239.

42 For a critique of ICL's denunciation of some crimes over others, see Baars, "Making ICL," 209.

43 On the messy and complex work of translation and interpreters in ICL mechanisms, see Jonneke Koomen, "Language Work at International Criminal Courts," *International Feminist Journal of Politics* 16, no. 4 (2014): 581–600.

44 The discussions in this section of the chapter are based on the findings of my PhD project, Biddolph, "Queering Governance."

45 Heathcote, *The Law*, 23. See also Baars, "Making ICL," 209; Vanja Hamzić, "International Law as Violence: Competing Absences of the Other," in *Queering International Law: Possibilities, Alliances, Complicities, Risks*, ed. Dianne Otto (New York: Routledge, 2018), 77–90; Philipose, "Prosecuting Violence," 160.

ICL's violence, which criminalises and incarcerates Othered populations. Second, I explore the interrelated legal violence of paternalism, which depends on ICL's denunciatory power to position legal actors as saviours of victimised groups.[46]

First, practices of denunciation at/of the ICTY are acts of juridical violence that unsettle the assumption that ICL is separate from, and instead only responds to, violence. By denunciation, I refer to the condemnation and judgment of individuals, populations, and behaviours at/by legal actors in sites of international law. The denunciatory practices of ICL not only attempt to make violence juridically legible, but they also seek law's 'miraculous seal of finality'.[47] This manifests in the guilty verdict, where '[i]ndividuals accused of crimes who appear in the courtroom will almost certainly be found guilty'.[48] The war crimes trial is a site through which (criminalised) violence and 'uncivilised' populations are made legible in and through law with judgment and sentencing providing a predictable and legally certain ending to the trial. These practices of denunciation and judgment are violent, often invoking racialised and/or civilisational logics of 'normal' and 'perverse', and instrumentalising these logics to enact carceral governance at both the international and domestic levels.[49] That is, 'bad' bodies are apprehended, comprehended, and mastered in and through the civilisational and paternalist practices of ICL.

At the ICTY, perpetrators were rendered legible through civilisational logics of Balkanism, which refers to the construction of the Balkans as inferior, uncivilised, and violent in contrast to (Western) Europe as superior,

46 See also Sarah M. H. Nouwen and Wouter G. Werner, "Monopolizing Global Justice: International Criminal Law as Challenge to Human Diversity," *Journal of International Criminal Justice* 13, no. 1 (2015): 161. These practices of juridical violence are not the only ones I found in my analysis of the ICTY. For example, legal actors at/of the ICTY engaged in practices of victimisation that reduced victim-survivors to feminised, homogenised, and silenced victims. Moreover, I also identified practices of excision, where the violence of Western actors and the victimisation of LGBTQIA+ persons were excised from the Tribunal's mandate. See Biddolph, "Queering Governance."

47 Immi Tallgren, "The Sensibility and Sense of International Criminal Law," *European Journal of International Law* 13, no. 3 (2002): 562.

48 Schwöbel, "The Comfort," 177. See also Frédéric Mégret, "The Anxieties of International Criminal Justice," *Leiden Journal of International Law* 29, no. 1 (2016): 197.

49 Grady, "Towards a Carceral Geography," 360. Grady notes that international criminal law funds domestic prisons and the prison-industrial complex by requiring States to house convicted ICTY defendants in their prisons. See also Oumar Ba, Kelly-Jo Bluen and Owiso Owiso, "The Geopolitics of Race, Empire, and Expertise at the ICC," *Oxford Research Encyclopedia of International Studies* (2023); Engle, *The Grip*; Mattia Pinto, "Of Sex and War: Carceral Feminism and its Anti-Carceral Critique," *London Review of International Law* 8, no. 2 (2021): 351–364.

civilised, and peaceful.[50] The Balkanist logics that organised the denunciation of individuals at the ICTY must be understood within the broader cis-heteronormative, racist, (neo)colonial, and Eurocentric practices of designating 'Other', 'Oriental', 'African', and 'Balkan' populations as uncivilised and violent in ICL.[51] The perpetuation of these logics is violent because they generalise and demonise whole populations. But they also initiate a suite of violent juridical effects, including criminalisation, incarceration, and 'the stripping of legitimacy – both political and personal – from the body of the war criminal'.[52] Practiced along a teleological path that ends in the guilty verdict, denunciation also obscures the uncertain and unending temporalities of justice for real lives and bodies subject to violence and international law.[53] As an international criminal tribunal, the ICTY was mandated to establish the criminal responsibility of individuals accused of violating international humanitarian law. In practice, this meant that the ICTY *was obliged to* denunciate individuals to make sense of and regulate violence.

Denunciation is violent because it relies on and reproduces pejorative, civilisational, and racialised logics of violence (about who commits 'illegal' violence) and because it enables the judgment, punishment, and incarceration of individuals. At the ICTY, denunciating practices constitute perpetrators as dangerous, hyper-heteromasculine sadists and vicious rapists, and in doing so, such denunciation authorises their arrest, indictment, prosecution, judgment, and punishment (i.e., incarceration). This is evident across many of the legal texts, with predicates such as 'sadistic', 'brutal', 'monstrous', and 'savage' framing descriptions of torture, sexual violence, and other acts of violence in the court transcripts and trial judgments.[54] The construction

50 Milica Bakić-Hayden and Robert M. Hayden, "Orientalist Variations on the Theme 'Balkans': Symbolic Geography in Recent Yugoslav Cultural Politics," *Slavic Review* 51, no. 1 (1992): 1–15; Elissa Helms, "East and West Kiss: Gender, Orientalism, and Balkanism in Muslim-Majority Bosnia-Herzegovina," *Slavic Review* 67, no. 1 (2008): 88–119; Federica Tarabusi, "Development, Balkanism, and New (Im)moralities in Postsocialist Bosnia-Herzegovina," *Focaal* 87 (2020): 75–88; Maria Todorova, *Imagining the Balkans* (New York and Oxford: Oxford University Press, 1997).

51 See, for instance, Neda Atanasoski, "'Seeing Justice to Be Done': The Documentaries of the ICTY and the Visual Politics of European Value(s)," *Transnational Cinemas* 9, no. 1 (2018): 68–85; Clarke, "Affective Justice," 244–267; Kamari Maxine Clarke, *Affective Justice: The International Criminal Court and the Pan-Africanist Pushback* (Durham: Duke University Press, 2019); Ann Sagan, "African Criminals/African Victims: The Institutionalised Production of Cultural Narratives in International Criminal Law," *Millennium: Journal of International Studies* 39, no. 1 (2010): 3–21.

52 Dauphinée, "War Crimes," 57.

53 Caitlin Biddolph, "Queering Temporalities of International Criminal Justice: Srebrenica Remembrance and the International Criminal Tribunal for the Former Yugoslavia (ICTY)," *Griffith Law Review* 29, no. 3 (2020): 401–424.

54 As part of the broader research project on which this chapter is based, I analysed selected texts from five ICTY cases: *Mucić et al.*, *Tadić*, *Brdanin*, *Kvočka et al.*, and *Delić*. For

of the perpetrator through denunciatory practices is violent because it feeds into and reproduces harmful civilisational logics. In the representations of crimes in the legal texts, perpetrators were made known and knowable through their 'Balkanness', with references to the ethnoreligious motivations and manifestations of violence evident throughout the ICTY texts. This is unsurprising, given the ICTY's mandate to investigate and prosecute crimes of genocide and crimes against humanity, which, in the case of genocide and persecution, requires discriminatory intent (i.e., along ethnical, racial, or religious lines) to be charged as such. However, in emphasising how crosses were carved into flesh,[55] how Bosnian Muslim detainees were 'forced to spit on the Muslim flag' and give the Serb salute,[56] and how in Bosnian-Muslim controlled camps, detainees were forced to say prayers from the Koran,[57] the ICTY constructed perpetrators as especially sadistic and deviant because their crimes were driven by and reflect an assumed 'Balkan' propensity for ethnic hatred. Certainly, the acts committed by these individuals must be recognised as violent and informed by inflammatory ethnoreligious and nationalist discourses. But the Tribunal reflected and reproduced these prejudices to the extent that all acts of violence were seen by the ICTY through a lens of ethnic division, which is itself a form of violence that homogenises Yugoslav populations and communities and informs international peacebuilding and reconstruction processes.[58]

Coupled with sexually humiliating crimes, such as when Muslim detainees were forced to take off their underwear so the perpetrator could see if they were circumcised,[59] denunciatory practices categorise and criminalise perpetrators through Balkanist logics of difference, sexual predation, and

examples of these practices of denunciation in the ICTY legal texts, see "Trial Judgment," *Prosecutor v Zdravko Mucić et al.*, Case No. IT-96–21, ICTY, November 16, 1998, www.icty.org/x/cases/mucic/tjug/en/981116_judg_en.pdf, paras. 1057, 1254, 1261, 1262, 1269, 1273, 1275; "Trial Judgment," *Prosecutor v Miroslav Kvočka et al.*, Case No. IT-98–30/1, ICTY, November 2, 2001, www.icty.org/x/cases/kvocka/tjug/en/kvo-tj011002e.pdf, para. 707. For the designation of perpetrators as brutally violent, see Clarke, "Refiguring the Perpetrator," 594.

55 Trial Hearing, *Prosecutor v Radoslav Brdanin*, Case No. IT-99–36, ICTY, March 3, 2003, www.icty.org/x/cases/brdanin/trans/en/030303IT.htm.

56 Trial Judgment, *Prosecutor v Duško Tadić*, Case No. IT-94–1, ICTY, May 7, 1997, www.icty.org/x/cases/tadic/tjug/en/tad-tsj70507JT2-e.pdf, para. 154.

57 Trial Hearing, *Prosecutor v Zdravko Mucić et al.*, Case No. IT-96–21, ICTY, March 27, 1997, www.icty.org/x/cases/mucic/trans/en/970327ed.htm.

58 The 1995 Dayton Agreement, for example, institutionalised the very same ethnic divisions the international community denounced, Aida A. Hozić, "Dayton, WPS and the Entrenched 'Manliness' of Ethnic Power-Sharing Peace Agreements," *LSE Women, Peace and Security Blog*, February 15, 2021, https://blogs.lse.ac.uk/wps/2021/02/15/dayton-wps-and-the-entrenched-manliness-of-ethnic-power-sharing-peace-agreements/.

59 Trial Hearing, *Prosecutor v Duško Tadić*, Case No. IT-94–1, ICTY, June 19, 1996, www.icty.org/x/cases/tadic/trans/en/960619IT.htm; "Trial judgment," *Tadić*.

monstrosity. In one example, Delić is described in the Trial Judgment as 'having a general sadistic motivation . . . driven by feelings of revenge against people of Serb ethnicity. Before raping Ms. Antić, he stated that 'the Chetniks were guilty for every thing that was going on'.[60] The Tribunal denounced this crime in a way that took as natural a 'Balkan' disposition for ethnic hatred and revenge, an assumption that made the rape legible as a horrific but expected crime committed by 'Balkan' perpetrators. To be sure, my critique of denunciation does not condone the commission of atrocities by these individuals. Instead, my queer orientation is attuned to the construction of and distinction between 'good' and 'bad' bodies in ICL and that these follow gendered and civilisational scripts. Logics of 'normal' and 'perverse' anchor these practices so that the perpetrator 'is made out to be "queer" in its dehumanizing sense, as variously unnatural, backward, effete/promiscuous, strange, underdeveloped, and uncontrollable'.[61]

Second, the violence of denunciation is paired with violent practices of paternalism at the ICTY and in ICL more broadly. The demonisation of Balkan perpetrators depends on the construction of the ICTY, and international law, as the acceptable, lawful response to violence. In justifications for the creation of the Tribunal, as well as throughout its operation, the ICTY was positioned in the legal texts as 'the only civilised alternative' to Balkan violence.[62] Judges and other legal actors were constructed as moral interveners providing justice and a means for 'restoring humane and peaceful conditions in that torn region and to alleviating the anguish and grief of those who have suffered and still suffer from armed conflict and brutality'.[63] Through paternalism, the former Yugoslavia and 'Balkan' bodies were infantilised and feminised, unable to achieve justice on their own.[64] In the 1994 Annual Report, the judges were positioned as 'ow[ing] a compelling moral obligation to the population of the former Yugoslavia' and that 'the ICTY fervently hopes to contribute, by its own means, to restoring humane and peaceful conditions in that torn region and to alleviating the anguish and grief of those who have suffered and still suffer from armed violence and brutality'.[65] Paternalist practices are violent for the same reasons that denunciation is a form of juridical violence. They enable the intervention of 'good' actors into the fates of 'bad' populations. Notwithstanding the deeply problematic reification of gendered and

60 Trial judgment, *Mucić et al.*, para. 1269.
61 Otto, "Queerly," 24.
62 ICTY, *Annual Report* A/49/342 – S/1994/1007 (August 29, 1994), www.icty.org/x/file/About/Reports%20and%20Publications/AnnualReports/annual_report_1994_en.pdf, 15.
63 ICTY, "Annual Report," 50.
64 See, for instance, ICTY, *Completion Strategy Report* S/2004/420 (May 24, 2004), www.icty.org/x/file/About/Reports%20and%20Publications/CompletionStrategy/completion_strategy_24may2004_en.pdf, paras. 26, 29.
65 ICTY, "Annual Report," 50.

civilisational logics of normal/perverse, paternalism is violence that distinguishes between acceptable violence (i.e., juridical violence, Western violence) and criminal violence (i.e., committed by racial and civilisational 'Others').[66] In the Yugoslav context, this was particularly evident in the ICTY's deliberate exclusion of the NATO air strikes and the bombing of the former Yugoslavia, as well as the inaction and failure of the United Nations Protection Force in preventing, and indeed enabling, the Srebrenica genocide.[67]

The assumption that ICL is a response to the ('uncivilised') violence of others reflects the 'ordering and mastering'[68] logics that constitutes this site. Through this Eurocentric perspective of law, actors who embody lawfulness are those of 'the "stable" world', and law functions as 'a "service" [by the "stable" world] to the "unstable" world'.[69] Qualities of good and evil that are mapped onto victims, perpetrators, and saviours are both product and productive of these paternalist and civilisational logics of ICL.[70] Violence can thus be 'comprehended' through the law, where gendered, racialised, and civilisational subjects of innocent victims, guilty perpetrators, and lawful saviours 'create consoling patterns of causality in the chaos of intertwined problems of social, political, and economic deprivation surrounding . . . violence'.[71] They stem from a desire to order, stabilise, and make certain[72] things that are very often uncertain and 'incomprehensible'.[73]

Through a reflection of the juridical violences of denunciation and paternalism at/of the ICTY, a distinction between ICL and violence is far from certain. Indeed, as Vanja Hamzić writes, 'law cannot *be* other-than-violence'.[74] My queer orientations have exposed and problematised the gendered, sexualised, racialised, and civilisational hierarchies of ICL so that to queer ICL is to see law as an 'exercise . . . of monopolizing violence as a legitimate tool of politics'.[75] While my reflections have so far traced the violence of ICL

66 See Dauphinée, "War Crimes," 50–51; Philipose, "Prosecuting Violence," 159; Engle, "Anti-Impunity," 1122; Gina Heathcote, "Article 51 Self-Defense as a Narrative: Spectators and Heroes in International Law," *Texas Wesleyan Law Review* 12, no. 1 (2005): 132; Heathcote, *The Law*, 22.

67 Sarah Wagner, "Identifying Srebrenica's Missing: The 'Shaky Balance' of Universalism and Particularism," in *Transitional Justice: Global Mechanisms and Local Realities after Genocide and Mass Violence*, ed. Alexander Laban Hinton (New Brunswick, NJ and London: Rutgers University Press, 2019), 42.

68 Eslava, "Istanbul Vignettes," 11.

69 Schwöbel, "The Comfort," 181.

70 On human rights discourse, see Makau Mutua, "Savages, Victims, and Saviors: The Metaphor of Human Rights," *Harvard International Law Journal* 42, no. 1 (2001): 201–245.

71 Tallgren, "The Sensibility," 561.

72 Santos de Carvalho, "The Powers of Silence," 13.

73 Tallgren, "The Sensibility," 594.

74 Hamzić, "International Law," 84, emphasis in original.

75 Tallgren, "The Sensibility," 594.

and the violence of assuming a distinction between law and violence, queering (un)certainty also involves seeing moments for disrupting and subverting this violence, a dynamic I explore later in my discussion of queer logics at/of the ICTY. Importantly, my queering of the law/violence binary has also illuminated how gender, sexuality, ethnicity, and race, for example, construct plural legal subjectivities, a discussion to which I now turn.

3.2 Gendered and Sexualised Legal Subjectivities

ICL attempts to produce homogenous legal subjects, and this is evident, for example, in the construction of cis-heteronormative and binary legal subjects as common sense.[76] However, there is nothing fixed or certain about this. Indeed, queer deconstructive perspectives have helped to illuminate the discursive construction of 'normal' expressions and practices of gender and sexuality in international law and that people are not only incredibly diverse but that they live plural, shifting, and simultaneous gendered and sexual realities.[77] Queer orientations, therefore, challenge the assumption that people conform to a fixed and certain (read: cis-heteronormative, binary) subjectivity in ICL and that bodies may be legible through plural gendered and sexualised meanings. At the ICTY, this manifested in several ways, such as through the construction of bodies as simultaneously (hetero)masculine and feminine (and/or queer).

My analysis of the ICTY revealed examples where bodies are legible through multiple and even contradictory gendered and sexual signifiers, evident in the simultaneous construction of victim-survivors as (hetero)masculine *and* feminine. For example, testimonies and representations of violence including men being beaten and kicked in the genitals,[78] men subjected to forced fellatio with other detainees,[79] and instances of detainees being forced

76 Biddolph, "Haunting Justice"; Sandra Duffy, "Contested Subjects of Human Rights: Trans- and Gender-Variant Subjects of International Human Rights Law," *The Modern Law Review* 84, no. 5 (2021): 1041–1065; David Eichert, "Expanding the Gender of Genocidal Sexual Violence: Towards the Inclusion of Men, Transgender Women, and People Outside the Binary," *UCLA Journal of International Law and Foreign Affairs* 25, no. 2 (2021): 147–201; Tamsin Phillipa Paige, "The Maintenance of International Peace and Security Heteronormativity," in *Queering International Law: Possibilities, Alliances, Complicities, Risks*, ed. Dianne Otto (New York: Routledge, 2018), 91–109.

77 David Eichert, "Decolonizing the Corpus: A Queer Decolonial Re-examination of Gender in International Law's Origins," *Michigan Journal of International Law* 43, no. 3 (2022): 557–593.

78 See, for example, Trial Judgement, *Prosecutor v. Radoslav Brdanin*, Case No. IT-99–36. ICTY, September 1, 2004, www.icty.org/x/cases/brdanin/tjug/en/brd-tj040901e.pdf, para. 498.

79 See, for example, Trial Judgement, *Tadić*, paras. 198, 206; "Initial Indictment," *Prosecutor v. Duško Tadić*, Case No. IT-94–1. ICTY, February 13, 1995, www.icty.org/x/cases/tadic/ind/

to kiss ethnic symbols and proclaim, 'I am kissing this Serbian soil. I'm a Serb bastard',[80] all worked to construct legal subjects as both masculine and feminine. Each of these examples depends on the perpetrators' and ICTY's assumption that the men are prefigured as masculine and that such acts of violence work to feminise them. Other examples, such as when two women undid a detainee's pants and threatened to cut his penis off with a razor blade[81] or when an older man was forced to walk around naked in front of teenage girls and 'sort of felt . . . not to be man' because of it,[82] position victim-survivors as both masculine and feminine – as masculine subjects who are also already transformed into pejoratively feminine ones.

The commission of these violent acts by the perpetrators depended on the assumption that these detainees were (hetero)masculine threats and that victimising them in these particular ways would render them submissive, feminine, and homosexual. These discourses of gender and sexuality relied on the valourisation of cis-heteronormative masculinity and manliness and the denigration of femininity and homosexuality.[83] They were also intertwined with discourses of ethnicity, religion, and nationalism, and this directly informed the commission of violence and its legibility at the ICTY. That the ICTY seemingly accommodated bodies that were rendered simultaneously masculine and feminine suggests that ICL has the capability to embrace more fluid understandings of gender. However, a closer reading reveals the cis-heteronormative assumptions the Tribunal reinforced and depended on in its interpretation of violence. Rather than approaching gender as multiple, fluid, and queer, the ICTY interpreted these acts as hyper-heteromasculine individuals perpetrating acts against assumed heteromasculine men to feminise them, evident in the Prosecutor's characterisation of such crimes as

en/tad-ii950213e.pdf, para. 5.1; "Trial Hearing," *Prosecutor v. Zdravko Mucić et al.*, Case No. IT-96–21. ICTY, July 7, 1997, www.icty.org/x/cases/mucic/trans/en/970707ED.htm.

80 Trial Hearing, *Prosecutor v. Radoslav Brđanin*, Case No. IT-99–36. ICTY, April 26, 2002, www.icty.org/x/cases/brdanin/trans/en/020426MH.htm; www.icty.org/x/cases/brdanin/trans/en/020426IT.htm.

81 Trial Hearing, *Prosecutor v Zdravko Mucić et al.*, Case No. IT-96–21. ICTY, March 17, 1997, www.icty.org/x/cases/mucic/trans/en/970317IT.htm.

82 Trial Hearing, *Prosecutor v Miroslav Kvočka et al.*, Case No. IT-98–30/1, ICTY, August 31, 2000, www.icty.org/x/cases/kvocka/trans/en/000831ed.htm; www.icty.org/x/cases/kvocka/trans/en/000831SC.htm.

83 For the devalourising effects of feminising violence, see Jessica L. Peet and Laura Sjoberg, *Gender and Civilian Victimization in War* (Abingdon and New York: Routledge, 2019); V. Spike Peterson, "Gendered Identities, Ideologies and Practices in Contexts of War and Militarism," in *Gender, War, and Militarism: Feminist Perspectives*, eds. Laura Sjoberg and Sandra Via (New York: Prager Security International, 2010), 17–29; Laura Sjoberg, *Women as Wartime Rapists: Beyond Sensation and Stereotyping* (New York: New York University Press, 2017).

'emasculating'.[84] Of course, the acts committed by these individuals are violent in and of themselves and were made possible by heterosexist assumptions held by the perpetrators. But while the ICTY did not actively promote these assumptions, it nevertheless (and perhaps unavoidably) reproduced them. The gendered and sexualised effects of these examples were violently cis-heteronormative and exclusionary because they foreclosed the reality that sexual and gender-nonconforming people exist and are subjected to targeted violence. But they are only made visible by taking plural discourses of gender and sexuality seriously in sites of ICL, and my queer orientation allows me to access the simultaneous ways in which bodies are configured as *both* straight and masculine *and* homosexual and feminine.

As I have elsewhere argued, gendered and sexualised legal subjectivities manifest at the ICTY through the simultaneous presence and absence of queer bodies.[85] This is evident, for example, in the ways that the Genocide Convention on which the ICTY Statute relied erases homophobic and transphobic violence, yet elsewhere, in a UNSC document issued just after the Tribunal's creation, the report explicates that 'violent crimes of a homosexual nature are not explicitly mentioned in international humanitarian law' but would still be applied at the ICTY.[86] Moreover, even as the Tribunal reified the straight, binary, and cis-gender legal subject as the common sense (evident in, for example, the assumption that 'homosexualising' acts of violence were committed against cis-heterosexual men), queer bodies are nevertheless present throughout the ICTY texts, at times explicitly rendered (as with the case of 'a well-known . . . homosexual'[87] being beaten) or else made invisible but still haunt ICTY proceedings.[88] There is more to be said about the assumed cis-gendered and straight embodiment of victims and perpetrators in ICL and the intersections of ethnicity, race, and other vectors of oppression in these sites, but the reflections I have offered here go some way to illuminating the unfixed, contradictory, and uncertain discourses of gender and sexuality that constitute legal subjects. ICL is uncertain, queer, and made meaningful through plural ways of knowing and being in the world. These insights are

84 Trial Hearing, *Prosecutor v Duško Tadić*, Case No. IT-94–1, ICTY, November 25, 1996, www.icty.org/x/cases/tadic/trans/en/961125IT.htm; Trial Hearing, *Prosecutor v Duško Tadić*, Case No. IT-94–1, ICTY, November 26, 1996, www.icty.org/x/cases/tadic/trans/en/961126ED.htm; Trial Hearing, *Prosecutor v Duško Tadić*, Case No. IT-94–1, ICTY, November 28, 1996, www.icty.org/x/cases/tadic/trans/en/961128ED.htm.

85 Biddolph, "Haunting Justice."

86 UNSC, *Final Report of the Commission of Experts Established Pursuant to Security Council Resolution 780* (1992) S/1994/674 (May 27, 1994), www.icty.org/x/file/About/OTP/un_commission_of_experts_report1994_en.pdf, 75.

87 Trial Hearing, *Prosecutor v Jadranko Prlić et al.*, Case No. IT-04–74, ICTY, May 1, 2007, www.icty.org/x/cases/prlic/trans/en/070501ED.htm.

88 Biddolph, "Haunting Justice."

also possible through a queer orientation that explores and embraces queer logics of law and violence, an (un)certainty in ICL to which I now turn.

3.3 Queer Logics

Contra to positivist approaches, ICL is not simplistic and uncontested but legible through strange, paradoxical, and queer logics. Here, I reflect on two ways in which queer logics manifest at/of the ICTY: through the reinforcement and subversion of cis-heteronormative discourses; and the co-existence of violence and kindness.[89] Each of these examples reflects the *both/and* of queer logics I introduced earlier in the chapter, of how bodies and practices in ICL are plural, singular, normal, and perverse all at once. There is nothing certain, then, about queer logics; they offer possibilities for reading international law queerly.

Queer logics organise representations of violence throughout the ICTY texts, both reinforcing and subverting dominant cis-heteronormative discourses in ICL.[90] One example concerns the testimony of a survivor who detailed the rape she was subjected to in the prison camp. During her testimony, she emphasised her resistance to the rape, stating: 'I defended myself'.[91] This statement can be read plurally. In one sense, it could indicate the survivor's insistence to prove to the court that the rape was unwanted, feeding into traditional gender discourses of bodily honour and integrity. At the same time, it could also reflect the survivor's desire to reclaim autonomy and move beyond the dominant portrayal of women as victims. Queer logics manifest here in the ways that gendered discourses of 'expected' sexual relationships and 'unacceptable' ones inflected her testimony *alongside* the resistance to and subversion of the feminised victim subjectivity. Queering (un)certainty in ICL thus offers opportunities to see the *both/and* of this encounter, as well as the openness and fluidity of these representations.[92]

89 These are just two examples, see also the queer logics of humour and violence in the testimony of a detainee resisting the three-finger Serb salute because he was missing a finger, Trial Hearing, *Prosecutor v Miroslav Kvočka et al.*, Case No. IT-98–30/1, ICTY, September 1, 2000, www.icty.org/x/cases/kvocka/trans/en/000901it.htm.

90 For examples of subverting violence while reproducing cis-heteronormative discourses of gender and sexuality at/of the ICTY, see Trial Hearing, *Prosecutor v Radoslav Brdanin*, Case No. IT-99–36, ICTY, September 5, 2002, www.icty.org/x/cases/brdanin/trans/en/020905IT.htm; Trial Hearing, *Prosecutor v Radoslav Brdanin*, Case No. IT-99–36, ICTY, June 3, 2002, www.icty.org/x/cases/brdanin/trans/en/020603IT.htm; *Kvočka et al.* 2000, Trial Judgment, *Kvočka et al.*, paras. 331–332; Trial Hearing, *Prosecutor v Miroslav Kvočka et al.*, Case No. IT-98–30/1, ICTY, February 29, 2000, www.icty.org/x/cases/kvocka/trans/en/000229it.htm.

91 Trial Judgment, *Kvočka et al.*, para. 554.

92 See also Trial Hearing, *Prosecutor v Radoslav Brdanin*, Case No. IT-99–36, ICTY, September 5, 2002, www.icty.org/x/cases/brdanin/trans/en/020905IT.htm; www.icty.org/x/cases/brdanin/trans/en/020905ED.htm, where one detainee, Omer, 'would not give in' after guards attempted

Queer logics also organise the simultaneous ways in which perpetrators in the ICTY texts embody kindness and violence, inhabiting the apparent contradiction of being *both* humane *and* violent.[93] In one example, a detainee was helped by one of the perpetrators during his torture: 'He brought a piece of cardboard and placed it under my face so that I could breathe. He brought me a cup of coffee so that I could drink. And at one point, he untied my hands as if to help me'.[94]

Instances of kindness such as these are in contrast to the demonisation of perpetrators in the denunciatory practices I discussed earlier in the chapter. However, the ICTY did not abide well by this complexity, even as such testimony was offered to the Tribunal. While the testimony reflects the uncertain and messy dynamics of ICL, the ICTY cleaved to a victim/perpetrator binary that only deals in the currency of innocence or guilt, with little space to imagine the nuances in between.[95] A queer perspective reveals the plural lives that constitute bodies in international law, of the complicated realities of legal subjects beyond the designation of 'good' and 'bad', of 'normal' and 'perverse'. In the previous example, as with others from the ICTY texts, kindness and violence co-existed and were entangled to the extent that violent acts of torture were enabled by the moments of reprieve offered by the perpetrator. Providing the detainee a chance to have a drink and respite from the violence was likely much welcomed, but the 'kind' person in question failed to stop the torture. Acts of care can thus be acts of violence. Here, the perpetrator embodied both violence and mercy, a queer logic that disrupts the binaries of ICL and assumptions about who constitutes the war criminal. Importantly, queer logics, as with the other (un)certainties I have explored, challenge the assumption of law as coherent, fixed, and certain. Queer orientations are alert to the fluidity and contingency of ICL and that within these (un)certainties, there are possibilities for reimagining law, or indeed moving beyond it, in more inclusive and queer ways.

4. Some Uncertain Conclusions

Queer orientations and approaches seek out uncertainties in international law. They destabilise assumptions that law is truth and that the authority and

to sexually torture and humiliate him by pouring hot tea over his naked genitals. Such an example reflects the bothness of subversion and violence: Of Omer who resisted humiliation, as well as the reinforcing (by the crime itself and by Omer's resistance to it) the cis-heteronormative motivation of the violence.

93 See for example, Trial Judgment, *Kvočka et al.*, paras. 331–332; Trial Hearing, *Kvočka et al.*; Trial Hearing, *Brdanin*, September 5, 2002.

94 Trial Hearing, *Prosecutor v Rasim Delić*, Case No. IT-04-83, ICTY, October 4, 2007, www.icty.org/x/cases/delic/trans/en/071004IT.htm.

95 See Mark A. Drumbl, "Victims Who Victimise," *London Review of International Law* 4, no. 2 (2016): 2–3.

decisions of legal actors are apolitical and uncontested. Importantly, queer perspectives expose and destabilise the intersecting gendered, sexualised, and racialised hierarchies and violences of international law. By embracing uncertainty, queer orientations seek out uncertain and plural pathways and question if, as a violent, carceral project, ICL can (ever) provide inclusive, open, and fluid possibilities for people in the wake of violence. Indeed, for queer abolitionists, any approach to ICL must be one of 'queer refusal of desires of incarceration, punishment, and policing',[96] a rejection of '"broken" systems'[97] that are 'built on the model of assigning individual criminal accountability . . . and guilt'[98] and 'imprisonment . . . [as its] primary sanction'.[99] Beyond critique, this perspective decentres the carceral certainties of ICL and seeks out alternative forms of justice,[100] such as 'bottom-up projects of political and economic redistribution',[101] and 'solidarity and mutual aid networks'.[102] Queering the (un)certainty of ICL reveals that law is itself violent, and thus the law/violence binary is far from certain, *and* that such uncertainty may invite 'more spiritual, emotional, relational, and embodied knowledge-seeking practices' outside the frame of ICL.[103]

I remain ambivalent about the project of ICL. I see it as an intimately political space, where questions of power, order, and violence are not just subjects that law responds to but are the practices through which it is legible as a form of global governance. I am joined by others too, both within and beyond the discipline of international law, in this queer, dissident approach to law and its violence.[104] As communities of knowing and doing law, the pluralist, feminist, postcolonial, abolitionist, and queer scholarship I have drawn on in this chapter remind me that reimagining international law might begin with efforts to dismantle its hierarchies, but it also entails finding more inclusive, nourishing ways of thriving beyond the gaze of ICL. In this way,

96 Martins and Coelho, "Notes," 219–220.
97 Alison Rose Reed, "'We're Here! We're Queer! Fuck the Banks!': On the Affective Lives of Abolition," *GLQ: A Journal of Lesbian and Gay Studies* 28, no. 2 (2022): 227–228.
98 Ba et al., "The Geopolitics of Race," 12.
99 Grady, "Towards a Carceral Geography," 360.
100 Sarah Lamble, "Queer Necropolitics and the Expanding Carceral State: Interrogating Sexual Investments in Punishment," *Law and Critique* 24, no. 3 (2013): 249. See also Nouwen and Werner, "Monopolizing," 157.
101 Silvana Tapia Tapia, "Human Rights Penalty and Violence Against Women: The Coloniality of Disembodied Justice," *Law and Critique* (2023): 19.
102 Martins and Coelho, "Notes," 219–220.
103 Tapia Tapia, "Human Rights," 19.
104 See, for example, Emily Jones, *Feminist Theory and International Law: Posthuman Perspectives* (Abingdon: Routledge, 2023); Ratna Kapur, *Gender, Alterity and Human Rights: Freedom in a Fishbowl* (Cheltenham: Edward Elgar, 2018); Lamble, "Queer Necropolitics," 229–253; Dianne Otto, *Queering International Law: Possibilities, Alliances, Complicities, Risks* (Abingdon and New York: Routledge, 2018); Rahul Rao, *Out of Time: The Queer Politics of Postcoloniality* (Oxford and New York: Oxford University Press, 2020).

my exercise in queering (un)certainty necessarily moves beyond the certain/uncertain binary. Instead, it seeks out ways of inhabiting and/or revelling in both, of understanding ICL as plural: as a site of violence and a form of justice for those victims and survivors who place faith in it. When ICL is *both* violent *and* holds out possibilities for more fluid and non-binary encounters, it is important to consider how queer international law can be[105] and whether spaces of openness and dialogue for people affected by violence might be beyond the law's reach. The queer approaches that orient this chapter imagine justice in uncertain, indeterminate, and speculative terms. Such uncertainty enables the envisioning of justice otherwise, of plural justices cultivated by communities affected by violence. As this is an intervention queering (un)certainty, I say this with ambivalence. I hold out hope that the plural, messy, and complicated practices and effects of violence – and the bodies which constitute them – can be recognised and valued both within and beyond international law. Revelling in uncertainty means sitting with the discomfort of no clear answers, but it also reveals the queer logics that sustain visions of peace, justice, and non-violent (or less violent) worlds.

105 Ratna Kapur, "The (Im)possibility of Queering International Human Rights Law," in *Queering International Law: Possibilities, Alliances, Complicities, Risks*, ed. Dianne Otto (Abingdon and New York: Routledge, 2018), 131–147.

Chapter 9

Uncloseting *Travaux*

Cris van Eijk[1]

1. Ambiguity Makes International Lawyers Uncomfortable

In this chapter, I attempt to understand what *travaux préparatoires* is and what it does within international legal doctrine from the perspective of queer theory. According to doctrine, international lawyers are allowed to rely on *travaux* to interpret a treaty provision in two cases. First, to 'confirm the meaning' of the provision using the general interpretive rule(s) of Article 31 of the Vienna Convention on the Law of Treaties (VCLT), or second, 'to determine the meaning' should said rule(s) leave the result ambiguous, obscure, 'manifestly absurd or unreasonable.'[2] Note the singular – in the VCLT, international legal 'meaning' is never plural. A clause can mean many things while we aren't looking, but it must eventually conform to one 'common' meaning and not flaunt its multiplicity in our faces. A clause that resists definition 'cannot . . . be accepted, because it would amount to . . . an uncertain and precarious situation.'[3] Therefore, 'it is the right and duty' of the international legal community to 'straighten out' such clauses.[4] Otherwise, they do not matter. Otherwise, *we* do not matter.

The idea is that somewhere in the VCLT-approved evidence pool lies one 'correct' common intention of the parties, waiting to be found.[5] The

1 I am forever grateful to Tamsin Phillipa Paige, Claerwen O'Hara, Di Otto, and Başak Etkin for their significant support and feedback. This chapter exists because of a conference held on the unceded and rightful homelands of the Woiworrung and Boonwurrung Peoples – always was, always will be.

2 Vienna Convention on the Law of Treaties, 1155 UNTS 331 (adopted May 23, 1969, entered into force 27 January 1980), article 32.

3 Advisory opinion, Jurisdiction of the European Commission of the Danube, [1926] PCIJ Ser B No 14, 27.

4 Hersch Lauterpacht, "Restrictive Interpretation and the Principle of Effectiveness in the Interpretation of Treaties," *British Yearbook of International Law* 26, no. 1 (1949): 77.

5 Panos Merkouris, "The 'Correct Interpretation' Premise in International Adjudication," in *Conceptual (Re)Constructions of International Law*, eds. Kostiantyn Gorobets, Andreas Hadjigeorgiou and Pauline Westernman (Cheltenham: Edward Elgar, 2022), 216–234; Kostiantyn

DOI: 10.4324/9781032645339-12

underlying assumption is that international law 'knows no gaps.'[6] Therefore, if an international lawyer should ever be 'confronted with an apparent gap,' it is their duty to 'fill the lacuna by all available means of interpretation.'[7] In this framing, the process seems strangely desperate, an urgent need to fill our voids with meaning and reason . . . *or else.*

This is because interpretation is more than a way of making international law matter – it makes international law*yers* matter, too.[8] Interpretation makes legal rules tangible, and interpretation happens because *we* do the interpreting. Doing so 'give[s] us the power and entitlement that we need in the profession to lay claim to authority vis-à-vis the people and the institutions we address.'[9] Interpretation is our marker of professional competence and the common thread that links our many interpretive communities into a discipline that 'feel[s] part of the same space and geography.'[10] Do it 'right,' and you enjoy all the authority of an international lawyer; do it 'wrong,' and you may be swiftly corrected.[11] Sometimes, the interpretive rules are loose enough that disciplinary correction never comes,[12] but they are exceptions, not the rule. There are countless examples, in both international adjudication and scholarship,[13] wherein the interpretive rules are wielded to discount

Gorobets, "Chasing the 'Correct Interpretation': Reply to Panos Merkouris," in *Conceptual (Re)Constructions of International Law*, eds. Kostiantyn Gorobets, Andreas Hadjigeorgiou and Pauline Westernman (Cheltenham: Edward Elgar Publishing, 2022), 235–239. See also Richard Gardiner, *Treaty Interpretation*, 2nd ed. (Oxford: Oxford University Press, 2017), 117.

6 Lauterpacht, "Restrictive Interpretation," 77; For Hart, this 'core of central meaning' was a fundamental characteristic of law itself: H. L. A. Hart, "Positivism and the Separation of Law and Morals," *Harvard Law Review* 71, no. 4 (1958): 614–615.

7 Sep Op Judge Lauterpacht, *Voting Procedure on Questions Relating to Reports and Petitions Concerning the Territory of South West Africa*, ICJ Rep 90 (1955), 96.

8 Duncan B. Hollis, "The Existential Function of Interpretation in International Law," in *Interpretation in International Law*, eds. Andrea Bianchi, Daniel Peat and Matthew Windsor (Oxford: Oxford University Press, 2015), 78–110.

9 Andrea Bianchi and Fuad Zarbiyev, *Demystifying Treaty Interpretation* (Cambridge: Cambridge University Press, 2024), 1.

10 Bianchi and Zarbiyev, *Demystifying Treaty Interpretation*, 6.

11 Michael Waibel, "Interpretive Communities in International Law," in *Interpretation in International Law*, eds. Andrea Bianchi, Daniel Peat and Matthew Windsor (Oxford: Oxford University Press, 2015); Stanley Fish, *Is There a Text in This Class?: The Authority of Interpretive Communities* (Cambridge, MA: Harvard University Press, 1980); Owen M. Fiss, "Objectivity and Interpretation," *Stanford Law Review* 34, no. 4 (1982): 739–763.

12 Peat concludes that Arts 31–32 were not intended to be disciplining rules, and outlines cases where they were not used as such. However, the many counterexamples leave it at best ambiguous when an interpretation may be corrected, which is effectively the same problem: Daniel Peat, "Disciplining Rules? Compliance, the Rules of Interpretation, and the Evaluative Dimension of Articles 31 and 32 of the VCLT," *NILR* 69 (2022): 221.

13 Preliminary objections, *Application of the International Convention for the Suppression of the Financing of Terrorism and of the International Convention on the Elimination of All Forms of Racial Discrimination (Ukraine v Russia)* ICJ Rep 558 (2019), para. 112;

or correct an 'incorrect' legal interpretation for overreliance upon historical materials. Moreover, interpretation has almost existential importance to the normative project of international law – to do interpretation 'wrong' in public is to risk the authority of the discipline at large.[14]

Articles 31–32 VCLT are often interpreted as prescribing a hierarchy of 'means of interpretation' in which *travaux* is 'ancillary.' *Travaux* here is an uncomfortable interpretive step that is tolerated so long as it knows its place. 'Reliance on a treaty's negotiating history,' an American Federal judge once declared, 'is a disfavored alternative of last resort.'[15] Its subordinance has been internalised by international lawyers as an almost religious refrain. Before we cite *travaux*, we must all acknowledge aloud that it is merely supplementary before proceeding to rely on it to give our treaties – and, in a sense, our discipline – meaning.

International lawyers have internalised the ancillary place of *travaux* as both an axiom and a process. In queer theory terms, interpretation is guided and constrained by various norms which qualify the boundaries of a 'correct' or' incorrect' interpretation. These include the norms provided by Articles 31 and 32 but also unwritten, assumed, and practised norms, like the implicit disciplinary understandings of what '*travaux*' means. But *travaux* is not ancillary just because Articles 31–32 VCLT say so; those provisions just provide us with an 'authoritative' basis through which to subordinate them. *Travaux* is ancillary because it is (re)enacted as such – it is made subordinate by people in the present tense. The way international law uses *travaux* is therefore *performative* – it is constituted by, and through, its enaction.[16]

This hierarchy of interpretive means is further contested by the VCLT's drafting history. As Mortenson explains, the VCLT's creators never intended to relegate *travaux* to lesser-than in either a hierarchical or methodological sense.[17] The separation of Articles 31 and 32 was intended to 'reconcil[e] the

Declaration of Judge Robinson, *Application of the International Convention for the Suppression of the Financing of Terrorism and of the International Convention on the Elimination of All Forms of Racial Discrimination (Ukraine v Russia)* ICJ Rep 658 (219), para. 7–8; Yulia Ioffe, "The Right to Family Reunification of Children Seeking International Protection under the Convention on the Rights of the Child: Misplaced Reliance on Travaux?" *IJRL* 34 (2022): 1.

14 Gleider Hernández, "Law's Determinability: Indeterminacy, Interpretative Authority, and the International Legal System," *Netherlands International Law Review* 69 (2022): 191.

15 *Sale v Haitian Centers Council, Inc.*, 509 U.S. 155 (1993), 194 (Blackmun J, dissenting).

16 Judith Butler, *Gender Trouble: Feminism and the Subversion of Identity* (New York: Routledge, 2011), 25.

17 Julian Davis Mortenson, "The Travaux of Travaux: Is the Vienna Convention Hostile to Drafting History?" *AJIL* 107 (2013): 780. See also, International Law Commission, "Draft Articles on the Law of Treaties with Commentaries," [1966] *Yearbook of the International Law Commission* II (1966) 40 (Waldock); International Law Commission, *Summary Record of the 33rd Meeting*, UN Doc A/CONF.39/C.1/SR.33, paras. 72–73.

principle of the primacy of the text . . . with the frequent and quite normal recourse to *travaux préparatoires*,' in an 'inherently flexible' manner.[18]

Let's begin with a preliminary question: what is 'queer'? Queer Studies is a stream of critical theory that adopts a broadly antinormative perspective to its object of analysis, often based upon the lived and embodied experiences of queer people.[19] A queer critique is a way of understanding a subject. That subject might concern queer or LGBTIQA+ people or not – what makes it queer is its approach rather than the subject matter. When used as a verb, 'queering' is a method that involves resisting categories, binary logics, and normative definitions.[20]

The meaning of 'queer' is necessarily fluid and ever-changing; it must be understood and re-understood in the context of its use. Judith Butler writes that queer must 'remain that which is, in the present, never fully owned, but always and only redeployed, twisted, queered from a prior usage and in the direction of urgent and expanding political purposes, and perhaps also yielded' over time.[21] For Noreen Giffney, queer is best defined by reference to what it does – it is 'here to set up something, a tool perhaps, that produces self-reflection and feelings of uncomfortability; a troublesome agent of rebellion.'[22]

Queerness often begins with questioning those implicit, 'falsely obvious' norms that 'go without saying.'[23] Dianne Otto writes that 'queer signals a curiosity about the conceptual and analytical underpinnings of international law's adjudication of the normal.'[24] This 'queer curiosity makes visible its [hetero]sexual ordering that is so taken for granted that it is considered "natural."'[25] Like petrification, the process is continuous and subtle. An assumption – by those with authority, whose assumptions can have disciplinary weight – might become 'common sense,' then the 'done thing,' and perhaps

18 International Law Commission, "Sixth Report on the Law of Treaties," *Yearbook of the International Law Commission* II (1966): 100–101, para. 20.

19 Robyn Wiegman and Elizabeth A. Wilson, "Introduction: Antinormativity's Queer Conventions," *Differences* 26, no. 1 (May 1, 2015): 1–25.

20 Gabrielle Simm, "Queering CEDAW? Sexual Orientation, Gender Identity and Expression and Sex Characteristics (SOGIESC) in International Human Rights Law," *Griffith Law Review* 29, no. 3 (July 2, 2020): 376.

21 Judith Butler, ed., "Critically Queer," in *Playing with Fire* (New York: Routledge, 1997), 19–20.

22 Noreen Giffney, "Introduction: The 'Q' Word," in *The Ashgate Research Companion to Queer Theory*, eds. Noreen Giffney and Michael O'Rourke (London: Ashgate, 2009), 1–13.

23 Susan Marks, "Four Human Rights Myths," in *Human Rights: Old Problems, New Possibilities*, eds. David Kinley, Wojciech Sadurski and Kevin Walton (Cheltenham: Edward Elgar Publishing, 2013), 229, albeit on radical critical methods in general.

24 Dianne Otto, ed., "Introduction: Embracing Queer Curiosity," in *Queering International Law: Possibilities, Alliances, Complicities, Risks* (Abingdon and New York: Routledge, 2017), 1.

25 Otto, "Introduction," 2.

eventually an implicit, unspoken rule. 'Because they are rarely called into question,' note Bianchi and Zarbiyev, 'certain links or associations become natural reflexes and end up being regarded as unassailable truths.'[26] For those often Othered by the unspoken or falsely obvious, asking 'silly' questions can 'highlight the instability of taken-for-granted meanings and resulting power relations.'[27] Asking is not only a path to new (legal) understanding(s) but also a reclamation of (disciplinary) authority.[28] The same unwritten rulebook that makes *travaux* seem obvious also prevents 'silly' questions about what it means *and* renders both as markers of disciplinary competence.[29] This is not a coincidence – it preserves and entrenches the authority of those who already wield it.

But questioning stops being queer if we start demanding prescriptive answers. 'Queer' contests norms, speaks the unspoken, and reveals contradictions in order to recognise and understand – *not* to rectify. Ambiguity has a complicated relationship with queerness. For many queer people, some ambiguities can be empowering refusals to be parsed or reduced by others.[30] But other ambiguities – let's call them *negative* ambiguities – function to prevent queer resistance to the implicit or unspoken norms that disempower them. Queerness entails a certain reliance upon, but also a resistance to, category and categorisation. Labels and umbrella terms have been important pathways to queer solidarity, community, and political recognition – especially for those beyond the L, G, or B. But queerness is also intrinsically anticategorical. For many queer people, there is perhaps an unspoken agreement that our labels have a limited shelf life, and they will obsolesce as soon as social realities allow.[31] This tension reminds us that the goal is not to expand *travaux*'s definitional boundaries merely for the sake of it but to render someday such bounds obsolete.

The problem this chapter addresses is not that *travaux* is ambiguous but that it is *negatively* ambiguous. It is trapped by our doubled refusal to recognise ambiguity and to reflect on our discomfort. The resulting status quo is not only 'unjust' in limiting which interpreters and histories can affect legal meaning but doctrinally absurd. *That* is what must be resolved.

26 Bianchi and Zarbiyev, *Demystifying Treaty Interpretation*, 4.

27 Kath Browne and Catherine J. Nash, eds., *Queer Methods and Methodologies: Intersecting Queer Theories and Social Science Research* (Routledge, 2010), 4, https://library.oapen.org/handle/20.500.12657/30031.

28 Dianne Otto, "'Taking a Break' from 'Normal': Thinking Queer in the Context of International Law," *Proceedings of the ASIL Annual Meeting* 101 (2007): 119.

29 Bianchi and Zarbiyev, *Demystifying Treaty Interpretation*, 44.

30 Lauren Wilcox, "Practising Gender, Queering Theory," *Review of International Studies* 43 (2017): 789.

31 Joshua Gamson, "Must Identity Movements Self-Destruct? A Queer Dilemma," *Social Problems* 42, no. 3 (1995): 390–407.

The title and crux of this chapter is (what seems to be) a silly question – one that may seem better fit in an introductory international law class than here, among such esteemed scholars. 'What is *travaux*?' To answer this, I will ask several more 'silly questions,' starting from the more specific – is *travaux* a specific kind of document, for instance – and moving to the general, such as whether records must exist to be valid *travaux*. While my perspective and position are both queer, I will answer these questions doctrinally by frequent reference to international case law. By pulling one thread and then another, we can unravel the normative matrix that quietly constrains our discipline, and show it in its absurdity.

2. '*Travaux*' Is Ambiguous

Travaux has no definition. The International Law Commission (ILC) did not want to give it one because 'to do so might only lead to the possible exclusion of relevant evidence.'[32] Instead, we have 'an omnibus expression which is used rather loosely.'[33] Describing it by example yields a list that boils down to 'anything that looks helpful'[34] to establish 'the objective proof of the intentions of the parties regarding the meaning of the terms employed in the treaty.'[35] This chapter uses '*travaux*' as an umbrella term for the Article 32 supplementary materials in general. Courts and tribunals have been remarkably inconsistent in distinguishing between drafting history, circumstances of conclusion, and 'everything else' listed in Article 32. For the International Court of Justice (ICJ), 'circumstances of conclusion' sometimes refer to broad generalisations of what the bench assumes the parties thought at a given historical moment,[36] while the World Trade Organisation (WTO) considers circumstances of conclusion to include specific relevant historical facts also.[37]

The following section is structured around increasingly general questions about the normative boundaries of *travaux préparatoires*, as sourced from international case law, ILC statements, authoritative commentaries, and textbooks. As will become apparent, these 'rules' are at best ambiguous, often obscure, and at times even absurd.

32 International Law Commission, *Report on the Work of Its 16th Session*, UN Doc A/5809, 205 (11 May–24 July 1964), para. 17.

33 R. Gardiner, *Treaty Interpretation* (Oxford: Oxford University Press, 2015), 144.

34 Gardiner, *Treaty Interpretation*, 112.

35 International Law Commission, "Draft Articles," 223, para. 26; *Iron Rhine Arbitration (Belgium/Netherlands)*, 27 RIAA 35 (2005), 48.

36 Dissenting Opinion of Judge Weeramantry, *Arbitral Award of 31 July 1989 (Guinea-Bissau v Senegal)*, ICJ Rep 130 (1991), 143.

37 *EC – Chicken Cuts, Brazil v European Communities* (WT/DS62/AB/R) WTO, DSR 19, 9295 (5 June 1998) [2005], para. 86; (WT/DS269/AB/R) [2005] WTO, DSR 19, 9157, paras. 238, 293.

2.1 Is Travaux a Certain Book or Volume?

The term '*travaux*' has become disciplinary shorthand for a treaty's official negotiation records,[38] or rather a *version* of those records – one curated by (usually White, Western, cisgender, heterosexual, male, and tenured) experts.[39] No matter how complete or helpful such resources are, they are inherently constrained by the curator's unspoken choices, biases, assumptions, timelines, and pressures at that moment in time – 'any intellectual process of narrativizing the past is always positioned.'[40] Limiting *travaux* to certain books or volumes titled '*travaux*' narrows history from a fluid, evolving field into a static archive that cannot change. It also continues international law's hallowed tradition of narrating our history almost exclusively in the voices of White, Western, cisgender, heterosexual, and tenured men.[41]

2.2 Is Travaux the Official Negotiation Record?

There is likewise a tendency to use *travaux* to mean the official negotiation records, often summaries or minutes.[42] When international lawyers do cite such records, we never consider them as constructed documents – made by people anonymised by time, working with limited resources, strict deadlines, and little support.[43]

38 Preliminary Objections, *Immunities and Criminal Proceedings (Equatorial Guinea v France)*, ICJ Rep 2018 (2018), paras. 96–98; Final Award, *Methanex Corporation v USA*, Part II, Chapter H (Aug 3, 2005), para. 25.

39 See, for instance, Marc J. Bossuyt, *Guide to the 'Travaux Préparatoires' of the International Covenant on Civil and Political Rights* (Leiden: Martinus Nijhoff, 1987); Lars Adam Rehof, *Guide to the Travaux Préparatoires of the United Nations Convention on the Elimination of All Forms of Discrimination Against Women* (Leiden: Martinus Nijhoff, 1993); Paul Weis, *The Refugee Convention 1951: The Travaux Preparatoires* (Cambridge: Cambridge University Press, 1995); Stefan Barriga and Claus Kreß, *The Travaux Préparatoires of the Crime of Aggression* (Cambridge: Cambridge University Press, 2012).

40 Thomas Skouteris, "Engaging History in International Law," in *New Approaches to International Law*, eds. José María Beneyto and David Kennedy (The Hague: Asser Press, 2012), 99–121.

41 Henry Jones and Aoife O'Donoghue, "History and Self-Reflection in the Teaching of International Law," *London Review of International Law* 10, no. 1 (2022): 86–93.

42 Decision on Resp Prelim Obj, *Daniel Kappes et al v Guatemala*, ICSID Case No. ARB/18/43 (March 13, 2020), 155 which included synonymising *travaux* with official negotiation records.

43 Memo from G.E. Yates to David Owen, Summary Records, 8th Session ECOSOC UNARMS S-0991-0001-21-00001 (Jan 24, 1949), 59-60; Memo from David Owen to G.E. Yates, UNARMS S-0991-0001-21-00001 (January 26, 1949), 57.

Summary records are not histories but 'highly mediated facsimiles of actual debates and texts.'[44] The UN Summary Record-making process was only codified in 1981.[45] Until then, the process was unwritten, informal, and *ad hoc* – and the 1981 Instructions only rendered the many invisible decisions involved *slightly* more visible. How many of the treaties we cite were negotiated before then? How many scholars have cited such records without any further questions?

A summary record began as notes by a precis-writer at a meeting, usually in either English or French, relying on the live interpretation for other languages. These notes were then drafted into summaries, edited, and then translated into the Official Languages 'as soon as possible.'[46] In practice, this process varied dramatically across UN bodies and between sessions, depending on available staff, resources, and time.[47] Whatever Conference Services staff could not do became the translators' problem later and added an additional layer to the interpretation-precis-summary-edit process.

Even verbatim records were constrained by exorbitant costs, technological capacity, and the split-second choices of interpreters and translators. Even the few UN committees entitled to verbatim records could not afford stenographers for each Working Language at every meeting. For one, the UN was not technically capable of Arabic or Chinese stenography for most of the 20th century.[48] Instead, verbatim records were usually taken in English and sometimes French;[49] statements in other languages were taken from live interpretation. Being longer, verbatim records were far more expensive to produce, edit, and print, so they were only translated into other Working Languages if absolutely necessary.[50]

44 Nathan A. Kurz, "'Hide a Fact Rather than State It': The Holocaust, the 1940s Human Rights Surge, and the Cosmopolitan Imperative of International Law," *Journal of Genocide Research* 23, no. 1 (January 2, 2021): 56.

45 UN Translation Division, *Instructions for Précis-Writers*, UN Doc INSTR/1/Rev.4 (September 1981). I am grateful to Boyd van Dijk and Nathan Kurz, "Hide a Fact," for this point.

46 See, for example, UN General Assembly Rules of Procedure, as amended December 1, 1963, A/520/Rev.7 (June 1964), Rule 56.

47 Report of the Secretary-General, UN Doc A/6675 (Oct 5, 1967), 4; UN General Assembly Res 2538 (XXIV), A/RES/2538 (XXIV) (December 11, 1969).

48 UN Secretary General, *Publications and Documentation of the United Nations*, A/C.5/1670 (June 27, 1975).

49 Report of the Secretary General, *Publications and Documentation of the United Nations*, UN Doc A/6675 (October 5, 1967), 4. Practice seemingly contradicted the Rules of Procedure, which also required Spanish and (from 1968) Russian: see, for example, UN General Assembly Rules of Procedure, as amended 1 Dec 1963, A/520/Rev.7 (June 1964), Rules 51, 55.

50 UN General Assembly Rules of Procedure, as amended 1 Dec 1963, A/520/Rev.7 (June 1964), Rule 55.

States were given limited periods to amend either record before its dissemination. For some, including the UN Secretariat, this was state approval of a given record's contents. But, the formal ability to amend the record did not always translate to reality in the busy life of a diplomat – especially for those with limited resources or staff. For example, in the 1960s, the UN gave states three working days to submit changes before their approval was presumed.[51] Delegates not working in English had even less time; they had to wait for the provisional records to be translated if they were translated at all. Consequently, the ICJ has previously held that 'oral statements and opinions not recorded in minutes or conference papers can apparently be regarded as a component of *travaux préparatoires* only in exceptional cases. They can, in any event, be considered only if made in an official capacity and during the negotiations themselves.'[52] However, as shown in what follows, later case law disagrees.

On some level, we all understand that many decisions in a treaty negotiation process – perhaps the most important ones – occur off the record. But crucially, that does *not* mean they were not recorded. Each negotiator had bosses to please, colleagues to brief, and other governmental divisions to keep informed. When we limit ourselves to only looking in certain places or at certain kinds of records, we imply that said records *are* the history. This suggests a definition of history that should not pass muster at a secondary school, much less a court of law.

It is one thing to rely on summaries where no better record exists – in *South West Africa*, both the court and Judge Jessup (in dissent) noted the limitations of using summary records as *travaux*.[53] But the ICJ continues to do so, even where verbatim records exist.[54] In *Legality of the Use of Force*, the ICJ primarily considered summary records as *travaux* but then decided they were too 'provisional' and 'cursory' to be useful.[55] Sometimes, it treats summaries like direct quotes.[56] In *Application of the Convention on the Elimination of*

51 See, for instance, UNGA, *Provisional Verbatim Record of the 864th Plenary Meeting*, UN Doc A/PV.86 (September 20, 1960), 3.

52 *The Question Whether the Re-Evaluation of the German Mark in 1961 and 1969 Constitutes a Case for Application of the Clause in Article 2(e) of Annex I A of the 1953 Agreement on German External Debts*, 19 RIAA 67 (1980), para. 34; Jurisdiction, *Maritime Delimitation and Territorial Questions (Qatar v Bahrain)*, ICJ Rep 6 (1995), paras. 40–41.

53 Judgment, *South West Africa (Liberia v South Africa)*, ICJ Rep 6 (1966), para. 77; Dissenting Opinion of Judge Jessup, *South West Africa (Liberia v South Africa)*, ICJ Rep 6 (1966), 361.

54 Joint Dissenting Opinion Judges Spender and Fitzmaurice, Preliminary Objections, *South West Africa* ICJ Rep 465 (1962), 218, fn 1; Advisory Opinion, *Legal Consequences of the Construction of a Wall in the Occupied Palestinian Territory*, ICJ Rep 136 (2004), para. 104.

55 Preliminary Objections, *Legality of Use of Force (Serbia and Montenegro v Belgium)*, ICJ Rep 279 (2004), para. 113.

56 See discussion of Jurisdiction, *Georgia v Russia*, *infra*; *Border and Transborder Armed Actions (Nicaragua v Honduras)*, ICJ Rep 69 (1988), para. 37; Preliminary Objections, *Equatorial Guinea v France*, ICJ Rep 2018 (2018), para. 98.

All Forms of Racial Discrimination (CERD) (Georgia v Russia), the court approached summary records like direct quotations and then concluded they were insufficiently clear to disprove its previous conclusion.[57] In *Maritime Dispute (Peru v Chile)*, the ICJ determined the minutes of a negotiation were *travaux* and not an agreement, exactly *because* they were a summary.[58] Increasingly, the ICJ does not excerpt records at all but instead cites only its previous interpretation of them, relying on, at best, a summarised summary.[59] The ICJ has only ever cited verbatim records for reasons other than treaty interpretation: to interpret the question at issue,[60] to assess subsequent UN Security Council practice of the UN Charter,[61] or as factual evidence.[62] It is only in the case of citing *travaux* for interpretation that the court constrains itself to summaries, and it has never explained why.

The implicit narrowing of *travaux* to mean summary records results in subtle but serious problems. As Kurz put it, 'summary records constitute a sieve, catching only a small number of particles which pass through their frame,' and thus we must 'supplement them with additional sources to better approximate the concerns that those involved in any international lawmaking process brought with them.'[63]

2.3 Is Travaux a Record Written by the Negotiating States?

If the purpose of *travaux* is to reveal the intent or common understanding of the treaty's drafters,[64] it follows that a document must be authored by most, or perhaps all, of those negotiating states in order to constitute *travaux*. This

57 Preliminary Objections, *CERD (Georgia v Russia)*, ICJ Rep 70 (2011), para. 147.
58 Judgment, *Case Concerning Maritime Dispute (Peru v Chile)*, ICJ Rep 3 (2014), paras. 54, 65–68.
59 Judgment, *Application of the Convention on the Prevention and Punishment of the Crime of Genocide (Croatia v Serbia), ICJ* Rep 3 (2015), paras. 137, 157; Preliminary Objections, *Application of the CERD (Qatar v UAE)*, ICJ Rep 89–97 (2021); *Request For Advisory Opinion by the Socio-Economic Rights and Accountability Project (SERAP)*, Adv Op No. 001/2013 (May 26, 2017), para. 34.
60 Advisory Opinion, *Application for Review of Judgment No. 333 of the UN Administrative Tribunal*, ICJ Rep 18 (1987), para. 44.
61 Advisory Opinion Separate Opinion of Judge Dillard, *Namibia*, ICJ Rep 153 (1971); Advisory Opinion Dissenting Opinion of Judge Gros, *Namibia*, ICJ Rep 153 (1971), 323; Order of 14 April 1992 Dissenting Opinion Judge El-Kosheri, *Lockerbie Incident (Libya v USA)*, ICJ Rep 200 (1992).
62 Judgment, *Paramilitary Activities (Nicaragua v USA)*, ICJ Rep 14 (1986), para. 88; Judgment, *Application for Revision of the Bosnian Genocide Case (Yugoslavia v Bosnia and Herzegovina)*, ICJ Rep 7 (2003), para. 50.
63 Kurz, "Hide a Fact," 56.
64 *Iron Rhine*, para. 48; *EC – Computer Equipment*, 5 DSR 1851 WT/DS62 (1994), para. 93; *China – Publications and Audiovisual Products*, WT/DS363 10 DSR 261 (2010), para. 405.

was the view of the tribunal in *Iron Rhine*, which held internal records from both parties and was not *travaux* because they only informed the parties' unilateral view at that point in time.[65] It is also a common conclusion by WTO dispute settlement bodies.[66]

However, there is rampant discrepancy across international case law as to whether *travaux* must be authored by all of the parties, most of the parties, some of the parties, or just one of them. Doctrine tells us the last is incorrect because *travaux* purportedly evidences the common understanding of the parties and, therefore, should not be unilateral.[67] As Waldock said, '[s]tatements of individual parties during the negotiations are therefore of small value in the absence of evidence that they were assented to by the other parties.'[68] Still, international courts and tribunals have, in many cases, cited records by a minority of drafters[69] or even records authored by just one state.[70] In *Generation Ukraine v Ukraine*, the applicant submitted a US internal State Department commentary as *travaux* for a bilateral investment treaty (BIT), to which Ukraine objected, arguing it established nothing about Ukraine's interpretation.[71] The Panel responded by noting that Ukraine had not 'tender[ed] any documents emanating from official Ukrainian sources,'[72] implying not only that *travaux* can include unilateral sources but that adverse inferences could be drawn from Ukraine's 'failure' to provide such sources in response.

It is important to consider the practical effects of this unwritten rule. For example, in the Preliminary Objections in *Somalia v Kenya*, the ICJ cited as *travaux* a note verbale from the Norwegian government to the UN Secretary General, and a presentation by the Norwegian Permanent Representative at an event unconnected to negotiations.[73] Norway was not a party to the relevant treaty or the dispute but had 'supported' Somalia in

65 *Iron Rhine*, para. 48.

66 *US – Softwood Lumber V (Article 21.5 – Canada)*, WT/DS264/AB/RW 12 DSR 5087 (2006), paras. 120–121; *US – Stainless Steel (Mexico)*, WT/DS344 2 DSR 513 (2008), para. 131; *China – Publications and Audiovisual Products*, WT/DS363 10 DSR 261 (2010), para. 405.

67 *Iron Rhine*, para. 48; Decision on Preliminary Objections, *Daniel Kappes & Kappes, Cassiday & Associates v Guatemala*, ICSID Case No. ARB/18/43 (March 13, 2020), 155, para. 155.

68 Waldock, "Third Report on the Law of Treaties," *YILC* 2 (1964): 58–59, 21.

69 Preliminary Objections, *Maritime Delimitation in the Indian Ocean (Somalia v Kenya)*, ICJ Rep 3 (2017), para. 127.

70 Preliminary Objection *Oil Platforms (Iran v USA)*, ICJ Rep 803 (1996), para.; Jurisdiction, *Border and Transborder Armed Actions (Nicaragua v Honduras)*, ICJ Rep 69 (1988), para. 37.

71 Award, *Generation Ukraine Inc v Ukraine*, ICSID Case No ARB/00/9 (September 16, 2003), paras. 15.4.

72 Award, *Generation Ukraine Inc v Ukraine*, paras. 15.4.

73 Preliminary Objections, *Somalia v Kenya*, para. 104; cf. *Re-Evaluation of the German Mark*, para. 34, defining *travaux* as sources 'made in an official capacity and during the negotiations themselves.'

negotiations – though Somalia characterised its 'support' as exclusion. For example, Norway 'frequently' failed to copy the Somalian government in key emails.[74] Still, the ICJ decided to emphasise Norwegian records – a bilateral note to the UN Secretary-General and a unilateral presentation made in an unofficial capacity – as decisive *travaux*. This effectively made Norway the voice of the common intentions of the two African states.[75]

The court then later cited as *travaux* a working paper from informal negotiations for the UN Convention on the Law of the Sea (UNCLOS) by a working group of nine states, including Australia, the United States, Luxembourg, and Belgium, in order to confirm the meaning of *Kenya's* reservation to UNCLOS.[76] By doing so, the court not only amplified a (Western-allied) minority of states over the many participants of UNCLOS negotiations; it drew from secret negotiations to which neither applicant *nor* respondent was invited. That seems rather far from the 'common intention of the parties' at which we started.

2.4 *Is Travaux a Record Written by States?*

There are, however, many cases in which courts cite *travaux* written by non-state actors. The key example, often accepted in the everyday practice of international legal interpretation,[77] is preparatory work by the ILC.[78] But other actors also feature, including documents by the International Committee of the Red Cross,[79] dialogues between the UN Secretary-General and UN organs,[80] the General Agreement on Tariffs and Trade Secretariat,[81] and expert committees.[82] International and non-state organisations are not neces-

74 Preliminary Objections Written Statement of Somalia, *Somalia v Kenya*, para. 2.20.

75 This is not to say states should rely only on their own records as *travaux*, but that foreign records are relevant not because they are convenient or readily available but as evidence of the parties' common understanding(s).

76 Preliminary Objections, *Somalia v Kenya*, 104; Judgment, *Somalia v Kenya*, ICJ Rep (2021), paras. 127–129.

77 For a discussion, see Panos Merkouris, "Debating the Ouroboros of International Law: The Drafting History of Article 31(3)(c)," *International Community Law Review* 1, no. 9 (2007).

78 Judgment, *Continental Shelf (Tunisia/Libya)*, ICJ Rep 18 (1982), para. 41; Separate Opinion Judge Jiménez de Aréchaga, *Continental Shelf (Tunisia/Libya)*, ICJ Rep 100 (1962), para. 42; *Avena (Mexico v USA)*, ICJ Rep 12 (2004), paras. 56, 86; Judgment, *Jadhav (India v Pakistan)*, ICJ Rep 418 (2019), paras. 69–70, 76–86.

79 Advisory Opinion, *Wall*, ICJ Rep 136 (2004), para. 95.

80 Jurisdiction, *Prosecutor v Norman*, SCSL-04–14-PT-026, TC 1 (March 3, 2004), para. 22 (citing discussions between the UNSG and UNSC as *travaux*).

81 *US–Gambling*, WT/DS285/AB/R DSR 12 (2005), 5797, paras. 196–197; *US–Sections 301–310 of the Trade Act of 1974*, WT/DS152/R vol 2, 815 (1999) para. 4.453.

82 Advisory Opinion, *Wall*, ICJ Rep 136 (2004), 175, para. 95; Preliminary Objections, *Serbia and Montenegro v Belgium*, para. 111; Judgment, *LaGrand (Germany v USA)*, ICJ Rep 466

sarily neutral actors; they are as capable of having intentions during treaty negotiations as states. Indeed, some might wonder why we pretend said intentions vanish when the same organisations craft negotiation records.

Sometimes, scholarship is cited as *travaux*. In his separate opinion to the ICJ's *Wall* Advisory Opinion, Judge Kooijmans cited Professor Frits Kalshoven as the interpreter of the *travaux*.[83] In *Aguas del Tunari*, an arbitration under the auspices of the International Centre for the Settlement of Investment Disputes (ICSID), the tribunal categorised testimony by Professor Nico Schrijver as (an interpretation of) *travaux*.[84] In the ICJ's *Ukraine v Russia* Convention on the Elimination of All Forms of Racial Discrimination (CERD) case, counsel for the applicant relied upon testimony from Professor Andreas Zimmerman to interpret the Convention Against Terrorism.[85] While an exhaustive analysis is beyond the scope of this chapter, it may not be a coincidence that all three academics were White, tenured, cis men with considerable disciplinary capital.

Another problem with relying on scholars as *travaux* arose in *Churchill Mining v Indonesia*.[86] Indonesia relied upon a Hague Academy course by Aron Broches as a record of *travaux* to the relevant BIT – but the claim cited was found to be inaccurate.[87] In reply, the tribunal noted that '[t]hrough a "citation chain" dating back to Broches, that interpretation has become "conventional wisdom". That wisdom is no evidence of the intent of the drafters.'[88] This led the tribunal to set the purported '*travaux*' aside. But had that argument been made before another court or panel, it may have succeeded unquestioned.

2.5 *Must Travaux Pertain to the Treaty at Issue?*

Generally, *travaux* must be part of the history of the treaty at issue, rather than another treaty. We interpret a treaty provision in its own context, given the treaty's specific object, purpose, and subsequent practice record.[89] Klab-

(2001), para. 105; *US – Softwood Lumber V (Article 21.5 – Canada)*, WT/DS264/AB/RW 12 DSR 5087 (2006), para. 120.

83 Advisory Opinion Separate Opinion of Judge Kooijmans, *Wall*, ICJ Rep 136 (2004), 219, para. 47.

84 Decision on Jurisdiction, *Aguas del Tunari v Bolivia*, ICSID Case No. ARB/02/3 (October 21, 2005), para. 269.

85 Oral Pleadings, *CERD (Ukraine v Russia)*, CR 2017/3 (March 8, 2017), para. 42.

86 Decision on Jurisdiction, *Churchill Mining & Planet Mining v Indonesia*, ICSID Case No ARB/12/14 (February 24, 2014), paras. 139–141.

87 Aron Broches, "The Convention on the Settlement of Investment Disputes Between States and Nationals of Other States," *Recueil des Cours* 136 (1972): 331.

88 Broches, "The Convention on the Settlement of Investment Disputes."

89 As explained in Provisional Measures, *MOX Plant (Ireland v UK)*, ITLOS Rep 2001 (December 3, 2001), 51.

bers, with an eye to the fundamentals, notes that '[d]oing justice in individual cases depends to a large extent on the context of those individual cases.'[90] However, international courts often refer to drafting histories of similar provisions from previous treaties. For instance, the ICJ regularly interprets its own Statute in light of the Permanent Court of International Justice's *travaux*.[91] Likewise, the court has several times cited *travaux* from treaties with entirely different parties[92] or an entirely different object and purpose.[93] For a court asked to determine a singular, conclusive legal meaning, it is certainly convenient to rely on the available sources. But even identical treaty provisions in different treaties were presumably concluded by different parties, with different intentions and understandings of their agreements, in different historical contexts. The verbatim transposition of a provision from one treaty to another is as likely to be a nondecision as an active choice informed by context.

2.6 Must Travaux Predate the Treaty?

It may seem uncontroversial to say that *travaux* must refer to records made before the treaty's conclusion, such as during negotiations.[94] But in practice, *travaux* has also been used to mean reservations produced during the treaty's signature,[95] from ratification months later,[96] or documents without any date at all.[97] Here, we see the distinction between using *travaux* as evidence of the common intention of the parties in concluding the treaty, which could conceivably be shown in records produced during or shortly after signature, and *travaux* as evidence of the decisions that went into certain words or provisions within a treaty, which would logically need to predate its conclusion.

90 Jan Klabbers, "International Legal Histories: The Declining Importance of Travaux Préparatoires in Treaty Interpretation?" *Netherlands International Law Review* 50, no. 3 (December 2003): 288.
91 Judgment, *LaGrand*, 105; Preliminary Objections, *Serbia and Montenegro v Belgium*, 103–112.
92 Preliminary Objections, *Alleged Violations of Sovereign Rights and Maritime Spaces in the Caribbean Sea (Nicaragua v Colombia)*, ICJ Rep 3 (2016), 28, 32, 47–48; Preliminary Objections, *Question of the Delimitation of the Continental Shelf (Nicaragua v Colombia)*, ICJ Rep 100 (2016), para. 26.
93 Preliminary Objections, *Equatorial Guinea v France*, ICJ Rep 2018 (2018), 99–101.
94 *Re-Evaluation of the German Mark*, para. 34.
95 *Judgment Border and Transborder Armed Actions (Nicaragua v Honduras)*, ICJ Rep (1988), 69, para. 38.
96 Preliminary Objections, *Territorial and Maritime Dispute (Nicaragua v Colombia)*, ICJ Rep 832 (2007), para. 116; Award, *Generation Ukraine*, paras. 15.4.
97 Judgment, *Frontier Dispute (Burkina Faso/Mali)*, ICJ Rep 554 (1986), para. 99; Decision on Jurisdiction, *Millicom International Operations and Sentel GSMSA v Senegal*, ICSID Case No ARB/08/20 (July 16, 2010), para. 72.

2.7 *Must Travaux be Written?*

The requirement that *travaux* be in writing seems fairly clear,[98] with the possible exception enabled by the broad adoption of digital recordings.[99] However, even then, the definition of 'written' is somewhat flexible; *travaux* has included an unattributed five-word scribble in a document's margins[100] and a pencil line on a map.[101] On the other hand, the ICJ has also found other pencil lines could *not* be *travaux*, with no clear reason why.[102]

International case law has also seemingly treated oral statements as *travaux*. In *Aegean Sea Continental Shelf*, the ICJ included a statement by the Turkish Prime Minister to the National Assembly in its analysis of *travaux*.[103] In his dissent in *ELSI*, Judge Schwebel cited Italian Parliamentary proceedings as part of the *travaux*.[104] And finally, the tribunal in *İçkale İnşaat v Turkmenistan* ordered the parties to submit relevant *travaux*, including witness testimony – seemingly implying that oral testimony could figure into *travaux* as well.[105]

2.8 *Must Travaux be Public?*

There is some disagreement as to how public a document must be to qualify as *travaux*.[106] Waldock had no issue referring to both 'unpublished, but accessible, *travaux préparatoires* as well as to published ones.'[107] In *Certain IT*

98 *Re-Evaluation of the German Mark*, para. 36; Anthony Aust, *Modern Treaty Law and Practice*, 3rd ed. (Cambridge: Cambridge University Press, 2013).

99 Olivier Corten and Pierre Klein, *The Vienna Conventions on the Law of Treaties: A Commentary* (Oxford: Oxford University Press, 2011), 855.

100 Judgment, *Frontier Dispute (Burkina Faso/Mali)*, ICJ Rep 554 (1986), para. 99.

101 Judgment, *Frontier Dispute (Burkina Faso/Mali)*, para. 103. Dissenting Opinion Judge Abi-Saab, *Frontier Dispute (Burkina Faso/Mali)*, ICJ Rep 554 (1986).

102 Judgment, *Sovereignty over Pulau Ligitan and Pulau Sipadan (Indonesia/Malaysia)*, ICJ Rep 625 (2005), para. 57.

103 Judgment, *Aegean Sea Continental Shelf (Greece v Turkey)*, ICJ Rep 3 (1978), para. 102.

104 Dissenting Opinion Judge Schwebel, *Case Concerning Elettronica Sicula (ELSI) (USA v Italy)*, ICJ Rep 94 (1989).

105 Award, *İçkale İnşaat Ltd Şirketi v Turkmenistan*, ICSID Case No. ARB/10/24 (March 8, 2016), para. 33.

106 Advisory Opinion, *Competence of the European Commission of the Danube Between Galatz and Braïla*, PCIJ Ser B No 14 (1927), 6, para. 32; *Re-Evaluation of the German Mark*, para. 34; ILC, "Draft Articles on the Law of Treaties, with Commentaries," *Yearbook of the International Law Commission II* (1966), 223; International Law Commission, *Summary Record of the 872nd Meeting*, UN Doc A/CN.4/SR.872 (June 17, 1966), para. 34; Ian Sinclair, *The Vienna Convention on the Law of Treaties*, 2nd ed. (Manchester: Manchester University Press, 1984), 144; Odile Ammann, *The Interpretative Methods of International Law: What Are They, and Why Use Them?* (Leiden: Brill Nijhoff, 2020).

107 Humphrey Waldock, "Third Report on the Law of Treaties," *Yearbook of the International Law Commission* II (1964): 58–59, para. 21.

Products, the WTO Dispute Settlement Body drew the line at public availability, discounting records to which only one party had access.[108] Likewise, in *Canfor v USA*, the Tribunal described *travaux* as 'negotiating records such as communications, explication notes, position papers or memoranda established during the negotiation of the Agreement and which were circulated among, discussed by or relied upon by the negotiating teams or by the drafting teams' and noted they were potentially 'pertinent to the issue of the common intention.'[109]

'Imagine now a treaty interpreter offering an interpretation based on a private letter of a negotiator,' Bianchi and Zarbiyev recently wrote.[110] 'It is unlikely that such interpretive moves would be recognized as a competent reading.'[111] But what feels like disciplinary common sense is not matched by practice – in fact, international courts and tribunals frequently cite records available to some or *neither* of the parties. In *Libya/Chad*, *travaux* included a *French* internal record;[112] in *Qatar v Bahrain,* it included two draft records submitted by Saudi Arabia and Oman;[113] and in *Aegean Sea,* it included multiple Greek internal records published 50 years after the treaty's conclusion.[114] At one point in the *Genocide Convention* case between Croatia and Serbia, Judge Owada referred in a Separate Opinion to the 'unpublished *travaux preparatoires*' of ICJ's *own Rules of Procedure* as interpretive guidance.[115]

This problem is central to investor-state disputes, as Judge Berman noted in *Empresas Lucchetti v Peru.*[116] In *Methanex v USA*, the Tribunal decided that, though the US could access *travaux* that Methanex could not, the onus was on Methanex to justify each record it sought *before* accessing it – otherwise, the 'scope of document production' on the respondent would be too burdensome.[117] Some tribunals have even issued remarkably broad procedural orders, even to states not involved in the dispute, including firm deadlines and – in a case between a private company

108 *EC – Tariff Treatment of Certain IT Products* (WT/DS375/R) WTO, DSR 4 (2010), 1567, paras. 7.577–79, 7.581.
109 Procedural Order No. 5, *Canfor v USA*, NAFTA/UNCITRAL (May 28, 2004), paras. 15–21.
110 Bianchi and Zarbiyev, *Demystifying Treaty Interpretation*, 30.
111 Bianchi and Zarbiyev, *Demystifying Treaty Interpretation*, 30.
112 Judgment, *Territorial Dispute (Libya/Chad)*, ICJ Rep 6 (1994), 55–56.
113 Jurisdiction, *Qatar v Bahrain*, paras. 41–42.
114 Judgment, *Aegean Sea Continental Shelf (Greece v Turkey)*, ICJ Rep 3 (1978), paras. 63–64.
115 Separate Opinion Judge Owada, *Genocide Convention (Croatia v Serbia)*, ICJ Rep 169 (2015).
116 Dissenting Opinion Judge Berman, *Empresas Lucchetti and Lucchetti Peru v Peru*, ICSID Case No. ARB/03/4 (September 5, 2007), para. 9.
117 Final Award, *Methanex v USA*, Part II, Chapter H (August 3, 2005), para. 19(ii).

and *Ecuador* – sentences like 'The Tribunal is not inviting argument from the French Republic.'[118]

Sometimes, such demands have enabled Global South states like Algeria to rely upon more complete or resourced archives to fill critical evidentiary gaps,[119] but third-state support is not always reliable. In *HICEE v Slovakia*, the Tribunal requested that the Dutch government furnish additional records to explain several public parliamentary Explanatory Notes in evidence.[120] Such evidence 'ought in principle to be readily available,' the panel insisted – but only Czech records were filed; the Dutch archives had nothing to submit.[121] Ironically, the modern system of archival organisation and the whole field of archival theory arguably began in Dutch archives for the *explicit* purpose of preserving documents 'so that they may serve as evidence.'[122] The takeaway is that states with access to the full(er) record, including third parties, may, for many reasons, find it advantageous to refuse to disclose records that adjudicators consider *travaux*.

In *Churchill Mining*, the Panel cited declassified British records as *travaux*, despite admitting their limited utility as evidence of the common intention of the parties.[123] Similarly, in *Generation Ukraine*, Ukraine noted that internal US records could not demonstrate Ukrainian intent.[124] 'This is certainly a fair and understandable reservation,' the Tribunal replied, 'but equally [Ukraine] did not tender any documents emanating from official Ukrainian sources.'[125] Again, this reads like a negative inference; the Tribunal then proceeded to treat the records as *travaux*, despite saying otherwise, and ultimately supported the (American) investor.[126] In *Clayton v Canada*, the Tribunal held that even if parties submitted subsequently declassified records as *travaux*, it likely would not affect its traditional interpretation of the North American Free Trade Agreement and so was not worth the effort.[127] This decision to prioritise legal certainty and interpretive continuity over fairness and histori-

118 Award, *Perenco Ecuador v Ecuador*, ICSID Case No. ARB/08/6 (June 30, 2011), paras. 83, 92–95, 242.
119 Award, *Orascom TMT Investments SARL v Algeria*, ICSID Case No. ARB/12/35 (May 31, 2017), paras. 107–108, 112.
120 Partial Award, *HICEE v Slovakia*, PCA Case No. 2009–11 (May 23, 2011), para. 126–131.
121 Partial Award, *HICEE v Slovakia*.
122 John Ridener, *From Polders to Postmodernism: A Concise History of Archival Theory* (Duluth: Litwin Books, 2008), 32; Samuel Muller, Johan A. Feith and Robert Fruin, *Handleiding voor het Ordenen en Beschrijven van Archieven (Manual for the Arrangement and Description of Archives)* (Groningen: Erven B. van der Kamp, 1898).
123 Decision on Jurisdiction, *Churchill Mining*, para. 212.
124 Award, *Generation Ukraine*, paras. 15.3–15.6.
125 Award, *Generation Ukraine*, 15.4.
126 Award, *Generation Ukraine*, 15.5–6.
127 Procedural Order No. 8, *Clayton et al v Canada*, PCA Case No. 2009–04 (November 25, 2009), 3.

cal accuracy coincidentally functioned to empower the party able to access classified records and control who else could do so.

2.9 *Must Travaux Evidence the Common Intention of the Parties?*

Apparently, the entire purpose of citing *travaux* is to help give meaning to uncertain terms by demonstrating the common intention of the parties.[128] However, international adjudicators have often cited records as *travaux* to evidence of the *absence* of said common intention. This is most common where the record is silent on 'important' issues that (according to the interpreter) 'should' have featured. In *Somalia v Kenya*, the ICJ dismissed Kenya's interpretation of a treaty with Somalia because a Norwegian diplomat who authored the *travaux* in question had not found Kenya's interpretation notable enough to mention.[129] Likewise, in the *Georgia v Russia* Preliminary Objections, the ICJ struggled to interpret a CERD provision because the drafters had found it sufficiently 'self-explanatory' that further explanation was not required.[130]

But courts have also set aside *travaux* exactly *because* it was too equivocal,[131] an implicit admission that comes *so tantalisingly close* to acknowledging that 'common' intent is fictive. This is partly due to confirmation bias – the interpreter, by misreading Article 32, locks themselves into a binary. Either the *travaux* confirms their prior conclusion, or it is irrelevant. As Judge Schwebel warns in his dissent to *Qatar v Bahrain*, '*travaux préparatoires* are no less evidence of the intention of the parties when they contradict as when they confirm the allegedly clear meaning of the text or context of treaty provisions.'[132]

After deciding that *travaux* is itself too ambiguous to resolve ambiguity, courts tend to walk one of two paths.[133] They may proverbially shrug, toss up their hands, and decide that the absence of evidence is evidence of absence,[134]

128 *Iron Rhine*, para. 48; *China – Publications and Audiovisual Products,* (WT/DS363) WTO, 10 DSR 261, (2010), para. 405.

129 Preliminary Objections, *Somalia v Kenya*, paras. 103–105.

130 Preliminary Objections, *CERD (Georgia v Russia)*, ICJ Rep 70 (2011), para. 146–147.

131 *Advisory Opinion on the Interpretation of the Convention of 1919 Concerning Employment of Women During the Night*, PCIJ Ser A/B No 50 365 (1932), at 379.

132 Jurisdiction Dissenting Opinion Judge Schwebel, *Qatar v Bahrain*, 39.

133 Some courts and tribunals use the third option to request *ex propria motu* that parties provide further records.

134 Preliminary Objections, *Continental Shelf (Nicaragua v Colombia)*, ICJ Rep 100 (2016), para. 30, 45; Judgment, *Equatorial Guinea v France*, ICJ Rep 300 (2020), para. 70; Concurring Opinion of Judge Diego García-Sayán, Judgment, *López Mendoza v Venezuela*, Inter-Am. Ct. H.R. Ser C No 233 (September 1, 2011), para. 16; Jurisdiction, *Qatar v Bahrain*, paras. 41–42.

or they might fill the gap with their own opinions without recourse to historical or legal sources at all.[135] Often, their results bear an uncanny resemblance to their initial conclusions.[136] When we decide, as Lord Steyn did, that in order to cite *travaux* 'only a bulls-eye counts. Nothing less will do,'[137] we narrow the parameters of our analysis until real results become impossible. It's also, some might add, a lazy approach to history.

2.10 *Must Travaux be a Record That Exists?*

At the very least, surely a document must *exist* to be *travaux*. Indeed, there are several cases in which the lack of an official record was held to preclude an Article 32 analysis.[138] But although international law 'knows no gaps,'[139] evidentiary records inevitably do. What then?

A record that no longer exists can be *travaux* if corroborated by written evidence[140] or oral testimony.[141] What about documents that may have never existed? After all, absence of evidence cannot be evidence of absence.[142] However, courts have previously interpreted legal meaning from sources that never existed or from general assertions of what the drafters thought or believed and called it *travaux*. In *CERD (Georgia v Russia)*, the ICJ made general and unsupported observations about the putative beliefs of the parties at the historical moment of a treaty's conclusion;[143] Judge Brower did the same in the Preliminary Objections of *Treaty of Amity*.[144] Compare this with, for instance, Saidiya Hartman's critical

135 For instance, Separate Opinion Judge *ad hoc* Brower, Preliminary Objections, *Alleged Violations of the 1955 Treaty of Amity (Iran v USA)* (February 3, 2021), 13; Preliminary Objections, *CERD (Georgia v Russia)*, ICJ Rep 70 (2011), para. 147; Judgment Declaration of Judge Kittichaisaree, *Case Concerning the Detention of Three Ukrainian Naval Vessels (Ukraine v Russia)*, ITLOS Rep (May 25, 2019), para. 4.

136 As noted in Joint Dissenting Opinion Judges Owada, Simma, Abraham, Donoghue, and Gaja, *CERD (Georgia v Russia)*, ICJ Rep 142 (2011).

137 As claimed by, *inter alia*, the ICJ in Jurisdiction, *Qatar v Bahrain*, paras. 41–42; Lord Steyn, *Shipping Company v Linden Management and ors*, AC 605 (1998), 623.

138 Jurisdiction, *Qatar v Bahrain*, para. 41; *India – Quantitative Restrictions* (WT/DS90) 5 DSR 1763 (1999), 98, paras. 57, 94; *United States – Sections 301–310 of the Trade Act of 1974* (WT/DS152/R) 2, 815, para. 4.451.

139 Lauterpacht, "Restrictive Interpretation," 77.

140 Judgment, *Frontier Dispute (Burkina Faso/Mali)*, ICJ Rep 554 (1986], paras. 100–105; Judgment, *Frontier Dispute (Benin/Niger)*, ICJ Rep 90 (2005], para. 54.

141 Partial Award, *HICEE v Slovakia*, paras. 30–33.

142 Preliminary Objections, *Continental Shelf (Nicaragua v Colombia)*, paras. 30, 45.

143 Preliminary Objections, *CERD (Georgia v Russia)*, para. 147.

144 Preliminary Objections Separate Opinion Judge *ad hoc* Brower, *Alleged Violations of the 1955 Treaty of Amity (Iran v USA)* (February 3, 2021), 13, para. 23.

fabulation, which also interprets history despite archival silences but by reference to nuanced and intricate archival work.[145]

In *Oil Platforms*, the ICJ observed that, though the United States had produced several internal records to support its interpretation, Iran had not done the same – and held that, had Iran interpreted the provision as such at the time, such documents *should* have existed.[146] In *Croatia v Serbia*, Judge Xue conducted a 'quick perusal of the drafting history' and found no record that contradicted her preferred interpretation.[147] Few historians would consider a 'quick perusal' of an archive sufficient – with the possible exception of those reviewing archive funding proposals. It also does not seem correct, as a matter of treaty interpretation, to read silence in the record as confirmation of an Article 31 interpretive analysis. In reality, states use treaty negotiation for many purposes. The resources they apply to the process may vary for many reasons, and they create or avoid creating records of the process for many reasons. For example, Skovgard Poulsen recounts Pakistan's discovery that it lacked all negotiation records for its BIT with Switzerland, and indeed most of its BITs,[148] because at the time, it considered such treaties to be little more than photo opportunities. This makes it hard to conclude with any certainty what a state 'should' have thought or recorded or to read too far into its archival silences.

Try as we might, we may not be able to resolve ambiguity in every instance, no matter how deeply we dig through history. This is uncomfortable, both because ambiguity scares us and because it reveals an ugly truth: interpretation is always, on some level, a process of creation and not discovery.[149]

3. Travaux Is Fluid – and That's a Good Thing

If by now *travaux* seems a tangled mess – indeed, if the word has lost all meaning – I have been successful in my queer aim to 'disturb, unsettle, [and] make strange.'[150] The issue is that when we turn to *travaux*, we don't

145 Saidiya Hartman, "Intimate History, Radical Narrative," *The Journal of African American History* 106, no. 1 (January 2021): 127–135.
146 Preliminary Objections, *Oil Platforms (Iran v USA)*, ICJ Rep 803 (1996), para. 29.
147 Declaration of Judge Xue, *Genocide Convention (Croatia v Serbia)*, ICJ Rep 381 (2015), 386, para. 18.
148 LN Skovgaard Poulsen, *Bounded Rationality and Economic Diplomacy: The Politics of Investment Treaties in Developing Countries* (Cambridge: Cambridge University Press, 2015), xiv–xv.
149 Anne Orford, *International Law and the Politics of History* (Cambridge: Cambridge University Press, 2021), 287–291.
150 Suzanne Lennon and OmiSoore H. Dryden, "Introduction: Interventions, Iterations, and Interrogations That Disturb the (Homo)Nation," in *Disrupting Queer Inclusion: Canadian Homonationalisms and the Politics of Belonging*, eds. OmiSoore H. Dryden and Suzanne Lenon (Vancouver: University of British Columbia Press, 2015), 16.

know what questions we're asking, and then we balk at answers that are as vague as our questions. When we consult *travaux*, do we want to understand the similarities and differences in spoken views of states, as expressed in the pre-approved (and often summarised) negotiation record? Or are we trying to understand how and why a given term came to be in a treaty? These are two distinct questions involving different sources and modes of analysis; likewise, their results will differ. Either way, it is hardly fair to treat *travaux* like a magic spell to resolve disagreements about what treaties mean and do.[151]

The question of what *travaux* means was perhaps best addressed by Esmé Shirlow and Michael Waibel, who raise many of the previously mentioned problems with specific reference to investment disputes, a context involving one party with greater access to records.[152] According to their proposed 'sliding scale' approach, an interpreter should consider four key criteria to assess what may be *travaux*: a record's temporal relevance, its availability, its 'collectivity' (whether it was authored or agreed upon by multiple parties), and its 'quality' (in terms of its authenticity, completeness, coverage, and consistency).[153] These are indeed among the most important factors we must keep in mind when interpreting a treaty provision through *travaux*.

However, the sliding scale approach is a way toward a solution, not the solution itself. It is only helpful as a tool to explicate the implicit questions and assumptions involved in the *travaux* analysis. One analogy, inspired by too long spent in campus queer advocacy, is the 'Genderbread Person,'[154] a model designed to visualise many different forms of identity and expression. Turning categories into spectra – a series of sliding scales – can help to *unpack, communicate*, and (ideally) *understand* the complex and nuanced parts of queer identities. But it remains a tool to visualise the solution, not the solution itself. It is useful, but it can become a trap if we forget that queerness uses categories to dismantle them. The map – or the Genderbread Person, or the *travaux* sliding scale – is not the image. In the same way, we must be cautious in applying a sliding scale approach to *travaux*, lest we trade one constraining implicit rule for a set of others.

By queerly unpacking and explicating the questions involved in a *travaux* analysis, we become better able to tailor our interpretive method to produce helpful results. As a legal method, *travaux* does not need queering because

151 Klabbers, "International Legal Histories," 286.

152 Esmé Shirlow and Michael Waibel, "A Sliding Scale Approach to Travaux in Treaty Interpretation: The Case of Investment Treaties," *British Yearbook of International Law* (forthcoming, first published March 13, 2021).

153 Shirlow and Waibel, "A Sliding Scale Approach."

154 Sam Killermann, "The Genderbread Person version 4" (2018), accessed April 2, 2024, www.itspronouncedmetrosexual.com/2018/10/the-genderbread-person-v4/.

(and here's a plot twist) travaux *is already queer*. Its meaning is fluid and ambiguous; its subject is undefined and resists systematic definition. As I have shown, *travaux* means different things in different situations – and that is the only way it makes sense. *Travaux* only *seems* coherent and definable because of the unspoken rules that constrain it – rules that we learn from our first lectures, perform throughout our professional lives, and reinforce as disciplinary markers of (in)competence. That is why asking silly questions can explicate and unravel these rules, revealing *travaux* in all of its powerful, ineffable queerness.

So far, our discipline's fear of ambiguity has prevented us from recognising *travaux*'s queer potential. Instead, we attempt to 'straighten' it into artificial coherence with a nebulous collection of unwritten rules – and because *travaux* is queer, these implicit rules must likewise differ from one use to another. Often, they will reinforce prior normative assumptions about (1) 'relevant' or 'important' historical sources, actors, and narratives and/or (2) established markers of authority, expertise, or power. This results in *negative* ambiguity because its 'ambiguousness' is felt differentially and qualified by various dynamics of social and disciplinary power. International lawyers privileged with certain markers of (disciplinary) authority – for instance, those who are White, male, cisgender, heterosexual and/or heteronormative, able, healthy, wealthy, positioned, or tenured – will (be more likely to) have asymmetrical power to determine whose voices and which histories can affect legal meaning. For them, *travaux* might not feel ambiguous at all because the implicit norms that constrain it both feel familiar and tend to operate in their favour. Meanwhile, for the rest of us, the unwritten rules of *travaux* will feel all the more ambiguous, and the professional consequences of doing it 'wrong' will be all the more consequential. Ultimately, the negative ambiguity that constrains *travaux* makes this a question of who is empowered with the authority to interpret not just law but also history – and who may decide when, which, and how history may affect legal meaning.

Solving the problem of *travaux*'s negative ambiguity will require us, as a discipline, to learn to recognise its queer ambiguity as positive. There are as many treaty-making processes as there are treaties, each involving wildly variant interests and actors.[155] It makes perfect sense to adapt our analysis accordingly; the key is that as we do so, we say what we're doing and why. But questioning and explication are only helpful if we can unlearn our disciplinary discomfort with uncertainty. As often as international lawyers benefit from the ambiguous meaning of *travaux* we are still unprepared for (and uncomfortable with) ambiguous results. But *travaux*,

155 *EC – Chicken Cuts, Brazil v European Communities*, para. 293: 'What should be considered "temporally proximate" will vary from treaty provision to treaty provision, and may depend on the structure of the negotiating process.'

however defined, may yield only further uncertainty, because *history is often uncertain*.[156] As Odile Amman notes, 'historical interpretation can be challenged for being indeterminate.'[157] This leaves the legal interpreter with a problem – what then? Indeed, several international courts and tribunals have dismissed *travaux* as inconclusive, either because it was silent to the question(s) they posed or because it offered several contradictory answers. For some, the risk that *travaux* may support multiple views or that it might not resolve ambiguity are additional reason to consider it supplementary.[158] Of course, the irony is that *international law* usually supports multiple views, and it is often ambiguous; that is exactly why we rely on *travaux* to begin with. Ambiguity is as endemic to international law as it is to history.[159] It is unfair to demand that history save us because our own discipline cannot.

4. Conclusion: The Problem Is Us

Membership in our invisible college is defined by invisible rules. As much as we subordinate the place of *travaux* in our ways of doing international law, as much as we insist to ourselves that it is merely supplementary, we depend on it to protect us from the spectre of ambiguity. This problem, which I have only slightly hyperbolised, should trouble us – and therefore, we should trouble the problem. This chapter has attempted to begin the process.

First, however, we must work to understand why ambiguity is so uncomfortable. As a starting point, I would suggest that *travaux* sits at the intersection of two unspoken fictions that our discipline would prefer to leave unpacked. First, the axiom is that parties to a treaty negotiation have equal power to affect the result. Second, they share one 'common understanding,' which we can discover using one prescribed method. We know these to be fictions, but we have yet to decide, as a discipline, what that means. As Orford writes, 'In the end, no other discipline or method can save us, analyse us, offer us therapy or sanctuary or sophistication or the moral high ground or escape from uncertainty or redemption.'[160] The problem is not in our method; it is us. Until we open ourselves to ambiguity, *travaux* will remain closeted, bound by invisible rules that privilege certain histories over others.

156 Orford, *International Law and the Politics of History*; Klabbers, "International Legal Histories," 270.
157 Ammann, *The Interpretative Methods of International Law*, 218.
158 Klabbers, "International Legal Histories"; Corten and Klein, *The Vienna Conventions on the Law of Treaties*, 857.
159 Orford, *International Law and the Politics of History*, 178.
160 Orford, *International Law and the Politics of History*, 320.

A queerer, more reflexive approach could allow us to better question the limits of our understandings better. How are our assumptions limiting our historical analyses? Could asking more specific questions yield more relevant answers? Which kinds of sources might help us to answer which kinds of questions? And, if our results are still ambiguous, (why) should that bother us? Is it fair for international lawyers to expect history to be any more determinate than law? And most fundamentally – why are we so uncomfortable with ambiguity?

Chapter 10

Queer Judging, Straight Up

The Queer Judge and Judicial Systems

Joanne Stagg

1. Introduction

Queer theorists, including the contributors to this volume, have long argued that law imposes and enforces cis-heteronormativity.[1] Though international law may formally arise from international agreements between states, judges and quasi-judicial officers bridge the space between that law and its application to participants in the international community (who themselves may comply with or ignore that application). In this role, international judges choose whether to impose or disrupt normativity, including cis-heteronormativity, in their judgments and reports. They speak the law into application and demonstrate, through their performance of judging, what law, impartiality, and the imposition of lawful authority mean. This chapter will examine what it means 'to queer'[2] judging and how the act of queering judging may make a difference to international law and international judging.

A judge does not need to be a member of the QUILTBAG+[3] community to engage in queer judging. Instead, I propose that a 'queer judge' is a judge of *any* gender or sexuality, who queers judging by applying the methods and spirit of queer theory to the process of judging – for example, by questioning

1 Cis-heteronormativity refers to systems and attitudes based on the assumption that assumes being cisgendered and heterosexual is normative and that sexuality, gender, and sexual orientation are based on assigned sex at birth.

2 The term 'queer' can be used several ways. It was once used as a slur for non-heterosexual or non-cisgender people, but now is used by some people as a self-descriptor of their gender or sexuality. It can be used as a verb, as a number of queer theorists do, to indicate the practice of questioning or making strange cis-heteronormative discourse or the practice of making spaces or discourses friendlier to queer people. It can also be used as an adjective for things such as 'queer theory' or for one who practices queering, as I do in this paper when I refer to 'queer judge/judging'.

3 QUILTBAG+ is an acronym similar to LGBTQIAA+. It means Queer, Unsure, Intersex, Lesbian, Transgender, Bisexual, Asexual/Aromantic, Gay, and other queer identities (the latter indicated by the "+"). I use it because it prioritises queerness generally and is easier to say than LGBTQIAA+.

DOI: 10.4324/9781032645339-13

norms and treating QUILTBAG+ people's lives as just as authentic and worthy as the lives and practices of cisgender or heterosexual people.

Through judging queerly, a judge has the scope to change not only the law but the practice and performance of the act of judging itself. Judging queerly may destabilise cis-heteronormativity, both explicitly and through a Butlerian performance of *the judge* by valuing non-normative members of society, challenging cis-heteronormative thinking, re-evaluating the place of emotion in public life, and prioritising justice over form.[4]

This chapter considers how this mode of judging can be enacted in international law, with particular attention to the 'consensus' and 'dissensus' judicial processes used by international courts and tribunals. The first part of this chapter is a short overview of queer theory as it pertains to law. The second part considers queer judging and the phenomenon of the queer judge. As part of this, I explore the tensions between traditional norms of judging and queerness in judging, observing how the navigation of this tension creates new Butlerian performances of the judicial role.

In the third part of the chapter, I situate my concept of queer judging within the two main models of judicial decision-making in international law: consensus and dissensus models of judging. I argue that challenging cis-heteronormativity in a dissent as part of the dissensus model of judging can allow the queer judge to directly contest their colleagues' assumptions about what is 'normal' in the context of gender and sexuality. At the same time, the use of the dissent to do so may position such queer judging as outside of legal norms, in much the same way that queer genders and sexualities are positioned as divergent by dominant cis-heteronormative discourses. Conversely, consensus approaches to judging may be able to accommodate queer judging by allowing the queer judge to use soft power to persuade their judicial colleagues to reconsider cis-heteronormative values, mirroring the use of soft power by queer communities in social contexts. Nevertheless, like dissensus judging, consensus judging comes with obstacles for queer judging. Specifically, the consensus model may result in the 'closeting' of queer perspectives to enable consensus, silencing outsider views through the presentation of cis-heteronormative discourses as unanimous and unchallenged.

2. Queer Theory

Queer theory arose in the late 20th century as a stream of critical theory that examines how society privileges and imposes cisgender heterosexuality over

4 Judith Butler, "Merely Cultural," *New Left Review* (1998): 37–38; Judith Butler, *Bodies That Matter: On the Discursive Limits of 'Sex'* (Abingdon and New York: Routledge, 2011), 176; Elena Loizidou, "The Body Figural and Material in the Work of Judith Butler," *Australian Feminist Law Journal* 28, no. 1 (2008): 37.

other modes of being. While it grew partly out of feminism's examination of gender and patriarchal power structures, queer theory is less bounded than many feminist approaches. Early queer scholar Eve Kosofsky Sedgewick explains queerness as 'the open mesh of possibilities, gaps, overlaps, dissonances and resonances, lapses and excesses of meaning when the constituent elements of anyone's gender, of anyone's sexuality aren't made (or *can't be* made to signify monolithically'.[5] In queer theory, this awareness of the fluidity and possibilities of queerness leads us to 'rethink the sexual in new ways, elsewhere and otherwise'.[6] That rethinking, in turn, allows us to examine not only sexual practices but also the way in which society, more generally, is structured around facilitating, encouraging, and enforcing heterosexuality and cisgender status. Building upon the work of Judith Butler,[7] queer theorists often use the postmodern technique of unpacking social structures to examine cis-heteronormative power structures and to consider how cis-heteronormativity could be challenged or replaced by queerness' 'mesh of possibilities' to create a more inclusive society for both QUILTBAG+ people and others affected by hierarchies that have their roots in patriarchy and cis-heteronormativity. Queer theorists have also critiqued 'homonormativity' – that is, the mirroring of heteronormativity *within* QUILTBAG+ communities in ways that naturalise and valourise heteronormativity while coercing queer culture into structures which replicate heteronormative social ordering and/or demobilise and depoliticise queerness in favour of respectability politics and consumerism.[8]

This chapter will draw from the work of Judith Butler, particularly their conceptions of performativity and 'law as written' versus 'law as experienced'.[9] Butler uses 'performativity' to describe the process in which we consciously or otherwise make, reinforce, or subvert social meaning through all of our behaviours, or have those social meanings performed upon us. As Butler defines it, performance 'is always a reiteration of a norm or set of norms, and

5 Eve Kosofsky Sedgwick, *Tendencies* (Durham, NC: Duke University Press, 1993), 7–8.

6 Teresa De Lauretis, "Queer Theory: Lesbian and Gay Sexualities an Introduction," *Differences* 3, no. 2 (1991): iii–xviii.

7 See particularly, Judith Butler, *Gender Trouble Feminism and the Subversion of Identity* (New York: Routledge, 1999); Judith Butler, *Undoing Gender* (London: Psychology Press, 2004); Judith Butler, *Bodies That Matter: On the Discursive Limits of 'Sex'* (Abingdon and New York: Routledge, 2011).

8 Lisa Duggan, "The New Homonormativity: The Sexual Politics of Neoliberalism," in *Materializing Democracy: Towards a Revitalized Cultural Politics*, eds. Russ Castronovo and Dana D. Nelson (Durham, NC: Duke University Press, 2002); Emma Genovese, "The Spectacle of Respectable Equality: Queer Discrimination in Australian Law Post Marriage Equality," *The University of New South Wales Law Journal* 46, no. 2 (2023): 655.

9 Butler, *Gender Trouble*; Robert Leckey and Kim Brooks, *Queer Theory: Law, Culture, Empire: Law, Culture, Empire* (London: Routledge, 2010); Judith Butler, *Antigone's Claim: Kinship between Life and Death* (New York: Columbia University Press, 2000).

to the extent that it acquires an act-like status in the present, it conceals or dissimulates the conventions of which is it a repetition'.[10] In this way, Butlerian 'performance' is not the same as 'performance' in the common meaning of the word – that is, chosen and deliberate behaviours. It involves the repetition of norms rather than the production of a 'spectacle', which is a deliberate portrayal of exaggerated forms of social behaviours, often to create meaning.

Butler's distinction between 'law as written' and 'law as experienced' further develops the concept of law as a form of performative act. 'Law as written' acts as a symbolic ideal.[11] 'Law as experienced', in contrast, is the law as performed and lived. It includes, but is not limited to, encounters with legal systems or law enforcement. It also includes the experience of living in a society shaped and informed by compliance with law so that even those who do not have direct experience of legal systems live inescapably under norms created by lawful and law-full society. Law, as written and as experienced, creates, enforces, implements, and is the instrument of hegemonic social norms and cis-heteronormative power structures.[12] Most importantly for this chapter, law and its processes can also create spaces for resistance to norms by defining what is normative and giving shape to what is forbidden or transgressive.[13] In my argument, by performing judging queerly, the queer judge may shift the normative concept of 'judging' to include questioning cis-heteronormativity, homonormativity, and social 'regimes of the normal', prioritising doing justice over technical compliance.

3. Queer Judging

3.1 Introducing Queer Judging

I argue that queer judging is the performance of judging using methods and insights from queer theory. Queer judges (that is, judges who use queer judging methods) do not themselves have to be a member of the QUILTBAG+ community. Rather, they are judges who interrogate and reject cis-heteronormativity in law and society. Similarly, a judge who is a member

10 Judith Butler, *Bodies That Matter: On the Discursive Limits of "Sex,"* Routledge Classics (Abingdon, Oxon and New York: Routledge, 2011), xxi.

11 Butler, *Antigone's Claim*, 20–21; Tamsin Phillipa Paige and Joanne Stagg, "Queer Approaches to International Adjudication," in *The Max Planck Encyclopedia of International Procedural Law*, ed. Hélène Ruiz Fabri (Oxford: Oxford University Press, February 2021), www.opil.ouplaw.com/home/mpil.

12 François Ewald, "Norms, Discipline, and the Law," *Representations* 30, no. Spring (1990): 138; Janice Nadler, "Expressive Law, Social Norms, and Social Groups," *Law & Social Inquiry* 42, no. 1 (2017): 60–75.

13 Michel Foucault, *The History of Sexuality*, vol. 1 (London: Penguin, 1990), 101.

of the QUILTBAG+ community may ascribe to cis-heterosexual norms and reinforce cis-heteronormativity, thereby failing to act as my idealised queer judge (though, by being non-cisgender or non-heterosexual in a profession which historically had been inaccessible to anyone known to be QUILTBAG+, they may still somewhat 'queer' that role in the sense of challenging past informal social restrictions on the sexuality and gender of judges).

3.2 *Performing Queer Judging*

Through the performance of the judicial role, judges create 'the judge' and 'judging' as epistemological categories, and queer judging reinterprets those performances. Foucault argued that disciplinary power created what he identified as 'the soul', saying it 'is produced permanently around, on, within, the body by the functioning of a power that is exercised on those that are punished'.[14] Butler takes this further, saying,

> the law is not merely internalised, but incorporated, with the consequence that bodies are produced which signify the law on and through the body; there the law is manifest as the essence of their selves, the meaning of their soul, their conscience, the law of their desire.[15]

Law creates the law's subject(s) and makes intelligible those who are subjectified by the law. It also creates categories of divergence from the law, including categories of social and juridical deviance, which have no shape until the law defines that which is outside the law or deviates from the law's norms. Law produces categories of those who interact with mechanisms of law, creating 'the litigant', 'the criminal' – and, most importantly for this chapter, 'the judge', marking them apart from those not immediately before the law. Law defines human rights, but also the humanity or inhumanity of legal subjects, or who is even (un)thinkable as human.[16]

The act of punishing or adjudicating creates both the category of 'the judge' and the possibilities of judging, enabling the individual person to become the judge. The law acts not only 'around, on, within' the body of those disciplined to change their self/soul but also 'around, on, within' the judge to make them a conduit of the power of law while informing and constraining

14 Foucault, *Discipline and Punish*, 29. Michel Foucault, *Discipline and Punish: The Birth of the Prison* (London: Allen Lane, 1977), 29.

15 Butler, *Gender Trouble*, 134–135.

16 Ratna Kapur, "Precarious Desires and Ungrievable Lives: Human Rights and Postcolonial Critiques of Legal Justice," *London Review of International Law* 3, no. 2 (2015): 270.

that which is necessary for that power and role. Butler considers how the judge is created through the performative act of judging, saying:

> though it may appear that the binding power of his works is derived from the force of his will or from a prior authority, the opposite is more true: it is through the citation of the law that the figure of the judge's 'will' is produced and that the 'priority' of textual authority is established.[17]

Thus, for Butler, the performative act of judging creates and recreates the figure and authority of the judge. Each time the judge enacts a law through the citation of prior law, the judge makes that law authoritative. This occurs through the act of treating that law as authoritative and by the judge claiming to judge with the authority of the jurisdictional forces, norms, or persuasive authority of international organisations behind them. Thus, the judge creates the meaning of their role, the meaning of law(s), and the scope of their authority. For law to then become 'law as experienced', it is adopted, even legitimised, and given power through acts not only of the judge or litigants but those who further act upon it, performatively legitimising it, submitting to it, and using it to regularise and discipline themselves and others (directly or through compliance with law's norms).[18]

For the queer judge, the idea that judging, the judicial role, and judicial authority are the product of performative acts creates both possibilities and constraints. By performing queerness in judging – that is, by applying insights from queer theory to the act of judging, the queer judge can decentralise cis-heteronormativity and legitimise the experiences and voices of traditionally marginalised groups. They can create a space to question norms and normalise questioning.

3.3 Constraints on Queer Judging

At the same time, the judicial role is necessarily constrained by both official limits and social constructions relating to the role of the judge and judicial power. The law, including relevant instruments investing the court with authority, delineates the official power and scope of any particular judicial role. The role of the judge and the performance of judging are also constrained by strong normative expectations relating to who can be a judge and how the judge must embody their role. Thus, the queer judge, in their performance of judging, must ensure their performance does not render them 'un-judged' or outside the normative boundaries of the judge construct, where their performance would become 'deviant' and therefore cease to be that of the judge.

17 Butler, *Bodies That Matter*, 171.
18 Ewald, "Norms, Discipline, and the Law," 139–141.

In this regard, the queer judge must enact a form of judicial respectability politics, even though to do so represents a departure from queer theory. To ensure that they maintain their own authority as a judge, as well as the authority of the judiciary generally, the queer judge cannot completely undermine the same cis-heteronormative patriarchal power structures and hierarchies which grant them power. When discussing writing queer alternative judgments, Sharpe has stated that this requirement to simultaneously rely upon judicial norms and traditions for authority, whilst critiquing cis-heteronormativity, means the queer judge 'proceeds into the fray with one hand tied behind one's back'.[19] The queer judge may therefore be critical but not truly radical. By working within existing power structures, their performance of judging can reinforce those very structures. As Smart has pointed out, the law cannot 'provide the solution to the oppression that it celebrates and sustains'.[20]

Paradoxically (queerly?), it is the queer judge's co-option of those power structures (using a position within intensely normative structures to challenge cis-heteronormativity) that may make their critiques of cis-heteronormativity effective. After all, a judicial voice may be effectively heard and authoritatively enforced when the voices of activists or protestors may not gain traction in the corridors of power. Thus, a restricted application of queer method may, in at least a limited way, still work to queer the content of law, even if it will never completely queer the institutions, imposition, or existence of law. The queer judge becomes one part of a spectrum of resistance that may require both insider and outsider agitation to effect social change eventually.[21]

As such, despite the constraints, I argue it is possible to queer the act of judging. The first step, as Sharpe has discussed, would be for the judge to interrogate or reject cis-heteronormativity.[22] However, queerness is more than the mere rejection of cis-heteronormativity. Queerness embodies and articulates the excess, difference, and 'open mesh of possibilities, gaps, overlaps, dissonances and resonances' that Sedgewick identified.[23] The queer judge would therefore be sensitive to the imposition of norms and that which is excess to, made different by, or dissonant with, those norms. They would interrogate those norms, not only where they are cis-heteronormative but also in other areas where norms are not intrinsic to the law, but also where they adhere to schemes of gender, race, disability/ability, and other normative

19 Alex Sharpe, "Queering Judgment: The Case of Gender Identity Fraud," *The Journal of Criminal Law* 81, no. 5 (October 1, 2017): 424.

20 Carol Smart, *Feminism and the Power of Law* (London: Taylor & Francis Group, 1989), 49.

21 Tamsin Phillipa Paige, "Resistance Breeds Contempt" (Deus Ex Machina: Law-Technology-Humanities Conference: Law Literature and Humanities Association of Australasia Conference 2023, Brisbane, 2023).

22 Sharpe, "Queering Judgment," 420.

23 Sedgwick, *Tendencies*, 8.

regimes. In addition to being open to departures from normative thinking, the queer judge would also bring a queer spirit of curiosity, pleasure, and even play to their thinking about the law.[24]

Some reasonably argue that the law, in its processes of regularisation inevitably suppresses diversity in its project of universalisation.[25] Though judging queerly does not disrupt the power structures of law, that does not preclude the use of courts and tribunals to queer cis-heteronormative *concepts* included within the law.[26] As Sedgewick argues in her later work, borrowing from psychoanalytical analysis, queering does not only have to take a critical (what she calls 'paranoid/schizoid') approach but can also take a reparative/depressive position that acknowledges the negative but uses 'middle ranges of agency' where one has 'the ability to be empowered or disempowered without annihilating someone else or being annihilated'.[27] Judging queerly uses that middle range of agency to make change possible, even where existing structures cannot be overthrown. The judge's queerness is not annihilated even when queer judging fails to annihilate repressive power structures. In addition, the queer judge may create a Butlerian performance of judging which challenges the idea that judging must suppress difference in favour of normativity, thereby undercutting existing processes reliant only upon regularisation, and queering the discourse of what it means to *judge*.

3.4 Queer Judging and Reimagining Emotion in the Courtroom

Queer judges may reject parts of the conventional model of judging. The traditional view of judging imagines the imposition of order by 'rational' judgment upon the irrational or chaotic dispute of the less rational (than the judge) parties, reinforcing dualities of rationality – law and order versus irrationality, chaos, and conflict. Such dualities have a long history of gendered application, in which order, rationality, impartiality, intelligence, intellect, active lawfulness, normative humanity, and similar traits are assigned to the cis-masculine, while chaos, irrationality, partiality, foolishness, emotion/instinct, being invisible to law, and abnormality are assigned

24 Dianne Otto, "Introduction: Embracing Queer Curiosity," in *Queering International Law: Possibilities, Alliances, Complicities, Risk*, ed. Dianne Otto (London and New York: Routledge, 2017), 1–11.
25 Wayne Morgan, "Queer Law: Identity, Culture, Diversity, Law," *Australasian Gay and Lesbian Law Journal* 5 (1995): 1.
26 Odette Mazel, "Queer Jurisprudence: Reparative Practice in International Law," *American Journal of International Law* 116 (2022): 10–15.
27 Eve Kosofsky Sedgwick, "Melanie Klein and the Difference Affect Makes," *South Atlantic Quarterly* 106, no. 3 (2007): 632–633.

to those who are feminine, queer or insufficiently masculine. In this duality, the judge must adopt rationality and impartiality to be authoritative – a performance that discursively positions the parties before them as perforce less rational, more partial, and more emotional. Thus, long-established models of judging assume particular types of hegemonic masculinity, in which logic, mental toughness, lack of emotion, and intelligence are all judicial traits.

Acknowledgment that judging does not necessitate rejecting emotion may be part of queering the judicial role. Traditionally, judges have been called upon to reject compassion as a distortion of the judicial role.[28] Emotion generally became suspect for many judges.[29] To banish any semblance of emotion, however, courts have traditionally treated some forms of emotion as rationality rather than emotion. This may include sympathy or fellow feeling for people who are normative and similar to those judges (often, until recently, middle-class white straight men in many jurisdictions, including international law). This exercise of empathy with the experiences of cis-heteronormative white men has historically been necessary for cis-heteronormative male judges to position cis-hetero male experiences, emotions, and habits as reasonable, non-emotive, normative, and central to law's narratives, expectations, and rules. At the same time, they have often decried reasoned decisions and arguments made by law's outsiders as emotional, irrational, or a special pleading.

The queer judge may both acknowledge that emotion already enters decision-making and agree with Nussbaum that compassion is essential to the existence of society.[30] Compassion and related empathy may let the judge see beyond the normative and their own lived experiences to hear those who have less normative lives without rejecting their stories as irrational or unreasonable. They may actively employ empathy for law's 'others' rather than rejecting their experiences as irrational or unlikely. Thus, the queer judge may be paradoxically more neutral in their willingness to consider wider viewpoints than their peers who centre cis-hetero-male-middle-class experiences as 'normal' and reject alternative narratives and experiences based upon little more than their failure to match cis-hetero social norms. In this way, the queer judge removes the fig leaf of 'rationality' or 'normality' from the emotional experiences of their peers.

28 Thomas Hobbes, *Leviathan: Or, The Matter, Forme, & Power of a Common-Wealth Ecclesiasticall and Civill*, Digitisation of 1st edn. (Andrew Crooke, 1651), 195; Dermot Feenan, "Law and Compassion," *International Journal of Law in Context* 13, no. 2 (2017): 134.

29 Sharyn Roach Anleu and Kathy Mack, *Judging and Emotion: A Socio-Legal Analysis* (London: Routledge, 2021).

30 Martha Nussbaum, "Compassion: The Basic Social Emotion," *Social Philosophy and Policy* 13, no. 1 (1996): 27.

3.5 Queer Judging as a Method for Examining Normative Presumptions

Building on the ability to hear narratives beyond the cis-heteronormative traditional stories of law, the queer judge may upend some of the traditional narratives of judging, including that only one outcome in each case is inevitable or natural. Queer judging requires the interrogation of normative statements about social hierarchies, gender roles, family formation, and social norms more generally. By being open to Sedgewick's mesh of possibilities, the queer judge can make normative presumptions explicit and open to question. They may expose the dissonances and resonances of 'law as written' as well as 'law as lived'. By making social norms explicit and being clear that they are merely one social discourse among many, queer judging allows other experiences, including queer life experiences, to become intelligible to law. Applying law and logic to queer litigants in open and neutral ways requires that life experiences and norms within the queer community can be recognised by the court and not constructed in ways which make minority litigants automatically suspect or outside the regimes of law. Although the law is putatively neutral, the queer judge can make it more objective by accepting that queer lives and queer litigants are as equally deserving of legal privileges and protections as cis, hetero, or masculine ones.

As stated previously, the queer judge may not necessarily be a member of the QUILTBAG+ community. One of the editors of this volume, Claerwen O'Hara, has also posited that one may unmoor queerness from being only about the lives of QUILTBAG+ people.[31] To be gender or sexually diverse is not necessary to embrace the possibilities of queer theory. To be straight is not to be incapable of queer thinking. Though being queer themselves may help the queer judge to more easily see instances of cis-heteronormativity, a straight judge may also be alert to the law's gendered and heteronormative discourses and bring a critical and curious mind to the application and making of law. Conversely, a judge who is a member of the QUILTBAG+ community may not fit my model of the queer judge if they have deeply internalised, and, as a result, now replicate and reinforce cis-heteronormativity and homonormativity.

When the queer judge engages in acts such as identifying normative presumptions, treating queer litigants as non-deviant, or bringing critique and curiosity to the law, the judge's performance of judging shifts the epistemological conceptions of *judge* and *judging*. Their performative acts, while being required to remain within constraints that reinforce judicial authority,

31 Claerwen O'Hara, "Consensus and Diversity in the World Trade Organization: A Queer Perspective," *AJIL Unbound* 116 (2022): 32.

may shift our understanding of the judicial role from one that unquestioningly accepts cis-heteronormativity and other oppressive norms to one that can interrogate normative constructions of society. This performance can lead to new constructions of the subject(s) of law and justice including queer and other oppressed groups, and expanding concepts of normative humanity and subjectivity to include those groups. By prioritising empathy, compassion, and justice, the queer judge may reorient courts to focus on just outcomes in an approach which privileges function (granting justice) over form. Though the judge may be enforcing traditional hierarchies (including that of judge, state, or police over litigants), they may also be breaking or bending cis-heteronormative, gendered, or other oppressive hierarchies in ways which may only be done by authoritative insiders.

3.6 *Queer Judging in the Real World*

There are no judges who precisely fit my model of the queer judge in either international or domestic law. However, some judgments and legal developments show how queer judging could operate. At the international level, Antônio Augusto Cançado Trindade is an example of a judge who prioritised humanity and empathy in his work on the Inter-American Court of Human Rights and later in the International Court of Justice.[32] Tribunal members in international people's tribunals, who often 'queer' both the process of judging and its outcomes,[33] come closer to fitting my model, but lack institutional judicial authority. In addition, participants in the Queer Judgments Project,[34] including Lucas Lixinski, whose contribution to this collection discusses his method of queer judging in the chapter "Rewriting Queer Markers of Identity: International Cultural Heritage Law, Criminalisation, and the Other,"[35] also queer judging outside the scope of judicial authority.

The English developments of equity and the law of negligence are arguably examples of queering strict applications of rigid norms to prioritise justice over form, especially Lord Aitkin's reliance on the empathetic 'neighbour principle'.[36] (While some may argue Lord Aitkin was merely applying

32 Patrick Robinson and Danilo B. Garrido Alves, "The Legacy of Antônio Augusto Cançado Trindade to Contemporary International Law," *Leiden Journal of International Law* 36, no. 2 (June 2023): 445–450.

33 Claerwen O'Hara, "In Search of a Queerer Law: Two People's Tribunals in 1976," *Australian Feminist Law Journal* 49, no. 1 (January 2, 2023): 17–38.

34 "Welcome to the Queer Judgments Project," accessed March 22, 2024, www.queerjudgments.org/.

35 Lucas Lixinski, "Rewriting Queer Markers of Identity: International Cultural Heritage Law, Criminalisation, and the Other," this volume.

36 *Donoghue v Stevenson* [1932] UKHL 100; 1932 AC 562. Aitkin J was the English Judge who effectively created the law of negligence in common law countries through his House of Lords decision in this case.

Christian principles of 'care for others', queerness does not require strict ideological boundaries and can include approaches that may be both queering one orthodoxy and simultaneously based in other dominant ideologies or systems of belief, such as Christian doctrine.) As another example, Justice Michael Kirby, the first publicly gay judge on the Australian High Court, challenged notions of masculine homophobia as normative in *Green v R*.[37] In that case, the High Court majority implicitly assumed that it was reasonable and understandable for a straight man to respond with frenzied murderous force to a homosexual advance. Justice Kirby highlighted in his dissent that the majority's reasoning relied upon positioning homophobic straight men as the normative standard of ordinariness in criminal law. Justice Kirby also pointed out that the defence would not be available for women who murdered men making non-violent unwelcome sexual advances. In doing so, he exposed the gendered heteronormativity of the majority reasoning and proposed neutral, non-homophobic, and non-gendered standards for the ordinary person.

4. International Judging Processes and Queer Judging

4.1 *Consensus and Dissensus Decision-Making in International Law*

International courts have two main models of judgment delivery: consensus and dissensus approaches. A consensus process occurs in multi-judge courts which deliver a single judgment arrived at by consensus among all judges. Courts that give consensus judgments include the WTO Appellate Body (prior to it ceasing operation in December 2019), UN human rights bodies (like the Human Rights Committee), and the European Court of Justice.[38] Consensus judgments are also common in domestic courts in civil law countries. Consensus is marked not necessarily by unanimity of reasoning but by the absence of dissent.

Dissensus approaches to judgment delivery, by contrast, allow split judgments, in which the majority judgment is the authoritative decision of the court, but other judges may write and publish a judgment which dissents in whole or in part from the majority judgment. Courts that allow dissenting

37 *Green v R* [1997] HCA 50; (1997) 191 CLR 334.

38 "WTO | Dispute Settlement – Working Procedures for Appellate Review," accessed March 9, 2024, www.wto.org/english/tratop_e/dispu_e/ab_e.htm; Dag Hammarskjöld Library, "Research Guides: UN Human Rights Documentation: Treaty-Based Bodies," *Research Guide* (United Nations. Dag Hammarskjöld Library), accessed March 9, 2024, https://research.un.org/en/docs/humanrights/treaties; "Presentation – Court of Justice of the European Union," *CURIA*, accessed March 9, 2024, http://158.167.241.123:8090/jcms/jcms/Jo2_7024/en/.

opinions may also have cases decided by consensus by the whole bench. A number of international courts use the dissensus system, including the International Court of Justice, the European Court of Human Rights, and the Inter-American Court of Human Rights.[39] This model is also more common in common law jurisdictions and European domestic constitutional courts.

4.2 *Consensus Decision Making and the Queer Judge*

There appears to be little direct interview-based research on the process used in international consensus-based courts to reach decisions, though Claerwen O'Hara and others have examined the effect of consensus decision-making between states in the WTO, consensus decision-making between the quasi-judicial members of the now defunct WTO Appellate Body, and the search for a 'European consensus' among member states in the European Court of Human Rights.[40] At the domestic level, Bricker has also interviewed judges about domestic consensus courts in Germany.[41]

Judges in consensus-requiring courts manage their work and judging activities to maintain good relationships with other judges since they know that good relationships are required to ensure that consensus discussions are effective.[42] Many judges in Bricker's study of consensus in German courts said that informal discussions, for example, over lunch, were critically important to the consensus process, both through discussions of joint cases and also other discussions which created amicable relationships between judges.[43] This fits with Lewis' examination of the WTO Appellate Body members' attempts

39 "Statute of the International Court of Justice," 1 UNTS 993 § (1945); "European Convention on Human Rights," n.d.; "Inter-American Court of Human Rights – Statute," *Inter-American Court of Human Rights – Statute*, accessed March 10, 2024, www.corteidh.or.cr.

40 O'Hara, "Consensus and Diversity in the World Trade Organization: A Queer Perspective,"; Claerwen O'Hara, "Consensus Decision-Making and Democratic Discourse in the General Agreement on Tariffs and Trade 1947 and World Trade Organisation," *London Review of International Law* 9, no. 1 (March 1, 2021): 37–68; Claerwen O'Hara, "Consensus, Difference and Sexuality: Que(e)rying the European Court of Human Rights' Concept of 'European Consensus'," *Law and Critique* 32, no. 1 (2021): 91–114. (2012): 1; Meredith Kolsky Lewis, "The Lack of Dissent in WTO Dispute Settlement," *Journal of International Economic Law* 9, no. 4 (2006): 895–931; Hélène Ruiz Fabri, "The WTO Appellate Body or Judicial Power Unleashed: Sketches from the Procedural Side of the Story," *European Journal of International Law* 27, no. 4 (2016): 1075–1081. Lewis and Ruiz have examined the use of judicial decision-making in the Appellate body of the WTO, while O'Hara concentrates on consensus in the WTO itself.

41 Bricker, "Consensus Decision Making."

42 Hélène Ruiz Fabri, "The WTO Appellate Body or Judicial Power Unleashed: Sketches from the Procedural Side of the Story," *European Journal of International Law* 27, no. 4 (2016): 1079.

43 Bricker, "Consensus Decision Making," 29–31.

to promote collegiality and positive relationships, particularly amongst those who wished to seek re-appointment.[44]

In addition to good judicial relationships, another key factor in achieving consensus is judicial leadership.[45] The consensus process often relies on presiding judges managing relationships with and disputes amongst their judges.[46]

Judges in consensus systems are often also acutely aware that they *have* to reach consensus, and 'therefore they do'.[47] They may decide it is not worth dissenting.[48] Further, Bricker found that judges who did not adopt common processes disagreed routinely with other judges, or failed to comply with established norms of judicial consensus processes may be held in disfavour by other judges.[49]

Secrecy is a strong feature of consensus-based court systems, whereby many courts neither record nor publish information about the negotiation process that led to the consensus decision or the identity of the rapporteur who prepared the judgment.[50] The public cannot be aware of individual judges' views or initial disagreement amongst judges. In consensus-based bodies, this secrecy and presentation of a single decision of the court without a record of disagreement is considered to strengthen the authority of the decision and the clarity of the law.[51]

For the queer judge, consensus decision processes create both opportunities and constraints. Where the process of consensus judging results in a single, authoritative statement from the court that includes queer reasoning, such as an embrace of difference and a disruption of cis-heteronormativity, as a result of the queer judge's efforts, then a queer perspective may end up being treated as authoritative. This would be a unique space in which QUILTBAG+ experiences are not treated as 'other' or as legally unintelligible.

44 Lewis, "The Lack of Dissent in WTO Dispute Settlement," 907–908, 913–915.
45 Bricker, "Consensus Decision Making," 29; Lewis, "The Lack of Dissent in WTO Dispute Settlement," 907.
46 Bricker, "Consensus Decision Making," 31.
47 Bricker, "Consensus Decision Making," 31.
48 Lewis, "The Lack of Dissent in WTO Dispute Settlement," 912.
49 Bricker, "Consensus Decision Making," 31.
50 Bricker, "Consensus Decision Making," 28.
51 Bricker, "Consensus Decision Making," 27; Dieter Grimm, "Some Remarks on the Use of Dissenting Opinions in Continental Europe," *Global Constitutionalism* (2008): I–1; John Henry Merryman and Rogelio Pérez-Perdomo, "The Civil Law Tradition, 3ª," 2007; Mathias Siems, "Comparative Law," 44–47. See also the express requirement for the former WTO Appellate Body contained in Article 17(11), Understanding on Rules and Procedures Governing the Settlement of Disputes, Marrakesh Agreement Establishing the World Trade Organisation, Annex 2, opened for signature 15 April 1994, 1869 UNTS 401 (entered into force 1 January 1995).

Even if the queer judge is not able to gain consensus from the other judges for a judgment that disrupts cis-heteronormativity explicitly, there are still spaces for the queer judge to influence the consensus process. The soft, non-hierarchical, non-official power of persuasion that is often seen as feminine, non-masculine, or queer is crucial to consensus decision-making. In a consensus-based model, other judges on the bench *must* engage with the queer judge. When each judge is aware that they *must* reach a consensus,[52] they are also aware that they must engage with the arguments of the queer judge, at least until an agreement is reached or they can persuade the queer judge of the validity of their own position. This is a unique opportunity for education and persuasion. Where other judges may not be aware of their own biases or have interrogated their own positions, being forced to grapple with alternative views, QUILTBAG+ life experiences, and/or challenges to cis-heteronormativity may help them to come to a richer understanding of both law and lived possibilities outside of cis-heteronormativity, producing a queerer judgment.

However, being marked as an outsider or as someone who will always be an educational resource to their colleagues may distance the queer judge from their colleagues in ways that other judges do not experience. To always be othered or expected to educate others can be exhausting for members of oppressed groups. It may also position them as the outsider or their knowledge as being only or primarily about minority status, rather than the queer judge being respected for legal subject matter expertise. This may make the queer judge's role more difficult at times when it is their doctrinal knowledge rather than their queerness upon which they wish to rely. It may also lead to them being taken less seriously by judicial colleagues, advocates, and international or national leaders.

Even more concerningly, the need to maintain relationships and reach a consensus may act to silence the queer judge. The need to maintain working and friendly relationships with judges with strongly cis-heteronormative views may require the queer judge to 'closet' their critiques of cis-heteronormativity and the gendering of laws. They may feel strong normative pressure to acquiesce to majority cis-heteronormative arguments or decisions. Their influence may be muted or silenced, in the same way that queers without strong social support may be muted, silenced, and closeted to allow them to maintain safety or employment.[53] They may thus be thrust into a judicial closet.

The identity or approach of the judicial rapporteur (that is, the one who writes the judgment) in a consensus court or tribunal may also affect the effectiveness of the queer judge. The rapporteur's pre-hearing consideration or

52 Bricker, "Consensus Decision Making," 31.

53 See, for instance, Eleanor Wilkinson, "The Emotions Least Relevant to Politics? Queering Autonomous Activism," *Emotion, Space and Society* 2, no. 1 (2009): 36–43.

draft judgments will usually guide the other judges on the issues relevant to the case since the rapporteur will select and highlight key issues in the case.[54] The rapporteur will also frame the discussion around those issues and their interpretation of the law and social norms relevant to those issues.[55] The selection of issues may, of course, be guided strongly by the arguments of litigants. However, the acceptance or interrogation of cis-heteronormativity and gendered assumptions in the litigants' arguments and judicial responses, or the acceptance or rejection of cis-heteronormativity in the interpretation of the law, will depend on the framing of issues by the rapporteur and in the subsequent judicial discussions as the court moves toward consensus. Where the queer judge is rapporteur, they may have substantially more scope to encourage their judicial colleagues to see beyond cis-heteronormative assumptions simply through their selection of focus for drafts or discussions. Where other judicial colleagues are the rapporteur, they may not even see how socially normative discourses may affect their framing of argument or interpretation of law. The queer judge may have to disrupt judicial harmony to seek a different framing.

Space for queerness of style or even acceptance of a QUILTBAG+ judge's life experience may depend strongly on the style of judicial management within court systems. Where judicial managers may make space for greater diversity and normative challenge as part of the consensus process, queer judges may have more freedom to queer the law. On the other hand, if judicial managers are interventionist in the consensus process and strongly committed to existing cis-heteronormative interpretations of the law, the queer judge may have little space to interrogate norms, challenge cis-heteronormativity or champion QUILTBAG+ concerns.

The queer judge who too strongly objects to existing norms of judging or law may become like the unpopular judge in Bricker's study: someone who is 'no longer working in that senate', possibly due to their unwillingness to comply with the work practices of other judges.[56] Like many queers who must mute their queerness when in straight company, the queer judge may need to practice respectability or remain closeted altogether, either in their sexuality, gender or ideas, rather than risk disrupting relationships that rely on lunchroom camaraderie and ease of negotiation to allow a court to be effective. In this way, the experience of the queer judge may mirror that of women in law who adopt or comply with legal hegemonic masculinity practices to achieve success.

54 Silje Synnøve Lyder Hermansen, "Building Legitimacy: Strategic Case Allocations in the Court of Justice of the European Union," *Journal of European Public Policy* 27, no. 8 (2020): 1217.

55 Hermansen, "Building Legitimacy: Strategic Case Allocations in the Court of Justice of the European Union," 1217.

56 Bricker, "Consensus Decision Making."

Even if the queer judge does not become a judicial outsider, they may find their voice and concerns effectively silenced in a system which requires them to reach a consensus to ensure the functioning of their court. Any disagreement ultimately risks fracturing relationships that must be conserved to successfully sway outcomes in other cases. To maintain disagreement does nothing but delay judgment. As Bricker reports, one judge said, 'in the end, "it is worthless to try to cause disagreement or be disagreeable because there is no way to make it public"'.[57]

This silencing has a further effect. The apparently unchallenged consensus means that the public does not see the concerns of the queer judge or their challenges to or departures from cis-heteronormativity if their judicial colleagues refuse to include those ideas in the judgment. Queers may see only reiteration of cis-heteronormativity in law. At worst, the judicial closet is locked from the inside, and outsiders do not see any of the queer possibilities of the law.

4.3 *Dissensus Decision-Making and Queer Judging*

Dissensus decision-making presents a different set of challenges for the queer judge. Dissensus systems may still have strong social norms and groups of judges that seek some level of consensus. To the extent that consensus is sought amongst judges, the features of consensus judging may still operate in dissensus systems. Queer judges may have some of the same opportunities to engage with their judicial colleagues as rapporteurs or colleagues who can educate their peers in discussions of potential joint judgments. However, dissensus-allowing systems may have additional difficulties and opportunities.

Judicial systems that allow dissents and separate judgments give queer judges a space to explicitly and publicly address cis-heteronormative approaches to the law and develop clear alternatives, even where their judicial colleagues refuse to consider such issues. In doing so, even if their dissent does not directly become part of the law, they reassure readers that at least one member of a court is aware of queer issues and is questioning cis-heteronormativity. Dissents may also have a longer-term persuasive effect.[58] Dissent reasoning may become persuasive within its own court over time and eventually be adopted in later majority decisions.[59] Even if not adopted in its own court system, reasoning in dissents may still have the potential to persuade governments and international organisations.

57 Bricker, "Consensus Decision Making," 31.
58 Lewis, "Dissent as Dialectic," 14.
59 Lewis, "Dissent as Dialectic," 14–15.

Where other judges may require a queer judge to comply with existing cis-heteronormative presumptions to allow a judgment in a consensus-based system, the possibility of dissent means minority positions are not completely closeted from the public marketplace of ideas. Rather, like a participant in a pride parade, the queer judge has a space for explicit queerness of ideas and expression, even if the majority exclude those ideas from mainstream representation. The queer judge may also hold other judges to account since lawyers and the public may see alternative judicial reasoning, allowing them to question why the majority of judges espouse unjust cis-heteronormative or gendered applications of the law.

The act of dissenting itself may be an act of queering. By refusing to closet dissent based on rejections of cis-heteronormativity and other normative orthodoxies, the dissenting queer judge holds space for the idea that law itself, like queerness, can't be made to signify monolithically. By being the outsider to a majority judgment, the queer judge performs judging as the creation of a space where differences can be tolerated and celebrated, giving new meanings to the act of judging – even if that changing Butlerian performance must retain other features of standard judicial performances to maintain legitimacy.

Like the pride parade participant, the queer judge's ability to parade dissent has all the queer risks of being seen as deviant and non-serious. The calling out of cis-heteronormativity in a judgment risks being seen as merely a 'special interest' outside the law, especially if it is from a judge who not only draws on insights from queer theory but who is a member of the QUILTBAG+ community. Like other claims for justice from law's outsiders, it may be seen as a special pleading, seeking exceptional favours, since it does not apply to the presumed normative human; the cis-gender white Western heterosexual male.

In arguing against cis-heteronormativity, the queer judge, like queers more generally, may be seen as a threat. While the queer judge may be able to embrace the discomfort of destabilising norms and the immense possibilities of queerness, their readers may be deeply threatened by what feels like destabilisation of safety in the form of law, norms, and order. Since their arguments destabilise the putative neutrality of cis-heteronormative patriarchy, those who rely upon that framework may project their own discomfort on the queer judge to claim that it is the queer judge (not them) who is emotional, irrational, or biased. They may see the queer judge's actual impartiality (in not privileging cis-heteronormativity or treating it as neutral) as a special interest claim.

Being seen as making special interest claims may threaten the queer judge's ability to perform the judicial role more generally. Being perceived as biased or non-serious will generally reduce the authority of a queer judge and potentially also their court and the judicial system as a whole. To perform judging and to incorporate queer perspectives, the queer judge must, therefore, generally ensure that they are meticulous and impeccably rigorous in their application of the law. Their questioning of orthodoxy must generally be done with care and with a clearly unquestionable use of legal reasoning and legal praxis to maintain their judicial authority. To do this, the queer judge must often 'out-judge' other judges, acting as a model minority member who is even better than their peers at the practice of judging.

However, no matter how brilliant a dissent may be, it can still be ignored. Unlike in consensus-based systems, majority judges are not forced to engage with the views of dissenting judgments. They can maintain cis-heteronormative discourses without having to incorporate minority views to reach consensus. They can exclude minority judges from decision-making processes, particularly informal processes of the sort that Bricker found so important to the consensus processes. Thus, by having public exposure to their ideas, the queer judge may paradoxically have less traction within their judicial community.

Dissensus decision-making can, unfortunately, also provide a space to attack queer judging from a dissent. In the 2021 *Vicky Hernandez* decision, the Inter-American Court of Human Rights found that, since the relevant convention was a living document that clearly included references to gender diversity, then:

> in the sphere of application of the Inter-American Convention for the Prevention, Punishment and Eradication of Violence against Women, there is also a reference to situations of gender-based violence against trans women, as in this case.[60]

Unfortunately, Judge Elizabeth Odio Benito wrote a partial dissent in this case, which denied the womanhood of Vicky Hernandez because she was a trans woman.[61] Based strongly on ideas promulgated by trans-exclusionary radical feminists (TERFs), Judge Odio Benito argued strenuously that the Inter-American Convention for the Prevention Punishment and Eradication of Violence against Women[62] did not apply to trans women as women because sex and gender are inextricably entwined. For Odio Benito, gender identity is something different from her biologically-based sex/gender nexus. She stated that since gender is the basis of patriarchal oppression, it is inextricably related to physical form, and the female gender is necessarily limited to cisgender women due to that history of gender-based oppression.[63] This

60 Judgment, *Vicky Hernández et al. v Honduras*, Case No. 422, Inter-Am. Ct. H.R. (ser. C) 26 March 2021.

61 *Hernández v Honduras*.

62 Inter-American Convention on the Prevention, Punishment, and Eradication of Violence Against Women, opened for signature 9 June 1994, 33 I.L.M. 1534 (1994) (entered into force 5 March 1995).

63 *Hernández v Honduras*.

reflects transphobic rhetoric often used by anti-trans and trans-exclusionary radical 'feminist' hate groups.[64] It seems to be a misunderstanding of research dating back to the 1980s, which divides sex (biological features), gender (innate sense of self within society's construction of gendered roles), and gender role (social role) such that a trans woman's gender can be female, even if she was assigned male at birth.[65] The use of dissents to continue to promote cis-heteronormative oppressive discourses and to oppose the queering of law is an ongoing risk of dissensus decision-making, even where queer judges can persuade many of their peers to re-examine cis-heteronormative thinking.

5. Conclusion

Judges who embody and enact queerness within the judicial role will change the performative act of judging. Embracing that change will not only allow recognition of QUILTBAG+ lives but also promote greater justice in the legal system. While queers have traditionally been positioned as social outsiders, judicial queers must work within the hierarchical and normative systems of existing judiciaries to disrupt cis-heternormativity and generate legal change.

There is no single measure of successful queer judging, as queerness is, by its nature, illimitable and everchanging. Thus, it is difficult to say whether a queer judge may be more successful in queering systems of consensus or dissensus decision-making. Arguably, the queer judge may make space for themselves, and for queer thinking, in either system. Within both, it is possible for the queer judge to challenge cis-heteronormativity from their peers, the litigants, and society more broadly. Both also allow for applications of law that may be destabilising for systems that privilege cis-hetero- or homonormativity.

Similarly, both consensus and dissensus methods of judging have the potential to 'other' or closet queerness. To maintain judicial authority, the queer judge must accept the legitimacy of judicial authority itself, including its hierarchical power, its imposition on litigants, and its role in creating the normative structures of 'law as experienced'. The queer judge must also perforce accept the legitimacy of laws which impose oppressions, including those which explicitly 'other' or oppress the QUILTBAG+ community. Consensus systems may enact restrictions through the need to maintain judicial peer relationships with those who oppose or are indifferent to queerness. They may

64 Ruth Pearce, Sonja Erikainen and Ben Vincent, "TERF Wars: An Introduction," *The Sociological Review* 68, no. 4 (2020): 677–698, 679–680; Tamsin Phillipa Paige and Joanne Stagg, "Queer Approaches to International Adjudication." Note, I placed 'feminist' in previous quotes since many TERF groups espouse sex essentialist ideas rejected by most feminist theorists.

65 *Hernández v Honduras*; Candace West and Don H. Zimmerman, "Doing Gender," *Gender & Society* 1, no. 2 (1987): 125–151.

also erase queer thinking by never making it part of the public record. At the same time, dissensus systems, while making it easier for queer thinking to be publicly articulated, may make it easier for the same queer articulation to be sidelined or reduced to mere spectacle. Such queer spectacles may function as a contrast to, or boundary for, cisgender heterosexuality, which may paradoxically reinforce the very cis-heteronormativity that it seeks to displace.

Thus, while there is a place for the queer judge to make change from within judicial systems, the need for queer activism and critique of the sort displayed by the other authors of this volume remains vital to push queer judges away from homonormative complacency and into spaces of more radical forms of queerness.

Part 4

Queering Ourselves

Experimenting with Genre in Legal Academia

Chapter 11

Repairing (the) International Law (Conference)

The Affordances of Theatre

Danish Sheikh[1]

1. Introduction

How can theatre assist in the project of queering international law? What follows is a brief reflection that unfurls this question across three intersecting threads.

The first of these picks up repair as an ethos that might inform ways of queering and practicing law. The second thread considers how *Contempt*, a theatrical production that I wrote and first performed in 2017, might serve as a way of conducting repair-work in relation to the law. Finally, I linger within a rehearsed reading of *Contempt* as part of the Queering International Law 2.0 workshop, which served as the precursor to this edited collection and its sibling collection, *Queer Encounters with International Law: Lives, Communities, Subjectivities*. Thinking about *Contempt* in the context of an academic workshop allows me to consider some of the affordances offered by the theatrical form in terms of practicing repair.

2. Repair

In 1995, a year after HIV-related deaths became the leading cause of mortality in American adults, Eve Kosofsky Sedgwick delivered a lecture[2] – which would eventually become a widely circulated essay[3] – that outlined her turn to what she called 'reparative reading'. At the peak of this pandemic, Sedgwick

1 I am grateful to Tamsin Phillipa Paige and Claerwen O'Hara for their excellent feedback on an earlier draft of this essay and to Dianne Otto for sparking the idea of incorporating a theatrical performance into the *Queering International Law 2.0* (*QIL 2.0*) conference. I am also grateful to Di and my other reader-performers at *QIL 2.0*: Juliana Santos De Carvalho, Laura-Jane Maher, Emily Jones, Odette Mazel, and Warisa Ongsupankul.

2 Ellis Hanson, "The Future's Eve: Reparative Reading after Sedgwick," *South Atlantic Quarterly* 110, no. 1 (2011): 101–119.

3 Eve Kosofsky Sedgwick, "Paranoid Reading and Reparative Reading, or, You're So Paranoid, You Probably Think This Essay Is About You," in *Touching Feeling: Affect, Pedagogy, Performativity*, ed. Eve Kosofsky Sedgwick (Durham: Duke University Press, 2003), 123.

DOI: 10.4324/9781032645339-15

had a conversation with the activist-scholar Cindy Patton that gave her pause. Speculation was rife at that moment about the possible origins of the virus that it might have been engineered in some way and was spread deliberately as a method of government control. Sedgwick asked Patton about her thoughts on the possible natural history of HIV. Patton's response: even if it were clear that the virus was a conspiracy, even if it was established that it was deployed to target gay men and drug users, that it proved their lives were held cheap –

> 'what would we know then that we don't already know?'[4]

For Sedgwick, this exchange represented some of the limitations of dominant forms of critical theoretical enquiry. The critique was often charged with an affective stance of paranoia.[5] Here, the critic's training attuned them towards discovering a range of harms in the texts they read and the world they inhabited. Sedgwick's contributions to queer theory up to this point had drawn upon and refined paranoid forms of enquiry, notably providing tools for deconstructing assumptions about gender and sexuality, which demonstrated the pervasive mechanisms of homophobia.[6] These tools unearthed crucial insights that animated queer activist struggles across the 80s and early 90s.[7] But then, as this exchange from 1995 tells us, the dominance of these critical tools began to constrain other potential lines of enquiry.

Sedgwick began to explore what these other lines of enquiry might be by elaborating on a project of reparative reading. The reparative impulse is one through which queer persons succeed in extracting sustenance from the objects of a culture whose avowed desire has been not to sustain them.[8] Through engaging in a practice of reparative reading, a critic could find unexpected, hopeful resources in the text they were engaging with.

Sedgwick's work on the reparative has circulated widely in literary criticism and queer theory in the United States, its two key reference points. It has also found resonances across various disciplines, including international relations,[9] historiography,[10] cultural studies,[11] psychology,[12] and legal

4 Sedgwick, "Paranoid Reading," 123.
5 Sedgwick, "Paranoid Reading," 123.
6 Eve Kosofsky Sedgwick, *Epistemology of the Closet* (Berkeley: University of California Press, 2008).
7 Hannah McCann and Whitney Monaghan, *Queer Theory Now: From Foundations to Futures* (London: Bloomsbury Academic, 2022).
8 McCann and Monaghan, *Queer Theory Now*, 150.
9 Rahul Rao, *Out of Time* (Oxford: Oxford University Press, 2020).
10 Anjali Arondekar, *For the Record: On Sexuality and the Colonial Archive in India* (Durham: Duke University Press, 2009).
11 Mireille Rosello, *The Reparative in Narratives* (Liverpool: Liverpool University Press, 2010).
12 Eduard Moreno-Gabriel and Katherine Johnson, "Affect and the Reparative Turn: Repairing Qualitative Analysis?" *Qualitative Research in Psychology* 17, no. 1 (2019): 98.

theory.[13] More recently, legal scholars have engaged with Sedgwick's work to consider how reparative readings might inform the analysis of legal texts[14] as well as queer engagements with the law.[15]

Michael Warner argues that reparative reading, as set out by Sedgwick, isn't so much a structured program of reading or a method as it is '(principled?) avoidance of method'.[16] In a more recent essay, David Kurnick draws our attention to the fact that Sedgwick's essay gives no concrete examples of how a reparative reading of a text might differ from a paranoid one.[17] These criticisms reflect a shared anxiety about the difficulty in performing reparative reading. They sit adjacent to another set of critiques about the solipsism of reparative reading. These include the notion of repair as a solitary enterprise,[18] as well as concerns about its implication in colonial, settler-colonial, and imperialist histories.[19]

Instead of attempting to lay out a structured program of reparative reading, I have suggested elsewhere that we might better approach repair as an ethos.[20] As Shane Chalmers and Sundhya Pahuja note in the *Routledge Handbook of International Law and Humanities*, an ethos 'denotes shared ways of doing things',[21] with an emphasis on the scholar's practical ethical positioning. Besides unmooring repair from the programmatic notion of a method, understanding repair as ethos allows us to think of it as a potentially collective act. A reparative ethos suggests that we might do repair better if we are able to conduct repair-work together. Paying attention to Sedgwick's reparative ethos allows us to consider how she trains herself and her readers

13 Brenda Cossman, "Queering Queer Legal Studies: An Unreconstructed Ode to Eve Sedgwick (and Others)," *Critical Analysis of Law* 6, no. 1 (2019): 16.

14 Janet Halley, "New Directions in Law and Literature," in *Paranoia, Feminism, Law*, eds. Bernadette Myler and Elizabeth Anker (Oxford: Oxford University Press, 2017).

15 Odette Mazel, "The Texture of 'Lives Lived with Law': Methods for Queering International Law," *Australian Feminist Law Journal* 49, no. 1 (2023): 71, 5; See also, Claerwen O'Hara, "In Search of a Queerer Law: Two People's Tribunals in 1976," *Australian Feminist Law Journal* 49, no. 1 (2023): 17. O'Hara explores 'alternative, queerer legal possibilities' in this paper in a manner that resonates with the techniques employed by practitioners of repair.

16 Michael Warner, "Uncritical Reading," in *Polemic: Critical or Uncritical*, ed. Jane Gallop (New York: Routledge, 2004), 18.

17 David Kurnick, "A Few Lies: Queer Theory and Our Method Melodramas," *ELH* 87, no. 2 (2020): 349.

18 See Loveday Hodson, "Queer Edens: Visions of Living with Human Rights," in this volume's sibling book, *Queer Encounters with International Law: Lives, Communities, Subjectivities*, eds. Tamsin Phillipa Paige and Claerwen O'Hara (Abingdon: Routledge, 2025).

19 Patricia Rachael Stuelke, *The Ruse of Repair: US Neoliberal Empire and the Turn from Critique* (Durham: Duke University Press, 2021).

20 Danish Sheikh, "Staging Repair," *Law Text Culture* 25, no. 1 (2021): 144–177.

21 Shane Chalmers and Sundhya Pahuja, "Introduction: Practice, Craft and Ethos: Inheriting a Tradition," in *Routledge Handbook of International Law and the Humanities*, eds. Shane Chalmers and Sundhya Pahuja (Oxford: Routledge, 2021).

to practice repair. These trainings include: noticing queer practice and lived experience, including the scholar's own experiences, and drawing out learnings for critical scholarship from watching these practices;[22] an attentiveness to affective responses to the materials that the scholar works with;[23] and building queer community by identifying a range of varied sources and reading practices, and by placing them in conversation with each other.[24]

One of the notable ways in which Sedgwick attempts to practice repair is by playfully employing different genres, such as poetry[25] and memoir,[26] to express a scholarly argument. If the orientation of paranoid critique is towards unearthing or uncovering something harmful within the text,[27] Sedgwick's genre transgressions allow her to occupy a different textual relation: that of placing ideas *beside* each other.[28] Something is loosened with this kind of orientation, allowing 'life, loves and ideas' to 'sit freely, for a while, on the palm of the open hand'.[29]

In the next section, I introduce you to a genre experiment of mine that assisted me in conducting repair.

3. Contempt

The impulse to repair emerges in the wake of disrepair. Something is broken, and the repair-worker attempts to mend it. To do repair well, it is helpful to start by identifying the thing that has broken.

My play *Contempt* was written as a response to a judicial decision in December 2013. That month, the Indian Supreme Court ruled that the colonial sodomy law, which had been used to persecute queer persons in India since the inception of the Penal Code in 1860, was constitutionally legitimate.[30] The judges maintained that lesbian, gay, bisexual, and transgender (LGBT) persons constituted a 'miniscule minority' such that even if their 'so-called rights were affected', the numbers were not enough to justify the invalidation of a law.

A number of things broke with this ruling.

22 Chalmers and Pahuja, "Introduction," 149.
23 Eve Kosofsky Sedgwick, "Melanie Klein and the Difference Affect Makes," *South Atlantic Quarterly* 106, no. 3 (2007): 625.
24 Eve Kosofsky Sedgwick, ed., *Novel Gazing: Queer Readings in Fiction* (Durham: Duke University Press, 1997).
25 Eve Kosofsky Sedgwick, *Fat Art, Thin Art* (Durham: Duke University Press, 1994).
26 Eve Kosofsky Sedgwick, *A Dialogue on Love* (Boston: Beacon Press, 2000).
27 Rita Felski, *The Limits of Critique* (Chicago: The University of Chicago Press, 2015).
28 Eve Kosofsky Sedgwick, *Touching Feeling: Affect, Pedagogy, Performativity* (Durham: Duke University Press, 2003).
29 Sedgwick, *Touching Feeling*, 3.
30 *Suresh Kumar Koushal v Naz Foundation*, Civil Appeal No. 10972 of 2013 (Supreme Court of India, 2013).

For one, the Supreme Court reversed a celebrated 2009 ruling of the Delhi High Court.[31] The 2009 decision, which had declared the sodomy law to be unconstitutional, transcended the domain of the courtroom and sparked public imagination. Queer pride parades and rallies would invoke choice phrases from the decision,[32] even as legal scholars considered how it might refigure the broader domains of equality and anti-discrimination law in India.[33]

If the Supreme Court's decision shattered these dreams, lawyers also suggested that it tore the fabric of constitutional law. As argued in subsequent petitions, the Court misconstrued and wrongly applied key constitutional tenets,[34] arriving at a decision that was so poorly reasoned it threatened the integrity of the institution.[35]

As a queer lawyer myself, this decision broke my faith in the possibilities of law. In the weeks and months that followed, I found myself returning to the transcripts of the hearings that led to the ruling. Across 500-odd pages, those transcripts relayed the back and forth between the large team of lawyers and the two-judge bench over a six-week period. I had been in the courtroom through these proceedings; I had watched it all. Returning to the transcripts was a painful but necessary process in trying to make sense of this moment. What had gone wrong in the courtroom? Why would the judges not listen? What else could have been done? What else could have happened?

There were multiple critical genres within which these questions could be explored, and I attempted many of them: the journal article,[36] the essay,[37] the NGO report,[38] and the blog post.[39] Each of these helped me in thinking through the decision, even as none of them provided fresh insight into some of the questions I had been grappling with. The first glimmer of that insight

31 *Naz Foundation v Union of India*, 160 Delhi Law Times 277 (High Court of Delhi, 2009).

32 Arvind Narrain, and Alok Gupta, eds., *Law like Love: Queer Perspectives on Law* (New Delhi: Yoda Press, 2011).

33 Tarunabh Khaitan, "Reading Swaraj into Article 15: A New Deal for all Minorities," *NUJS Law Review* 2 (2009): 419–432.

34 *Revision Petition in the matter of Suresh Kumar Koushal v Naz Foundation* (2014) 1 SCC 1, accessed February 1, 2024, https://orinam.net/377-supreme-court-review-petition-process-explained/.

35 Siddharth Narrain, "We Dissent," *Kafila Online* (December 12, 2013).

36 Danish Sheikh, "The Road to Decriminalization: Litigating India's Anti-Sodomy Law," *Yale Human Rights and Development Law Journal* 16, no. 1 (2014).

37 Danish Sheikh and Siddharth Narrain, "Fundamental Rights and Wrongs of the Supreme Court," *Economic and Political Weekly* 48, no. 52 (December 2013).

38 International Commission of Jurists, *"Unnatural Offences": Obstacles to Justice in India Based on Sexual Orientation and Gender Identity* (February 2017), accessed June 30, 2024, https://www.icj.org/india-end-rampant-discrimination-in-the-justice-system-based-on-sexual-orientation-and-gender-identity/#:~:text=The%2060%2Dpaged%20report%20%E2%80%9CUnnatural,imputed%20sexual%20orientation%20and%20gender.

39 Danish Skeikh, "Curing the Koushal Malady," *Oxford Human Rights Hub*, April 30, 2014, https://ohrh.law.ox.ac.uk/curing-the-koushal-malady/.

emerged as I continued to parse through the transcripts of the hearings. Repetitions in argumentation became clearer, patterns of dialogue began to form, and dramatic themes emerged.

The text that emerged from this process was a theatrical rendition of the Supreme Court hearings. I edited the numerous weeks of transcripts into four short scenes, each following a different line of argument made before the judges, tracing it to the point that it failed. The dramaturgical attention I paid allowed me to note the numerous points at which the judges deflected arguments about the impact of colonial sodomy on queer persons, constantly pushing the lawyers to return, in Sisyphean fashion, to the text of the law. At this point, *Contempt* was an experiment, but an experiment rooted largely in paranoid critique. In using the genre affordances provided by theatre to get at the heart of what had gone wrong in the Court, I was ultimately still trying to uncover and prove a thing I knew to be true – that the judges did not want to listen to queer voices, that they did not consider queer persons equal citizens.

Parallel to this process, I had been conducting a different kind of genre experiment. I had been rewriting the affidavits presented in the Court that testified to the impact of the sodomy law on queer persons. I'd found that these affidavits were weighed down by the formal confines of legal language, and I wanted to see how these queer lives could be narrated differently before the law. I'd also been exploring stories that had not been brought before the Court because they did not neatly fit into the arguments generated by the lawyers. 'Exploring' is an important word here – I was writing my way through uncharted terrain, uncertain of what I wanted to find. Jill Stauffer observes that reparative reading entails an openness to surprise and to the possibility of being unsettled.[40] That openness is also what might allow for the improvisation of new responses to injustice that might otherwise not have been fully comprehended by pre-existing remedies. My genre experiment was cultivating this aspect of repair's ethos.[41]

At this point, the play that I was writing already made the violence of the courtroom visible. I did not want to leave it there, however. Yes, something lawful had been broken, and yes, it was important to bear witness. But I didn't want to perpetuate the silence that the Court had attempted to impose. I wanted to talk back, and I wanted to do this not through pointing out the Court's silencing tactics.

Eventually, I altered my orientation to the text. I took the transcripts from these hearings, and I placed them *beside* the queer voices that had gone unheard. I juxtaposed the Supreme Court hearings with the stories of queer Indians that I had been exploring and rewriting. The placement of the stories echoed the courtroom proceedings, where affidavits were read out to the judges, testifying

40 Jill Stauffer, *Ethical Loneliness: The Injustice of Not Being Heard* (New York: Columbia University Press, 2015).

41 Stauffer, *Ethical Loneliness*, 70.

to the impact of the sodomy law in the everyday lives of queer individuals. In my play, the affidavits were celebratory accounts of resisting the law.

In the years since I have written it, *Contempt* has been performed at largely two different kinds of venues. One set of performances has been conducted within theatrical spaces, directed by theatre practitioners other than myself. Another set of performances have made their way into university spaces, largely law schools, mostly directed by me.[42] Both these kinds of performances have involved extensive rehearsals with actors at varying levels of expertise. Most of these performances have been staged in India.

Beyond these performances, *Contempt* has also been realised through rehearsed readings. These have often been conducted at university spaces and, in one instance, within a library. The relative ease of putting up a reading as opposed to a full-fledged show has allowed *Contempt* to travel beyond India, with performances in Colombo, Kathmandu, London, Melbourne, and Tilburg. It has also allowed the play to enter spaces that are not traditionally within the domain of theatre.

The reading that took place at *Queering International Law 2.0* fell within this third category. Performances are informed by their context. A text means something different as it travels across different spaces. What did it mean to perform this show in this space at this time? I will now go on to consider what bringing this play within the context of an academic conference might have offered.

4. Queering the Conference

Deakin Downton. Level 12 of a multi-tower office complex in Collins Street, Melbourne. Everything glistens in this building, including the touchpads that replace regular buttons outside the elevators.

We are clustered around multiple tables in the conference room that hosts the Queering International Law 2.0 workshop. Everyone wears a face mask except for the performers, who sit at a table towards the center of the room, closest to the 'stage'. Five chairs on the stage, empty at the start, are to be filled gradually as the play proceeds.

Emily Jones steps up centerstage. 'I love you', she reads. 'These words come way too easily for me'.

I register these words as their writer, as a fellow performer, and as an audience member.

The performance of Contempt *has begun.*

Queering International Law 2.0 (*QIL 2.0*), as the name suggests, was a follow-up to a 2015 gathering in Melbourne. The initial *Queering*

42 I describe these performances in greater detail in the following essay: Danish Sheikh, "Performing Contempt," *Indent*, November 13, 2019, www.indent.in/present-continuous/2019/11/13/contempt.

International Law conference was convened by Dianne Otto. The conference enabled the coalescing of a queer legal community across the international law academy, leading to, amongst other things, a significant edited collection.[43]

As I have noted in the previous section, to do repair well requires us to start by acknowledging what has broken. The Call for Papers for *QIL 2.0* was framed by its convenors, Tamsin Phillipa Paige and Claerwen O'Hara, through an identification of the range of queer disappointments in international law since the 2015 gathering. Paige and O'Hara noted developments ranging from the rise of a transphobic 'feminist' movement that justifies exclusion through reliance on international law alongside global crises such as the pandemic, where public health responses continue to reify the monogamous, coupled unit. At the same time, the convenors opened up the space for conducting repair-work, asking participants to explore the 'possibilities, alliances, complicities, and risks' within international law's future.[44]

As the papers in this edited collection will demonstrate, the gathering brought together scholars from a range of geographies and positionalities. Panels followed conventions held within the conference genre: short paper presentations, commented upon by a discussant and then opened to audience questions for further discussion. The rehearsed reading of *Contempt* was an attempt by the convenors to play with the conference format. This, too, might be considered an attempt to do repair-work in relation to the conduct of the international law conference. Schramm, Santos de Carvalho et al. note that the exclusionary nature of academic spaces can often be exacerbated by the configurations of academic conferences that 'promote a division between the presenter and the audience, fostering an adversary logic of academic exchange'.[45] Reflecting on their attempts to push back against these combative modes of conference-ing through queering an international law conference, they describe their attempts to focus on mutual exchange and pleasure within the site of the conference. This endeavour includes attempts at changing the physical configuration of the conference to enable conversation between speaker and audience, as well as troubling the boundaries between the critical and creative through making for sharing art pieces, performances, and manifestos. Through programming *Contempt* within the slot of a conference panel (as opposed to an evening post-official-programme slot),

43 Dianne Otto, ed., *Queering International Law: Possibilities, Alliances, Complicities, Risks* (Abingdon and New York: Routledge, 2018).

44 Tamsin Phillipa Paige and Claerwen O'Hara, "Call for Papers: Queering International Law 2.0," *Australian and New Zealand Society for International Law*, accessed March 26, 2024, https://anzsil.org.au/resources/CfP-Queering%20Internaitonal%20Law%202.0[12].pdf.

45 Bérénice K. Schramm, et al., "Doing Queer in the Everyday of Academia: Reflections on Queering a Conference in International Law," *AJIL Unbound* 116 (2022): 16.

the convenors were asking participants to engage with the creative on the same register as the critical.

The reading was positioned early in the afternoon on the first day of the gathering, coupled with a short poetry reading by Laura-Jane Maher. Maher also participated in the play reading, along with myself and a number of other participants in the conference: Juliana Santos De Carvalho, Emily Jones, Odette Mazel, Warisa Ongsupankul, and Dianne Otto. The active involvement of multiple conference participants in this reading was an important gesture towards thinking of repair in a more collective mode as an ethos that we might cultivate together. I might have been the named playwright behind the show, but the performance was a separate entity, co-created with these six other participants. The setup of the room aided this participatory element: while one set of performers occupied the space otherwise held by the presenters, others were embedded within the audience. The divisive boundary between speaker and audience that Schramm, Santos de Carvalho et al. describe was blurred.

As I have noted earlier, texts shift in their meaning as they travel. One of the elements that I found had amplified in this context was this particular courtroom exchange early in the play:

Lawyer: Your lordships I am telling you that this was the intent of the law, and that these are the people who the law was originally created to persecute.

Judge 2: But how do we know this?

Lawyer: By looking at the origin of the law. By looking at how it has made its way into the Indian Penal Code. Your lordships, if we go back in time, the first recorded mention of sodomy in English law was in two medieval texts that prescribed that sodomites should be burnt alive. Then, when secular laws began to come into place in England, you had the Buggery Act in the 16th century.

At this point, instead of allowing the lawyer to continue offering vital historical context, the judges interrupt, asking why the Court should be concerned with asking what happened in England in the 16th century. The lawyer attempts to explain by noting the importance of context and the colonial imposition of silence on matters of queerness. The exchange leads up to this moment:

Lawyer: Except that the British were so concerned about not naming the identity, about not drawing people's attention to this particular social group that they said, and I quote – 'We are unwilling to insert in the text anything which could give rise to public discussion on this revolting subject – '

Judge 2: Speaking of inserting counsel, please go back to this carnal intercourse question.

When *Contempt* is performed in India, the post-show conversations rarely bring up this moment. Audience questions tend to revolve around the track record of the individual justices and the manner in which judicial benches in India are composed, comparing the judgment to other contemporaneous decisions on queer rights in the country, amongst others. Other conversations pertain to the manner in which lawyers relate stories before the courtroom and the ways this might be reformed. There is an interest in the immediate and the particular, which possibly follows from how the judgment's impact is more visceral and more of a lived reality for the audience members. Indian audiences are also more attuned to the institutional vagaries of the Supreme Court.[46]

When *Contempt* moves outside India, the framing of these questions tends to broaden. Empire takes centre stage, often because of a shared colonial inheritance with different audiences. The set-up of the judiciary is different, and legal conventions shift, but what is shared is a sense of the ongoing impacts of colonisation. I noted this with a Sri Lankan audience in Colombo and a diasporic South Asian audience in London. Now, at a conference on queering international law that has brought together international lawyers from a number of regions across the world, I notice it yet again. A moment of recognition surges around the room. I register the shake of a head from my right, an exasperated half-laugh from further behind.

Shared histories of violence can also mean shared histories of resistance. I am particularly struck by this thought as I watch Warisa Ongsupankul's reading of the testimony of a transgender woman, Kokila. Earlier that day, Warisa presented a paper examining international human rights law as it related to children and non-normative sexualities. The presentation featured a series of pictures from Warisa's own childhood growing up in Thailand, offering us a poignant reflection on the stakes within her work.

Now I watch Warisa speak in the words of Kokila, a trans woman who was subjected to brutal rape and torture in Bengaluru in 2004. Kokila filed an affidavit testifying to this experience before the Court, as part of a broader submission on the impunity that the sodomy law afforded to perpetrators of sexual violence against queer persons. In the transcripts, Kokila's testimony is interrupted by the judges and questioned, amongst other things, for its veracity. In *Contempt,* the scene plays out in a similar manner until Kokila's character decides to interrupt in turn. She breaks out of the narrow confines of legal storytelling and spins a personal narrative about the pleasure she takes in inhabiting her name and, by extension, her identity. The moment does not take away from the brutality of the violence she has experienced.

46 Gautam Bhatia, *The Transformative Constitution: A Radical Biography in Nine Acts* (Noida, Uttar Pradesh, India: HarperCollins Publishers India, 2019).

Rather, it suggests we approach Kokila's personhood in a more capacious manner instead of being defined by an act of violence.

Rahul Rao asks us to consider the spatial imaginaries through which 'certain places are imagined as locations of homosexual freedom and others as locations of homophobia'.[47] Rao observes these distinctions on a world map generated by an international NGO: 'red' areas which are relatively behind in their legal journeys and 'green' countries which have leaped ahead to same-sex marriage.[48] The maps tend to privilege formal legal provisions over the lived experience of queer subjects. In doing so, they are unable to capture how queer individuals and communities resist and reshape the law through their everyday lives. These are often fleeting moments, difficult to capture within a limited cartographic imaginary. But in this space, watching Warisa inhabit another persona, I start to imagine alternative maps composed around queer resistance in the global South. I consider how these various moments of resistance might speak to each other about what might be shared.

There are other moments where the persona of the conference participant contrasts with the persona of their theatrical counterpart in potentially generative ways. On stage, I watch Odette Mazel reading for the role of Swapna. Later in the conference, Mazel will go on to present her own work on queer reparative practice. Mazel's work runs parallel to mine, focusing on reparative elements of Australian engagements with law reform.[49] We orient repair differently in our work, with my focus directed more towards an act of queer dissent that might be cons idered lawful. As Mazel reads the story of a queer love that ends with two lovers jointly committing suicide, I think about a point at which both of us might converge. Sometimes, repair is impossible. Sometimes, the only remotely reparative position is to sit within a space of grief.

The reading goes on. Dianne Otto is seated next to me, inhabiting the villainous role of the judge with relish. It is particularly joyful to watch Otto in this mode, with the weight of her pioneering work having served as the precursor to this gathering. I think about a piece that Mazel has written about Otto's engagements with the law, oscillating between critique and hope.[50] Here we sit, watching and conducting a performance that is also caught within this oscillatory moment.

47 Rahul Rao, "The Locations of Homophobia," *London Review of International Law* 2, no. 2 (2014): 169.

48 Rao, "The Locations of Homophobia".

49 Odette Mazel, "Queer Jurisprudence: Reparative Practice in International Law," *AJIL Unbound* 116 (2022): 10.

50 Odette Mazel, "The Texture of 'Lives Lived with Law': Methods for Queering International Law," *Australian Feminist Law Journal* (2023): 1.

The form of scholarly writing and that of the conference presentation can make it difficult to inhabit reparative positions. Often, an argument must be advanced, which implicitly amounts to having to defend a position against objections, real or imagined.[51] The vulnerability that repair-work asks for[52] can be difficult to manifest. Genre experiments with academic forms such as theatre serve as one way to counter some of these inherent difficulties in scholarly exchange. Enfolding these experiments into a generous and collegial gathering, such as the one put together by the convenors of *Queering International Law 2.0*, further harnesses their potential towards building and nurturing scholarly community.

51 See, for example, James Boyd White, *Justice as Translation: An Essay in Cultural and Legal Criticism* (Chicago: University of Chicago Press, 1990). White reflects on how some of the worse impulses of scholarly writing emerge from having to meet imagined objections.
52 Eve Kosofsky Sedgwick, *Touching Feeling: Affect, Pedagogy, Performativity* (Durham: Duke University Press, 2003).

Index

For Product Safety Concerns and Information please contact our EU
representative GPSR@taylorandfrancis.com
Taylor & Francis Verlag GmbH, Kaufingerstraße 24, 80331 München, Germany

www.ingramcontent.com/pod-product-compliance
Ingram Content Group UK Ltd.
Pitfield, Milton Keynes, MK11 3LW, UK
UKHW020009200926
475702UK00015B/2552

* 9 7 8 1 0 3 2 6 4 5 3 4 6 *